EDUCATIONAL PSYCHOLOGY

EDUCATIONAL PSYCHOLOGY

Edited by
Dr. R.K. Pruthi

D P H

DISCOVERY PUBLISHING HOUSE
NEW DELHI-110002

First Published - 2004

Reprinted - 2017

ISBN: 978-81-7141-767-4

Educational Psychology

Published by:

DISCOVERY PUBLISHING HOUSE PVT. LTD.

4383/4B, Ansari Road, Darya Ganj

New Delhi-110 002 (India)

Phone: +91-11-23279245, 43596064-65

Fax: +91-11-23253475

E-mail: discoverypublishinghouse@gmail.com

sales@discoverypublishinggroup.com

web: www.discoverypublishinggroup.com

Printed at:

Infinity Imaging Systems

Delhi

PREFACE

This book is mainly intended for use as a textbook for Indian universities in educational psychology. It is designed to show college students/teacher how through the application of psychological facts and principles, educational procedures can be made more effective.

Attempt has also been made to examine psychological facts and principles and their implications for education.

I wish to express my thanks to my friends/scholars who have given me valuable help in preparing this work and from whom I have borrowed ideas and articles.

My publisher and his staff have worked hard, they deserve my readers love and patronage.

R.K. Pruthi

Contents

1

Introductory

DEFINITION OF PSYCHOLOGY

The Subject Matter of Psychology: Psychology is designed by William James as "the science of mental life, both of its phenomena and of their conditions." It studies such phenomena as feelings, desires and different modes of cognition. The student of psychology tries to know mental facts, classifies them in certain categories, and makes an attempt to determine their causes. Psychology in the past was a speculative science. The psychologist sat in his room and it reflected on his mental states. But modern psychology is approximating in its methods and procedure to natural sciences like biology and physics.

Psychology as a separate branch of study is more than 2000 years old. It was the genius of Aristotle that gave birth to this science. Yet in its modern form it is one of the latest of all mental disciplines. It has been changing its meaning from time to time. Rudolf Goeckel whose book on the subject was published in 1590, named it as *Psychologia*. This word is built up from *Psyche* meaning "soul" and *Logos* meaning "talk about" or "science of" Thus psychology meant "the science of soul". By soul was meant a being dwelling in the body which could at times even leave the body and go on a sojourn. A more advanced view regarded soul as "a vital principle inhabiting and animating each human body and somehow the ground of each individual's experience".* But psychology did not make much progress so long as the thinkers did not give up their theological bias. Soul in the theological or metaphysical sense is an entity inaccessible to scientific investigation.

* McDougal, An Outline of Psychology, p.10.

Psychology in the eighteenth century was conceived of as the science of mind. But according to one school the mind itself was nothing but an assemblage of ideas. Thus the "Associationist School" of Hume, Mill and Bain constructed a psychology without a soul. Hume said, "all we know directly is the stream of ideas and what we call the mind or soul is a mere empty stage which we innecessarily assume to exist as the scene upon which the ideas play their part.*

He further says that mankind are "nothing but a bundle or collection of different perceptions, which succeed each other with an inconceivable rapidity, and they are in a perpetual flux and movement". The Buddhists of India, who were psychologists of an advanced type also regarded mind as a perpetually changing stream of ideas.

Psychology was regarded later as "the science of consciousness". According to James our mental life is a stream. We have to study this "stream of thought" as we directly know it. But to define psychology as the science of consciousness is, in a way, misleading. In the first place, the definition is not comprehensive enough, for psychology these days studies not only our conscious mental life but the unconscious also. Besides, it studies the relation of conscious life to bodily behaviour. In the second place, "consciousness", as McDougall points out, is a word that has "the form of a substantative which cannot be used as a verb" and "allows us to forget that it stands for the fact of being conscious of something, and that it implies someone who is conscious of something, and that it implies someone who is conscious of that thing."

Thus we see that the definition of psychology as the science of mind or the science of consciousness is too narrow and even misleading. Most of the writers on the subject, however, retain

---

* "For my part", says Hume "when I enter most intimately into what I call myself, I always stumble on some particular perception or other, of heat or cold, light or shade, love or hatred, pain or pleasure, I never can catch myself at any time without a perception, and *never can observe anything but the perception.* When my perceptions are removed for any time, as by sound sleep, so long am I insensible of *myself,* and may truly be said not to exist, And were all my perceptions removed by death, and could I neither think, nor feel , nor see, nor love, nor hate after the dissolution of the body, I should be entirely annihilated."
Treatise on Human Nature, Chap. On Personal Identity.

the definition of psychology as the science of mind inspite of the inadequacy of the definition. Thus McDougall defines psychology as "the science of human mind, positive and empirical". The word "positive" is added to distinguish it from normative sciences like ethics and logic, and "empirical" to mark the fact that psychology relies on the method of investigation common to all natural sciences.

The latest definition of psychology is that it is "the science of human behaviour". Thus McDougall defines psychology in his *Physiological Psychology* as "the positive science of conduct or behaviour". It is the science which aims "to give us better understanding and control of the behaviour of the organism as a whole". This definition lays stress on objectively observable facts, the facts of outward behaviour or bodily action in which mental activity expresses itself. It is free from many of the logical and other difficulties involved in other definitions.

The Behaviourist School of psychology understands the term 'behaviour' in a sense different from the one held by McDougall. McDougall would not discard the hypothesis of the mind as something different from "the brain" or the body.* According to the Behaviourists, psychology has nothing to do with consciousness or mind. It is like every other natural science objective and experimental. Every law of psychology is verifiable even as the laws of other sciences are verifiable through observation and experiment. Its subject matter is the behaviour or activities of human beings. Behaviourism discards consciousness because the factual data required for a natúral science cannot be provided by it. As the facts are not available for objective study, they may well provide speculations for a philosopher but they cannot advance the progress of a science.

Psychology thus gradually lost one by one the various entities it postulated.** The psychologist is no longer an introvert,

* "The *mind*, then, of the individual organism is that which expresses itself in his experience, and in his behaviour: and we have to build up our description of the human mind by gathering all possible facts of human experience and behaviour, and by inferring from these the nature and structure of the mind." *An Outline of Psychology*. p. 35.

** The changing attitude towards the subject is very cogently put by. Woodworth thus: 'First psychology lost its soul. Then it lost its mind, then it lost consciousness; it still has behaviour, of a kind.' *Psychology*, p. 2.

but rather an extrovert. From being the study of an intangible entity called soul, it has become a study of the most tangible facts of bodily behaviour. According to some writers the change has been responsible for the great advance made in the subject. The various ramifications of psychology are due to it. At least educational psychology and child psychology are greatly indebted to Behaviourism. But for the objective attitude that Behaviourism brought to bear on psychological studies, the vast amount of educationally valuable data could not have been collected. Obviously the child mind cannot be introspectively studied, and whatever light reflection on one's experience may throw on the facts of child behaviour, certainly it is objective study of the behaviour as such that is truly the basis of child. psychology or educational psychology.

METHODS OF PSYCHOLOGY

Introspection: The peculiar method which psychology adopts to collect its data is commonly known as introspection. It consists in trying to understand the nature of mental phenomena by looking within one's own mind and analysing them as they actually exist in any state of consciousness. Thus, for instance, if I want to know the nature of anger, I must look within myself when anger comes, try to know the peculiarity of the experience, and watch the manifestation of the phenomena. Similarly while studying the process of attention, the psychologist has not only to attend to the object, but he has also to attend to his own mental state of attention. It is only thus that the conditions of attention, the strain involved in attention, and several other features of attention are determined.

Various objections have been urged against the desirability of using this method. First, the method is so difficult that only a very few trained individuals can use it. All scientific investigations require looking out for the data, here we have to do just the reverse. Secondly, the mind in watching its own working most necessarily have its attention divided between two objects—on the one hand, the mental operation itself which is observed, and on the other, the object to which the mental operation is directed. It is doubtful whether these two operations can be done by the mind simultaneously. It is urged that the actual experience is bound to disappear when one tries to observe and study it. The very act of observing tends to change the experience. As William James puts it, "The attempt at introspective analysis is like seizing a top to catch its motion." Thus introspection necessarily becomes retrospection or a study of the memories of the events that are either past or passing away. Thirdly, as the data are not available for verification to everyone the method is regarded by some psychologists as "subjective" and, as such, it cannot be a basis of a science.

These objections are really very difficult to meet. As a matter of fact psychology remained at a very elementary stage, so long as introspection remained the sole method of approach to the subject. It is only when observation and experiment began to supplement the work of introspection, that, the science grew to such an enormous extent.

But, however difficult or inadequate the introspective method may be, no psychologist can dispense with it altogether. The only way that we can understand the thoughts and feelings or motives of action of other men is by knowing how they rise in our own minds. There is only one individual whom I know directly and that is myself, others I know only indirectly. I interpret their behaviour in the light of my own experience known through introspection. It is true that a training is required to be able to introspect, but so does every science require training. As for the difficulty of availing of the data, it is actually overcome by minds that have a proper training. Retrospection substantially helps introspection in collecting data. These data are supplemented by what we observe in the behaviour of other men and what they express. Lastly, it is wrong to say that the method is subjective. Though the psychologist directly studies his own inner experience, he always compares it with the experience of others, and is not satisfied till he has attained to an objective point of view. "It is not the isolated observation which is of importance in introspective psychology but rather the accumulation of a vast number of observation, each helping others; introspection to be effective for the advancement of science, most like other modes of observation, be carried on by a number of experts in co-operation.* The introspective method,

* Stout: *Manual of Psychology*, p. 5.

though it is regarded as the peculiar method of analytic psychology, cannot be dispensed with in any psychological investigation. "Introspection", says Williams James, "is difficult and fallible; and that the difficulty is simply that of all observations of whatever kind."* Here James puts the difficulties of introspection in a line with the difficulties of collecting data through any other methods of scientific investigation. Hence a body of systematised knowledge built up through this peculiar method of study adopted by psychology can claim to be a science.

Observation: Observation of the behaviour of others is also recognized as an important method of psychological study. Psychology, these days, is becoming a natural science instead of being a speculative one, and it makes use of all those methods of investigations which are used by natural sciences to collect their data. By carefully observing the behaviour of human beings, we can know what is going on in their minds. This is particularly the case when some emotion is aroused in the minds of any person. When anger or fear is aroused, the individual invariably shows signs of his feelings in his external behaviour. However we may try to repress the external manifestations of anger, somehow our feelings are betrayed by our behaviour. Then the problem of conditioning of a reflex, that of habit formation or modification of an instinct, the problem of interest and attention, of memory, of delinquent behaviour of children and fatigue can all be studied through observation. It is regarded as an objective method as against introspection which, as pointed before, is often stigmatised by some as subjective.

The method of observation has proved of special value in the field of educational psychology. The method of introspection here has only a secondary value. Hence these days this method has developed a special technique. Unless a person receives a previous training in the technique of the method he cannot observe the child.

To observe the child he should first *get rid of his own prejudices* about his nature of abilities. He should proceed to observe him with an open mind. Parents for this reason cannot

* *Principal of Psychology*, Vol, 1. p. 192.

properly observe their own children. They proceed with certain prejudices either in favour of or against some children who are unfit to make a proper observation of their behaviour.

The second requisite of scientific observation is that the subject should not be allowed to become aware of the fact that he is being watched. He must be observed in perfectly natural sitting. This means that the child should not know the fact of his being observed else his behaviour would become artificial. For this the psychologist has to mix himself with the children sufficiently so that they might begin behaving in perfectly natural way in his presence. So long as the psychologist is a stranger to them he cannot properly observe them. To keep the naturalness of behaviour among children, the psychologist has sometimes to observe them secretly. The psychologist hides from the view of the children and then notes their behaviour. For this in America and England one-way screened glasses are used. Children are allowed to stay in a room and to act as they please. They are then observed without their becoming aware of the fact of observation.

Thirdly, the psychologist has to make note of observed facts just at the moment that observation occurs. If he does not do so, important fact slips from memory and what he recalls later is not the exactly observed fact but something similar to it mixed up with his own prejudices. For this the observer has to learn short hand and in the notebook put down separately the observed fact and his own interpretation of it.

Experiment: The experimental method, the basis of experimental psychology has been used enormously in recent years. An experiment is observation under known or determinate and pre-arranged condition. Rate of learning, remembering and forgetting, transfer of training, span of attention, onset of fatigue, and several other mental phenomena are in this way measured by experiments. Sometimes large statistics are prepared relating to the experiments, and then the method is known as the *statistical method*. The experimental method has played a very important part in developing the science of education.

The conducting of experiments in the field of educational psychology requires a very specialized training. Psychological experiments can be conducted only by experts. The result of an experimenter is very often vitiated if the experimenter does not take necessary precautions. A psychological experiment is not the same thing as an experiment in physics or chemistry. In the latter sciences there is no question of any modification in the data by the fact of their being under artificial conditions. But in the case of psychology we experiment with human beings whose behaviour becomes modified under the very condition of experiment. Hence great caution has to be taken to make the subject as easy as possible and make him behave in the way as he would do under natural conditions.

Much experimental work is being done these days in mental testing. The conducting of the experiments which determine that mental capacity of different types of children, not only require much psychological data, but it also requires much mathematical ability and insight. Without this mental tests cannot be standardized. The administration of these tests and the interpretation of results also require great psychological ability.

The experimental method has advanced educational psychology and the science of education a great deal. But there are limitations of this method. Every phenomena of child behaviour cannot be experimented upon and for some we have to simply wait and watch the child when he naturally acts in a particular way. Further the results of psychological experiments are not as reliable as the results of experiments in physical science. But with proper caution we can get a great deal in the study of human mind with the help of this method.

Comparative Method: Psychologists study not only human behaviour but they study animal behaviour also, for very often, as pointed out before, a study of the latter throws much light on the former. This way of studying human behaviour is known as the *comparative method*. It has given rise to comparative psychology. Thus, for instance, a psychologist studies the behaviour of wasps, birds and animals to know whether instincts can be modified by experience of whether instinctive actions involve the use of intelligence.

Psycho-analysis: A few decades ago a new field of psychology has been discovered, requiring the use of a new method for its study. As a matter of fact, as the fields of psychology increase new methods are invented to study them. Psycho-analysis studies the unconscious mind of an individual; psycho-analysis is the name both of the specialized knowledge about the unconscious mind as well as the method by which that knowledge is acquired. Now psycho-analysis is regarded as a new science.

The use of psycho-analysis as a method of mental study requires much technical knowledge and training. The unconscious mind of an individual tries to hide itself from the conscious and it requires much insight and alertness to find out what its desire, feelings and intentions are. One has to dive deep into the inner recesses of an individual's mind in order to know what he really feels or desires in himself. Such a study has to be made whenever abnormality of behaviour is noted in the case of any person.

The psycho-analysis studies the automata, dreams, slips and omissions and various symptoms that characterize the conduct of an abnormal person. Through the study of these he tries to form an idea of his inner troubles. Psycho-analysis has proved specially valuable to medical profession. A teacher cannot become a psycho-analyst. Yet a general knowledge of the science helps him to anticipate and forestall troubles that might arise in the conduct of any individual child. Most children become mentally uneasy before they become mischievous or sick. A teacher can note the growing uneasiness in the child and by devoting greater attention to him, he can make his mind easy.

BRANCHES OF PSYCHOLOGY

Psychology now has several branches. Thus we have Individual Psychology or General Psychology, Social Psychology Abnormal Psychology, and Animal Psychology. These names are given according to the data which the particular branch of psychology studies. Names are also given according to the peculiar method of investigation followed. Thus we get Analytic Psychology, Genetic Psychology, Experimental Psychology, Comparative Psychology and Educational Psychology. It is worth our while to explain the terms used to name the several branches of the subject more fully.

Individual or General Psychology studies the various mental processes and behaviours of an individual more or less in isolation from the group in which he lives. Social Psychology deals with the behaviour of individuals in relation to society. Thus, for instance, there is an inherited tendency in every animal to imitate others. This innate tendency is studied in general psychology as well as in social psychology, but whereas the former studies the origin, the development and modification of this tendency from the point of view of the individual, the latter studies it from the point of view of the group. The latter is more concerned with the characteristic manifestations of this tendency and the law of its working in society. It tries to reveal its social significance.

Abnormal Psychology studies the individual as he thinks, feels and behaves in an abnormal state of mind; it studies, in other words, his abnormal thoughts, feelings and modes of behaviour. Such phenomena as dissociation of personality, insanity, hysteria, fixations, obsessions, and dreams form the subject-matter of the study of Abnormal Psychology. *Psycho-analysis* which also studies abnormal phenomena of the mental life of an individual is an offshoot of this science. The former has developed into a science only in the present century and its study is proving to be of much value to the educators.

Animal Psychology or *Comparative Psychology* studies the behaviour of animals in different situations. This study has proved of immense value as throwing light on the origin and development of certain tendencies which we find in a very modified and complicated form in a man. The true nature of our instincts is knows in this way.*

---

* Sandiford has devised a very good diagram to enable one to remember the various divisions of the subject. The diagram is given below:

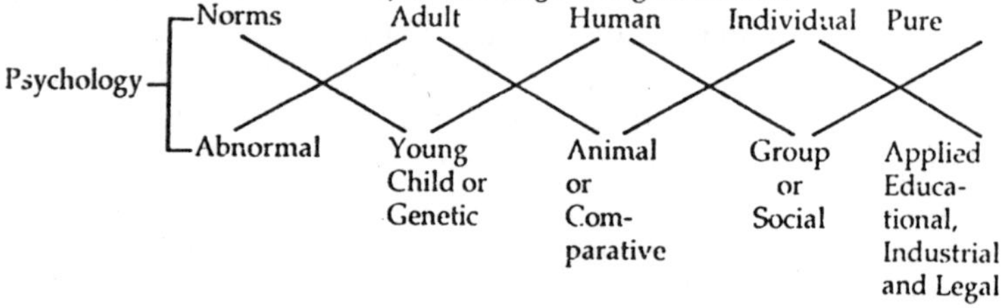

"Each term in the upper line is contrasted with the one immediately below it—Normal with Abnormals; Human with Animals and Pure with Applied. The lines and the crosslines indicate the various combinations which are to be found". The chief divisions, of the subject are—Normal Psychology, which studies the behaviour of normal adults and normal children, Abnormal Psychology which studies the behaviour of abnormal adults and abnormal children. Similarly there are other branches—Adult Psychology, Child Psychology, Human Psychology. Animal Psychology, Individual Psychology and Applied Psychology. Of course, these divisions are not absolutely exclusive of each other.

SCOPE OF PSYCHOLOGY

Psychology according to Stout deals with immediate experiences such as perceiving, attending, feeling, desiring, imagining etc. These immediate experiences may be subjective or they may be objective—that is, they may be such as are not capable of being pictured before consciousness, or they may be capable of being pictured, but here the use of the terms subjective and objective, marks off only a relative difference. There is, on analysis, found no fundamental difference between the two kinds of immediate experiences. One thing, however, marks distinctly the subject matter of psychology from the subject matter of other sciences. Psychology studies human experience primarily; it studies the conditions of the arousal of that experience only secondarily. Thus psychology is interested in what is perceived only insofar as it is related to the process of perception.

Human experience has three fundamental characteristics. All experience is a knowing, a willing and a feeling. Some psychologists emphasise one characteristic and point out that others are subsidiary to it. Others emphasise the importance of other characteristics. The Presentationists and Associationists (Herbart and Hume) emphasise the knowing side and think that mind is an assemblance of ideas; action and felling are determined by knowledge. There are others—those belonging to the *Hormic School,* such as McDougall, who assert that all knowing occurs in subservience to action. At the root of all life there is a will to self-expression. It is due to this fundamental urge that the conative or affective mental structure is developed. *The will to live,* which is responsible for all phenomena of life is eternally active, It evolves, according to Shopenhauer, *the understanding* to gratify its inner carvings.

Leaving the controversies aside we may accept the conclusion arrived at by all the schools that human consciousness has all the three elements—knowing, feeling and willing or cognition, affection and conation, They characterise all awareness. Hence we have to study the mind in its three above-mentioned aspects. The whole field of psychological study may be generally represented by the table given below:

Human Mind

- Cognition
  - Attention
  - Sensation
  - Perception
  - Imagination
  - Memory
  - Conception
  - Judgement
  - Reasoning
- Conation
  - *Inherited tendencies*
    - Reflexes
    - Instincts and General Tendencies
  - *Acquired tendencies*
    - Habit
    - Character
- Affection
  - Feeling
  - Emotions
  - Moods
  - Sentiments

A few decades ago psychology studied only the conscious process of the human mind; but now the field of psychological study has immensely widened due to the researches of the psycho-analysts regarding the unconscious processes of human mind. To-day psychology studies both the conscious and unconscious realms of our mind. The latter is ever expanding itself; new light is thrown by workers in this field practically every day about the true nature of our minds and its processes.

PSYCHOLOGY AND EDUCATION

In developing the theory of Education and in improving the practice of teaching, psychology is playing these days an increasingly important part. Every day experimental psychology is bringing out results which are immensely influencing our educational practice. Teachers have begun taking interest in the study of psychology and educational authorities everywhere have deemed it necessary for all the teachers to undergo a formal training in the training colleges, and learn psychologically sound methods of instruction before beginning their professional career.

In the past, however, the attitude of teachers towards psychology was that of indifference or even of positive repulsion. It was thought that a teacher cannot become more efficient in his art by his knowledge of psychology. Teaching requires practical skill and not introspective study of mental processes. The teacher who is given to introspection is likely more to be a failure than a success in profession, for his introvert attitude would be a hindrance to his progress in teaching and controlling children. Some philosophers also hold the view that far from psychology being helpful to education, the teacher's indulgence in psychology is positively detrimental to its cause. The attitude of the psychologist is analytic, whereas that of the educationist or the teacher is synthetic. The teacher is essentially an artist, a creator and not an analyser or dissector of his material. The teacher's attitude has to be that of an idealist, whereas the psychological attitude is a realistic one. The teacher sees the child in terms of what he ought to be, whereas the psychologist sees the child as he is. The teacher, therefore, will cease to be a source of inspiration if he becomes a psychologist.

The above arguments have a certain amount of validity. But they simply prove that the teacher has not to turn himself into a mere psychologist, and reduce his class-room to a psychological laboratory; he has to be a man of high ideals who believes in the nobility of his profession; he has to help the child to manifest the divinity in him. But his knowledge of psychology is not a hindrance to this. He has to be skilled in his art, but his skill will bring forth better results if he does not merely follow the rule of the thumb, but consciously makes use of the principle he has learnt through a deeper insight into human nature. It is, of course, true that a good teacher may not have much knowledge of psychology and a good student of psychology may be an indifferent teacher; for the ability to teach depends not merely on the information which psychology gives about the working of human mind, it equally depends upon individual resourcefulness. A good student of psychology may not have that amount of resourcefulness which a skilful teacher has. Yet the knowledge of psychology will certainly prevent the young teacher from committing many blunders and learning the art at the cost of the students.* Again the rule of the thumb sometimes

* "The science of logic," says Williams James "never made a man reason rightly, and the science of ethics (if there be such a thing) never made a man behave rightly. The most such sciences can do is to help us to catch ourselves up and check ourselves, if we start to reason to behave wrongly: and criticise ourselves more articulately after we have made mistakes. A science once lays down lines within which the rules of the art must not transgress, but what particular thing he shall positively do within those lines is left exclusively to his own genius. One genius will do his work well and succeed in one way, while another will do as well quite differently; yet neither will transgress the lines."—*Talk to Teacher*, p. 8.

does not work, and then sound psychological principles must be there to guide a teacher.

Those people, who urge that since the psychological attitude is analytic it would destroy the synthetic attitude of the teacher, ignore the facts of history. The two attitudes are not altogether incompatible with each other. Pestalozzi and Herbart were great idealists and yet it is they who aimed at psychologising education. Science does not necessarily hinder art–rather with scientific insight gained, the artist raises himself to a higher level and makes his work of eternal value. In the case of education it has proved true beyond all doubts—*The Child Study Movement* has helped the cause of education more than any theorising ever did.

The child is the material with which the teacher has to work and if he does not know the nature of his material well, he is not likely to succeed much in his undertaking . The teacher should not be merely a master of his subject, believing that somehow the knowledge he possesses will trickle down to his pupil, but he should also know thoroughly child nature and the method of communicating his knowledge according to his needs. As John Adam said, "The verb of teaching governs two accusatives, one the person and another the thing—the teacher taught John Latin; the teacher should know John as well as Latin".

The knowledge of psychology, it is true, does not help us in determining the aim of education, for this we have to look to moral philosophy for guidance. The formulation of the aim of education depends upon the aim of life as one conceives it. But in telling whether a particular aim is attainable or is to remain ever in the clouds, it is psychology that will help us. Even rules of moral conduct have to be framed, keeping a due regard to the excellences and failings of human nature as we know them through psychology. Psychology also helps in knowing how far the aim has been actually realised by us. Whatever may be conceived as the aim of education for the achievement of the aim, modification of the behaviour of the individual will always be necessary. Now in successfully modifying the behaviour of the individual, with the least expenditure of energy and time, psychology surely proves very helpful. It is also helpful in understanding the hidden motives of any kind of behaviour, and we can modify these only with a sound knowledge of psychology.

The teacher with a knowledge of psychology will handle the child better. If he knows the nature of the child well, that is his innate endowments, the laws of his mental development, the home and the school influence on him, how character is formed, he will do more good to him than is otherwise possible. The importance of psychology to education has increased due to the recognition of individual differences emphasis on motivisation, encouragement of spontaneity in the child, and a consideration of the child's total personality. Until quite recently education was meant mainly for the average child. The individual difference received scant recognition. If an individual did not fit into a uniform social order he was segregated. The subnormal child and the genius received little consideration. All attention was given to normal child.

Now this attitude has changed. The educator now pays heed to the individual differences and aims to perfect each individual after his kind. The child's spontaneity is encouraged. He is not forced to learn lessons, rather his interest is awakened in the subject and then he is merely guided in the process of self-education. The student's tastes and aptitudes are now carefully studied and work suitable to each student is given to him. All this implies a careful study of the child mind.

In the actual practice of teaching also, the knowledge of psychology proves very useful to a teacher. He has to awaken the child's interest in the subject taught, so that it may be easily learnt by him. For this he must know the natural inclinations of the child and work in a manner so as not to conflict with the child's nature.

A teacher is entrusted with the task of educating the child put under his care. He has to direct the physical and mental growth of his pupil in such a way as to make him a useful and effective personality in the world. Every community has a certain ethical or standard of efficiency and this the educator has to enable the child to realise. One of the means of the realising this ideal is to instruct the child in the way he has to live, to impart information to him and thus to communicate to him the social traditions and beliefs of the age. Usually it is this process of instruction and imparting information that goes by the name of education, and it is with this that the teachers are generally concerned. Psychology can be of immense value to the teacher in the task of instruction.

The above, however, is a very restricted view of education. In the more comprehensive sense, it includes instruction, but it includes many things more . Education is the cultivation of all the moral, intellectual and physical powers. In its widest sense it includes all the influences which act upon the individual from infancy to the grave. "Education," says Raymont, "is the process of development in which consists the passage of a human being from infancy to maturity, the process whereby he gradually adopts himself in various ways his physical, social and spiritual environment".* If we take such a comprehensive view of education, we can at once see that no one is qualified to undertake that sacred task who is ignorant of the laws that underline the growth of human personality.** It is with these laws that psychology acquaints a teacher. The child is a book, said Rousseau, which the teacher has to learn from page to page. Education is concerned not only with imparting knowledge which the teacher has under his command, but it is also concerned with the formation of the right habits of thought and action, cultivation of proper tastes and development of character in a child. The teacher cannot realise these objects of education without a knowledge of psychology. Children who are mishandled in early life grow up as unhealthy personalities. The early impressions of our life are the most enduring of all and if the child, due to the teacher's ignorance, receives wrong impression about any thing, he carries them with himself all his life and they do him great mischief Similar is the case about his

---

* *Principles of Education* , p.4.

** "Education" says Morgan. "is no longer merely drilling the child so that he can read certain skilled acts, solve so many arithmetic problems, know so many historical dates and names, and recite so many lines of poetry. It is all these but it is a vast deal more. It is the development of every phases of the child's life so that he becomes a unified and integrated-personality".

"A good educational task is not accomplished when one is trained to be good scientist, if he cannot get along with any one because of his irascible disposition. One is not the best type of person if, when he meets an unusual difficulty, he throws a temper tantrum, banks some one else, gets sick, sits and day-dreams".

"In other words, we have added to our task in the education of the child the goal of mental hygiene. We must develop the child to meet his difficulties squarely rather than by the adoption of some silly 'defence mechanism designed to deceive himself and others as to his true worth.'—*Child Psychology*, Chap.1.

feelings and the direction of his active nature. Many complexes* are formed in the early life of children or undesirable sentiments are developed which cannot be easily removed.

SPECIAL FUNCTION OF EDUCATIONAL PSYCHOLOGY

Educational psychology on the one hand is connected with Education which is a Normative Science and on the other with Psychology which is a Positive Science. Education is purposive and has to believe in the ability of an individual to his destiny. At least it believes in the capacity of the teacher to mould the behaviour of the child so as to make him a more effective citizen of the world. Psychology on the other hand is deterministic. Given certain conditions certain results are bound to follow. Psychology regarded education itself as a kind of environment which along with heredity shapes the destiny of an individual. For psychology there is no freedom of will and where scientific Psychology as such receives emphasis in education, the latter itself becomes deterministic. This deterministic attitude of the Psychologist has sometimes a very unhealthy effect on the education. The education can do the highest good to the child so long as he believes that the child has a free will that can reshape the whole of his nature and that the teacher himself can

* Hadfield in his book *Psychology and Morals* (page 158), tells us of a peculiar case of a distinguished barrister of Germany, who used to experience, on occasions, a very severe pain in one of his feet. He could not know the cause, and eminent doctors also failed to diagnose the disease. He finally approached a psycho-analyst, who through analysis discovered a hidden complex in the mind of the barrister. In his early childhood, while coming to the school, he saw on the road a man with badly crushed foot. He was moved by a feeling of pity and horror, and his mind was so engrossed with the scene that not only was he late to the class that day, but he could not answer properly the question put by the teacher. The teacher rebuked and chastised him for his unusual conduct. The boy felt much humiliation and as he was a brilliant boy his feeling of shame and humiliation, was intense. This feeling could find no expression in his early life and so it remained repressed for a long time till it worked itself out in the form of the foot-ache. The barrister experienced pain only when he lost a law a suit. The feeling of the horror for the crushed foot had become in his early life associated with his feeling of self-abasement. The pain of the crushed foot, however, had been now transferred from the seen person to himself. So the pain occurred whenever there was a feeling of self-abasement.

This is extraordinary case. It, however, brings into clear relief what occurs to the mind of the child whenever there is a great convulsion of his feelings. Teachers have to learn lessons from all such cases. Pain increases in intensity, as Schopenhaur points out, as man grows in intelligence and genius suffer from pain most.

do much in bringing about that change. Just as the belief in a free will is the *sin-qua-non* of Ethics so too it is of education and the more a teacher is sincere in education the less he will put his faith in the finding of pure scientific empirical psychology. Psychology as a handmaid of education is good, as its matter, it is bad.

The more intelligent a child is, the more delicate is his nervous system. It cannot withstand rude shocks. Hence the teachers must be very careful while dealing with such children. An angry word from the teacher sometimes does more harm to a child than all the good that may have been done by him during several years of his teaching. The career of many a promising child is spoilt through a careless handling of him. We may be meaning good to him all the while and yet due to the ignorance of the child's mind we may do him irreparable harm.

Hence a great care is to be taken in handling the child; all this requires a good knowledge of psychology.

Exercises

1. What is the subject matter of psychology? Can we define Psychology as the science of human behaviour?
2. How can we best study the mind of the child? Point out the difficulties of the observation method?
3. How can we experiment with the child mind? What precautions must be taken to make any experiment successful?
4. A person may be a good psychologist but an indifferent teacher. Discuss.
5. What is the exact value of the study of psychology to a teacher? Can the work of a teacher be improved by the study of psychology?
6. What help does psychology offer in class management and in maintaining discipline in the school? Give examples of errors that a teacher ignorant of psychology may commit in handling superior, backward and naughty children of the class.

7. "The verb of teaching governs two accusatives—one the person and another the thing."—Bring out the pedagogical significance of the statement.

References

1. Woodworth: *Psychology,* Chap. I.
2. Stout: *A Manual of Psychology* Chap. I.
3. Hadfield: *Psychology and Morals.*
4. Homer Lane: *Talks to Parents and Teachers.*
5. Dumville: *Child Mind,* Chap. I.
6. Sandiford: *Educational Psychology,* Chap. I.
7. James: *Talks to Teachers,* Chap. I.

2

General Nature of Development

"At each moment of life, any person is in process of changing into something a little different from what he now is. The whole pattern is changing, and it is important to keep in mind at one time both the fact of pattern and the fact of change. What the pattern at any stage will be depend upon the individual from his present surroundings. But it depends also on his own *response*, both to what has gone on before and to the influences that are acting upon him now. A person to some extent shapes the pattern of his life by the choices and decisions he makes at successive stages. Once a choice has been made and its effects built into the developing structure, it can never be eradicated. Development is a one-way street."[1]

Perhaps no better theme than this quotation could be found for a discussion of human development. First of all, it suggests that education should be broadly rather than narrowly conceived. Education may be thought of, from one point of view, as the process of attaining basic skills such as those involved in reading, writing, speaking, and computation. It may be thought of as acquiring knowledge of geography, history, science, and other subjects. It may be conceived more generally as "learning to think."

However, there is more to individual development than this. It is a many-sided process. Not only are intellectual aspects of a child's development important in education, but also the social and emotional phases of his changing personality. Thus,

1. L.E. Tyler, "Theoretical Principles Underlying the Counselling Process." *Journal of Counselling Psychology*, V, No. 1 (Spring. 1958), 6.

education may be thought of as attaining emotional stability. It may also be considered as the process of coming to terms with other people—learning to live in many kinds of groups and communities. It should also be conceived as the process by which the individual comes to terms with himself—becomes aware of his strengths and his limitations and arrives at a concept of himself.

All these aspects of development are interrelated and interdependent. It is fruitful in studying the individual and in portraying the process of development to describe the changes in terms of broad categories. But it is important to remember that to some degree this kind of description and interpretation is artificial. To understand the child, the adolescent, or the adult, it is necessary to see him as a person possessing a certain *pattern* of development and, at any moment, exhibiting uniqueness in relation to his fellows.

It is customary, too, in writing about human development, to discuss it in stages. But in dealing with a child at any one stage in his education, it is easy to overlook the *process* that underlies a change in his behaviour, and thus to fail to realize that what he does at one time is the product of change over a long period. This principle pervades every phase of development.

Although the fact (but not always the nature) of physical growth is apparent, and the progressive ability of the child to master more difficult tasks is taken as evidence of some underlying developmental process, teachers do not so readily understand that acquisition of specific behaviour patterns, such as knowledge of word meanings, is also a matter of development, of progression. Or, if they consider some process of growth necessary for the emergence of such functions as walking, they may fail to see the fact of development in such mental functions as concept formation.[2] Too often educational practice is based on the tacit assumption that desired behaviour takes form full-blown, so to speak, or is quickly produced through the medium of some psychological maid-of-all-work like repetition.

---

2. See, for example, the following study of the development of the breadth and depth of concepts; D.H. Russell, *The Dimensions of Children's Meaning Vocabularies in Grades Four Through Twelve* (University of California Publications in Education, XI, No. 5 [Berkeley, 1954]), 315-414.

Learning—a developmental process: It is generally understood (although the implications for guiding learning are all too frequently disregarded) that the attainment of skill is a process of progressive adaptation from an initial stage where the movements are awkward and poorly coordinated to one characterized by economy of movement and smoothness of organization. It is not so generally recognized that other than sensorimoter types of learning also involve a developmental process. It has been shown, however, that children's number concepts and their ways of dealing with concrete numbers change from rather primitive to progressively more mature stages.[3] The development of a typical pupil's ability to apprehend a number picture such as ... takes several clearly defined steps. He is likely first to count the dots to determine the number. Somewhat later he may distinguish a group within the total, and count the remainder, as 4, 5, 6, 7, 8 (partial counting). The next step is that of recognizing successive groups, as 4 and 2 and 2 (grouping). Finally he may be able to apprehend it as two 4's (multiplication).

The same study also revealed that children's success in learning the simple addition combinations is "largely conditioned by the level of ability attained in dealing with concrete numbers, or, in other words, by the degree of completeness and fullness which characterizes their concepts of numbers."[4] The child may carry over to the solution of the combinations the more-or-less mature methods he used with number pictures, namely, counting, partial counting, grouping, and multiplication and conversion. Success in learning the additive combinations is clearly related to the development of meaning for numbers.

These data provide excellent illustrations of the fact that concepts take form through a process somewhat comparable to that involved in the development of skill. In spite of this fact, textbooks and teachers bombard the pupil with a vast array of abstract terms and expressions for which he has developed no meanings, or, at best, very inadequate ones. Teachers, forgetting

3. W.A. Brownell, *Development of Children's Number Ideas in the Primary Grades* (Supplementary Educational Monographs, No. 35 [Chicago: University of Chicago Press, 1928]), p. 110.
4. *Ibid.*, p. 288.

that their own familarity with meanings is the subtle product of extensive and progressively organized experience, apparently expect pupils to apprehend abstractions with one inclusive act. Children's meanings, on the contrary, develop with experience through a complex process of analysis and synthesis, of expansion and restriction. Throughout the elementary—and secondary—school periods, meanings change in breadth (they encompass many more details or particulars) and also in depth (they represent more profound relationships).[5]

Personality traits and development: Failure of parents and teachers to recognize that a developmental process operates in the acquisition of important personality traits results frequently in persistence of childish levels of reaction. If they forget that "psychological weaning" takes a long time and should begin early though gently, parents and teachers may perpetuate the dependence of childhood and dispose youth to timidity in facing an adult world. A mother who coddles her child by ordering his life in comprehensive detail from babyhood through adolescence should not be surprised if he cannot meet the demands of adult life aggressively when he reaches chronological manhood. When the teacher takes the responsibility for the pupil's learning for twelve years, there is little reason to expect the student to assume it as a college freshman. Parents who dance attendance upon a child from babyhood to adolescence are likely to find that the twenty-year-old is as egocentric as he was at two. The achievement of self-dependence and the escape from excessive egocentricity are not the product of magic wand waving, but of a long and continuous process of development.

Genetic study of behaviour is necessary:. The foregoing illustrations of developmental processes should indicate the futility of trying to understand the nature of development merely by making cross-section analyses of behaviour of different groups of children at successive chronological periods. Increments of development may not reveal the process, which McGraw declares can be observed only by directing attention, in the case of certain motor skills, to "the movements which give rise to an organized behaviour-pattern, as well as the chronological sequence in which

5. Russell, *op. cit.*

behaviour-patterns reach maturity."[6] Development does not ordinarily proceed by leaps from one stage to another, but by a process of continuous change, one phase merging into another by almost imperceptible degrees. The genetic approach to psychology will be most fruitful as research is devoted to the continuous study of the *same individuals* in the *process* of development. Development is an attribute of the dynamic, integrated experience of a living organism.

Questions of status are important in education, but questions of the rate, limit and process of development are more important. To facilitate adequate educational adjustment, for instance, we need to know a pupil's mental age (status), but it is still more essential that we should predict as accurately as possible the *rate* of future mental development. For this reason, the intelligence quotient—the ratio of mental age to chronological age—is an invention of the first magnitude in educational psychology. It is important to remember, however, that prediction of mental development is imperfect at best, and that it is particularly so in the case of some individuals.

Although it is difficult to predict all aspects of later development, education at best always has a future reference. Teachers should ask such questions as the following: What is the probable length and character of the child's schooling? How rapidly will he develop in various ways in relation to other children of the same age? What special aptitudes may he have? What vocational and avocational plans are consistent with his capacities? How can his educational experiences contribute most effectively to the all-round development of his personality?

The developmental process has been characterized recently as "the actualization of potentialities." This actualization requires choice and self-limitation, and a resolution of realities and possibilities. Thus, one writer has explained: "At a later stage, all sorts of possibilities for personality development are ruled out by the fact that the individual spends his earliest, most formative years in a certain kind of family, in a certain geographical location, belonging to a certain kind of sub-culture.

6. M.B. McGraw, *Growth* (New York: Appleton-Century-Crofts, Inc., 1935), p. 4.

At still later stages, each choice that the person himself makes actualizes some possibilities but rules out many others. Thus if he commits himself to an attempt to make a career in music, and really takes it seriously, he will probably never be an athlete, although his neuromuscular structures would originally have made either line of specialization possible."[7]

In a very real sense, then, life is determined in considerable part by what one is able to do and what one decides to do, at a series of choice-points. If a high-school student chooses to take shorthand and typewriting instead of mathematics, he will later find certain educational opportunities and the careers that depend on them closed to him. One of the purposes of counselling is to aid the student to anticipate the future consequences of the choices he must make at all stages of his educational experience.

Education and development: Educational activities are valuable to the extent to which they stimulate and guide desirable forms of development, to the extent to which they help the individual to realize, as fully as realities permit, his potentialities. Education should be concerned with the development of individuals, all of whom are different, each of whom is unique, and each of whom has to some degree a peculiar course of growth. Mass methods of education and arbitrary standards of accomplishment easily obscure the extent of individual development, or mercifully disguise the lack of it. The success or failure of a school system cannot be estimated in comparisons of local averages with national norms in standardized school achievement tests. Educational results must be expressed in the extent to which individual children have developed in proportion to their potentialities, not in terms of "averages."

GENERAL CHARACTERISTICS OF DEVELOPMENT

Insight into the nature of development is fundamental to an understanding of teaching and learning. Although it is difficult to compress the results of many studies of particular aspects of development, it is possible to describe the general character of the process. The remainder of this chapter will be

7. Tyler, L.E., *op. cit.*

devoted to a discussion of some of the characteristics that have the widest applicability to the management of educational affairs.

Development is the product of the interaction of the organism and its environment: *Traits are not exclusively hereditary or environmental.* Development has been defined as a "process resultant from a constant flux or interchange of energies within an organism and energies within its environment."[8] Intrinsic forces, inherent in the genetic constitution of the individual, make up his "heredity".[9] Extrinsic or environmental forces are those influences brought to bear upon a new organism from the moment it is created. Although these two sets of factors that condition growth may be theoretically distinguished, it is not possible to describe any trait exclusively to heredity or environment. Some characteristics presumably take form more as the results of inherent growth factors than of *special* conditions of environmental stimulation, but it is nevertheless necessary to remember that no growth is possible without some stimulation, no development conceivable without an environment. Jennings made this interdependence of hereditary and environmental influences clear when he wrote:

> That which is directly inherited, in the way that property is inherited, that which is passed bodily from parent to offspring—is the set of genes, with the accompanying cytoplasm:—certain substances in certain combinations, which, under certain conditions, give rise to the individual, having certain later characteristics. With the same set of genes, different environmental conditions may induce the production of diverse characteristics.... There is then no thorough-going distinction in kind between diversities producible by gene differences and those producible by environmental differences. Characteristics do not fall into two mutually exclusive classes, one hereditary, the other environmental.[10]

It is probable that the genetic constitution, the particular combination of genes in the chromosomes of the new organism

8. McGraw, *op. cit.*
9. There is no space here for an outline of the main facts of genetics. The student who is unfamiliar with the basic data concerning the transmission of hereditary characteristics should consult recent texts in the field.
10. H.S. Jennings, *Biological Basis of Human Nature* (New York: W.W. Norton & Company. Inc., 1930), p. 133.

sets the limits and the general direction of development. But it is the interaction of these forces and those in the environment that produces development and that may profoundly influence many aspects of individual behaviour.

Responsiveness to environment: Some aspects of development seem to be more the product of intrinsic than environmental factors. Anatomical growth, for example, is one, but even this phase of development is not entirely independent of extrinsic conditions, for extreme environmental factors may influence the growth of structure.

Other aspects of behaviour are apparently conditioned in very considerable degree by the kind of environment in which the individual lives. For example, there are very few if any native interests. The intensity, the persistence, and the variety of interests are greatly influenced by such factors as: (1) the richness and variety of experience, in and out of school; (2) the stimulation of parents, teachers, and other persons who also engage in a variety of interesting and worth while activities; (3) encouragement, positive directions, and successful performance.

The development of language also depends upon environmental stimulation. It has been discovered that children who come from homes of higher socio-economic status surpass those of inferior level in "length of sentences used, frequency of questions, proportion of remarks involving adapted information, and vocabulary."[11] Studies have also revealed that the language of only children develops more rapidly than that of children who have brothers and sisters, and that between the ages of two and five, "singletons" acquire language abilities more rapidly than twins. These facts have been interpreted in the following fashion:

> Apparently the only child imitates the speech of adults who are far along in the linguistic process; the single child imitates the speech of older brothers and sisters who are a little farther along; twins or triplets imitate each other and develop poor linguistic form as well as poor articulation. In the light of these facts, one wonders whether the examples of language usage furnished by parents and associates in the home and play situation may not

11. A.T. Jersild, *Child Psychology* (4th ed.; Englewood Cliffs, N.J.: Prentice-Hall, Inc., 1954), p. 415.

> be of more importance as determiners of spoken language than is school instruction....[12]

Social behaviour is likewise responsive to the demands and sanctions of the social groups in which the individual participates. The growing child will develop competitive and cooperative behaviour in the proportion and in the degree to which these patterns of action are the means of attaining his goals, and to the extent to which the social groups of which he is a member reward him for one or the other or both forms of response. It is increasingly apparent that competitive tendencies have no more foundation in original nature than cooperative ones; the acquisition of specific competitive and cooperative activities is the product of response to the social context. From a careful study of the development of sympathetic and social behaviour in children the following conclusions emerged:

> ...we have no a priori basis for expecting sympathetic behaviour to be more dependent upon learning than is angry behaviour. At least, distress when others are distressed seem primitive, naïve, and reasonably universal, without inculcation by adults. In both anger and sympathy, techniques of response are learned from grown-ups and child associates; the situations to which one may respond with the techniques thus acquired are also learned, and in each case the culture determines the amount as well as the character of the responses...We may indeed say in general that sympathetic behaviour increases relatively in any individual or group, and in so far as the situation is conducive to it.[13]

The nature of group organization is reflected in the activities and attitudes of the individualized members. When a club of junior-high-school boys was organized on "autocratic" lines, with a dominating adult leader who made all decisions and gave authoritative directions, the members tended to work alone rather than together in small groups; they exhibited antagonistic attitudes toward one another, and though outwardly

12. J.E. Anderson, "Child Development and the Growth Precess," chap. 1 in *Child Development and the Curriculum*, Thirty-eighth Yearbook of the National Society for the Study of Education (Bloomington, Ill.: Public School Publishing Company, 1939), p. 33. Quoted by permission of the Society.
13. L.B. Murphy, *Social Behaviour and Child Personality* (New York: Columbia University Press, 1937), pp. 296, 298. Reprinted by permission of Columbia University Press.

submissive, acquired strong resentment toward the person in control. The members of a democratically organized group, on the other hand, when encouraged to work out plans cooperatively with the adult leader, showed more spontaneous group activity, friendly and constructive relationships, and more wholehearted interest in the task.[14]

The effect of environmental factors upon intelligence: The development of intelligence seems to be very much less susceptible to control by environmental conditions than the development of interests, language abilities, and patterns of social behaviour. The notion of the stability of rate of development of intelligence has long been embodied in the doctrine of the relative constancy of the intelligence quotient. Recent research, however, has indicated that there may be a considerable amount of fluctuation in an individual's intelligence quotient on retesting over a period of time. It will suffice here to quote from Anderson who makes the following statement:

> Perhaps a conservative statement would be that, although intelligence is in large part determined by hereditary components, it is modified or changed in some degree by environment factors. The environment determines in large part the extent, degree, and manner in which the innate potentialities of children are realized, and the manner in which hereditary capacities are put to work. In general, the more stimulating an environment is, short of extreme pressure, the better are potentialities realized.[15]

Admitting that the limit and direction of mental development are laid down in the constitution of the organism at the time of fertilization, it is important for educators to predict as early as possible (provided they revise their predictions repeatedly as new data are obtained) the general nature of these directions and limits; to be constantly on the alert for evidence of special aptitudes that may be nourished; and to ask themselves constantly what experiences will lead to the greatest realization of each child's potentialities.

---

14. R. Lippit, "An Experimental Study of the Effect of Democratic and Authoritarian Atmospheres" (University of Iowa Studies in Child Welfare, Studies in Topological and Vector Psychology I. [Iowa City: University of Iowa Press, Feb., 1940]), pp. 45-195.
15. Anderson," Child Development and the Growth Process," *op. cit.*, p. 35. Quoted by permission of the Society.

Development is a continuous and gradual, rather than a salutatory, process: If one should observe a random sampling of eighth grade boys and girls, he would be struck by what seem to be decided differences between adolescence and childhood. Most of the girls, and a somewhat smaller proportion of the boys (because, in general, girls develop earlier than boys) would show some of the superficial traits of early adolescence—the girls in the giggling, boy-conscious, show-off stage; the boys in the awkward, grinning, self-conscious period of growth. The remainder, usually smaller in stature and more childish in their reactions, would seem curiously out of place in this group. They have not yet crossed that indefinite area in one side of which lies childhood and, on the other, adolescence. The differences between individuals in two well-differentiated stages of development seem to be pronounced, so much so that it was once believed that development was characterized by rather sudden transformations. But when the construction of reliable physical and mental tests made possible the measurement of the same individuals at successsive intervals, investigators were struck with the essential continuity and gradual nature of the developmental curves of both physical and mental functions. It must be admitted that continuity of the process is more impressive when individual growth curves are thrown together into a composite picture. Individual curves usually show considerably more fluctuation, and may now and then show a rather pronounced change.

The statement that development is continuous does not mean that it may not be more rapid at some periods than at others. Neither is it inconsistent with the fact that different traits develop at different rates and reach the limit of development at different times. The fact remains that, in spite of these fluctuations in development, manifestations of behaviour are the product of extensive underlying preparation and maturing. If one compares the mature with the immature status, tremendous contrasts result. When the process is investigated and the dynamics of development are charted, the progressiveness of change is sharply delineated. Terms like "expansion" and "emergence" are more applicable to the actual developmental course than those suggesting sudden transformations. This means that the customary process of distinguishing developments stages, and of dividing education into pre-school, kindergarten, primary, intermediate, junior-high-school, and senior-high-school periods is one of convenience only—a convenience, however, that often results in obscuring the gradual movement of the child from one of these arbitrary levels to another, the emergence of new behaviour from what has gone before, and the great variability among pupils in any one grade or level in mental age, reading ability, mathematical ability, social adjustment, and other characteristics.

Reference to Table 2.1 reveals at a glance the different rates at which certain traits develop. Although the child in question had a chronological age of 108 months, she had the mental development characteristic of a typical 134-month-old child and about the same level of reading ability.

Table 2.1 Cross-sectional data for girl, G1, at a chronological age of nine years[16]

Function measured	*Abbreviation*	*Age equivalent in months*
Height	H.A.	160
Reading	R.A.	130
Weight	W.A.	156
Strength of grip	G.A.	130
Ossification of hand and wrist	Ca.A.	135
Mental capacity	M.A.	134
Dental eruption	D.A.	119
Organismic age[17]	O.A.	138
Variability	A.D.	11.7
Chronological age	C.A.	108

16. W.C. Olson and B.O. Hughes, *Child Behaviour and Development* (New York: McGraw-Hill Book Company, Inc., 1943), chap. 12, "Growth of the child as a whole."

17. The concept of "organismic age" as used here is of doubtful meaning or value. It suggests more unity of development than the evidence justifies, and it arises out of an additive process that belies the term "Organismic." See F.T. Tyler, "Stability of Intra-Individual Patterning of Measures of Adjustment During Adolescence," *Journal of Educational Psychology* XLVIII (Apr., 1957), 217-226; and F.T. Tyler," Concepts of Organismic Growth: A Critique," *Journal of Educational Psychology*, XLIV (Oct., 1953), 321-342.

Figure 2.1 shows the developmental pattern of a "socially competent, mentally retarded girl" whose mental and educational development lagged behind her physical growth and social development. (For meanings of abbreviations, see Table 2.1)

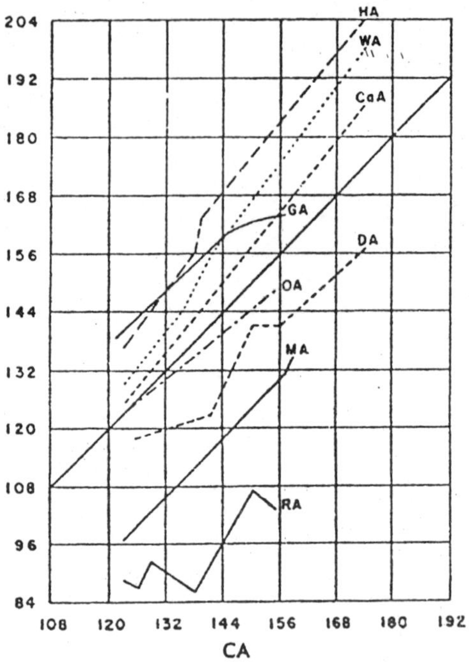

Fig. 2.1 Patterns of development for a socially competent, mentally retarded girl. *For meanings of abbreviations see Table 2.1. (From Olson, W.C. and B.O. Huges, "Concepts of Growth—Their Significance to Teachers," Childhood Education, 21 (Oct., 1944), p. 565).*

The child has many "ages:" The principle that various aspects of the personality may grow at different rates—or that one may develop at the expense of the other—has made chronological age an unreliable basis of estimating maturity. It saves the school principal or superintendent much friction with certain families in the community if entrance to school is made dependent on reaching a minimum chronological age, but this method of admission creates severe problems of curriculum adjustment for the first-grade teacher. Data on mental age, "physical age," "social age," "emotional age," and so on, are imperative for the adequate adjustment of children to the school environment at every level of education. Constant acceleration of the mentally gifted child will soon place him in a foreign community as far as his physical and social development are concerned. The dull pupil who lags farther and farther behind others of his own age may be fairly well classified mentally, but ultimately becomes something like a giant among the Lilliputians. The dull, retarded child may exercise unfortunate leadership among younger children because of his greater social and emotional maturity. Or, the oversized boy may take cut his resentment at his retardation by acting the bully and the brute. Perhaps even a more frequent result is elimination from school as a result of lack of interest, embarrassment at classification, and growing demand for participation in a grown-up world.

Inconsistencies in development are illustrated in persons who are fairly mature in many ways, but who still exhibit certain emotional reactions distinctly childish in level. Some college students, undeveloped in making choices and taking the consequences thereof without flinching, run for protection behind mother's skirts or dad's gruff voice when the first storm breaks. Many a grown woman manages her husband by recourse to a poorly disguised temper tantrum expressed in pouting, easy weeping, or constant nagging. The variations of the same childish means of getting one's desires satisfied are no less impressive in the behaviour of the male. The fraternity reunion is probably one of the best places to observe fixated emotional adolescence in the middle-aged.

Development of ability in problem-solving: An extremely significant corollary of the principle of continuity in development may be stated as follows: *Although traits develop at different rates, and reach their maximum at different times, simultaneous rather than serial development of broad mental functions is the rule.* Educational practice, however, would seem frequently to be based on a decidedly contrary assumption. For instance, although the young child has been thought capable of sensorimotor and associative learning to the extent of acquiring specific skills and information, it has often been assumed that he is incapable of problem-solving behaviour. There has been a pervasive belief, furthermore, that reasoning abilit, makes its appearance suddenly, and that it is primarily, if not entirely, the result of hereditary forces.

These doctrines have been in large part responsible for: (1) making the elementary school a drill school: (2) making a sharp distinction (in theory at least) in educational aims and methods of instruction between the grades and high school, and (3) neglecting systematic instruction in problem-solving.

Research, however, has shown that even the pre-school child is capable of problem-solving behaviour. One investigator[18] studied the problem-solving behaviour of forty-four children, ranging from nineteen to forty-four months of age, in a series of situations somewhat comparable to those used by Köhler with his chimpanzees.[19] One series of situations called for placing a block, a chair, a block turned on its perpendicular side, or a block piled on top of a box in such a way as to secure a suspended toy. For the second series, the children were placed in a play pen with the toy outside. To get the object, the child was required to reach through the bars with a stick, to substitute a broom for the stick, to use a short stick to reach another longer one, which in turn could be used to procure the toy, and to place two parts of a fishing rod together for a tool. Seventy-two per cent of the total possible number of solutions actually occurred. The solutions showed evidence of ability to recognize the problem, and to perceive and employ means for reaching the goal. The author declared that no matter what types of response to the problem situation was made, the behaviour culminated in a solution only when insight was attained.

Another study also showed that young children can discover and employ principles in the solution of problems.[20] The subjects were pre-school and orphanage children ranging in age from three years, six months, to seven years, ten months. It was necessary to discover an associative principle and transfer

18. A. Alpert, "Solving of Problem-Situations by Preschool Children" (Contributions to Education, No. 323. [New York: Teachers College, Columbia University, 1928]).
19. W. Köhler, *Mentality of Apes* (New York:) Harcourt, Brace & Company, 1926).
20. K.E. Roberts, "Learning in Pre-school and Orphange Children: An Experimental Study of Ability to Solve Different Situations According to the Same Plan" (University of Iowa Studies in Child Welfare, Vol. VII, No. 3 [Iowa City: University of Iowa Press, 1933]).

it in solving new situations. One of the most interesting results was that no relation existed between the number of trials in solving the first problem situation and the number necessary to master necessary the fourth and seventh, which were quite different from the first. Apparently the rapidity or slowness with which the principle was mastered in the beginning made no difference in its immediate transfer to new situations.

As the concepts of development should imply, competence in problem-solving increases with age. The young child is handicapped by meager experience, by inadequate language development, by inability to perceive subtle likenesses and differences, by lack of skill in overt behaviour, and so on. *But on his level of development,* the child is capable of rational behaviour. This fundamental truth should mean that at no stage should education be exclusively fact-getting or problem-solving. It means that insightful methods of learning should be employed to maximum extent at all times, that learning at every level should be creative and purposeful, and that discovery and verification should be substituted wherever possible for passive acceptance and rote memorization. If the acquisition of problem-solving ability is, like other functions, the result of a developmental process, is there not reason to believe that competence in this field is definitely conditioned by the adequacy of stimulation and learning activity throughout the developmental period? The sort of training that should facilitate the development of problem-solving ability cannot be detailed here, but it is fairly certain that competence in reasoning, though heavily dependent, perhaps, on genetic inheritance, does not appear by magic, or achieve maturity overnight.

Development of many functions proceeds most rapidly in this early years of life: *The mental development curve:* Although research has shown that after birth different bodily tissues show very different growth courses (see Fig. 2.2), it is nevertheless generally agreed that in infancy the rate of general physical growth probably is more rapid than at any subsequent time.[21]

The curve of growth of the body as a whole shows rapid progress in the early years, followed by a period of lesser rate,

21. J.A. Harries, C.M. Jackson, D.G. Paterson, and R.E. Scammon, *The Measurement of Man* (Minneapolis: University of Minnesota Press, 1930).

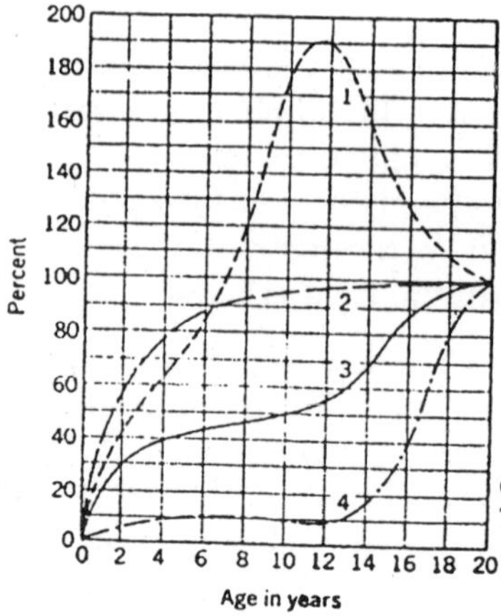

Lymphoid Type 1.
Thymus. Lymph-nodes intestinal lymphoid masses.
Neural Type. 2.
Brain and its parts, Dura, Spinal cord, Optic apparatus, many head dimensions.
General Type, 3.
Body as a whole, External dimensions (with exception of head and neck), Respiratory and digestive organs, Kidneys, Aorta and pulmonary trunks, Spleen, Musculature as a whole. Skeleton as a whole, Blood volume.
Genital Type, 4.
Testis, Ovary, Epididymus, Uterine tube, Prostate, Prostatic urethra, Seminal vesicles.

Fig. 2.2 Postnatal growth. Curves drawn to a common scale by computing their values at successive ages in terms of their postnatal increments (to 20 years). *(From Scammon, R.E. "The Measurement of the Body in Childhood," in the Measurement of Man, page 193. By permission of the University of Minnesota Press, publishers.)*

until another acceleration occurs ordinarily between twelve and fourteen. The course of mental development is still somewhat obscure. It is clear that at three years, the sense organs have reached a very high degree of functioning. At birth, the nervous system has attained one-fourth and at the age of six nine-tenths, of its adult weight. It is true that this rapid growth of the nervous system after birth does not necessarily mean that intelligence develops at a corresponding rate, but the results of mental measurements and studies showing the rapid development of behaviour in early years seemingly support the hypothesis of early acceleration of mental development. The problem of determining sceintifically the shape of the mental development curve is complicated by the difficulty of locating a zero-point, and also by the difficulty of constructing measuring instruments that employ a constant unit of increment of mental ability. The use of different mental tests and different methods of scaling these tests have resulted in different development curves. It is possible, also, that measurement of different aspects of mental development will show unlike curves.[22] Many of the curves that have been plotted, however, have taken a negatively accelerated form, something like the hypothetical one in Fig. 2.3. Figures 2.4 and 2.5 show curves suggested by Thurstone and Thorndike, respectively, which tend to support the conclusion that mental development is most rapid in early years.

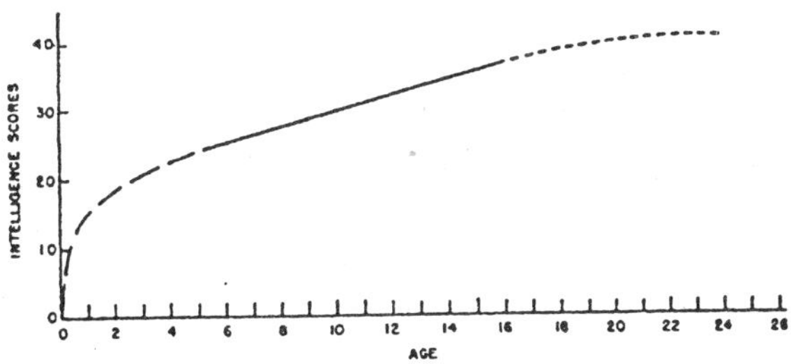

Fig. 2.3 Composite growth curve. The spaced part of the line is based on the work of Gesell; the solid part, upon numerous measures of growth as taken with group and individual intelligence tests; and the dotted part, upon the work of Thorndike. *(From Jordan, A.M., Educational Psychology, page 341. By permission of Henry Holt and Company, publishers.)*

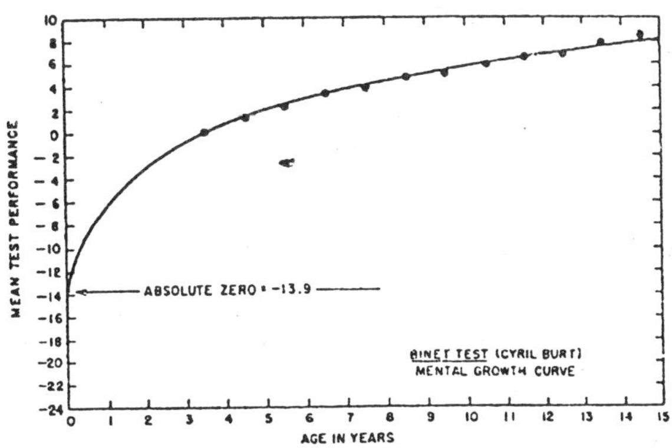

Fig. 2.4 Mental growth curve for the Binet Test. (From Thurstone, L.L., "The Absolute Zero in Intelligence Measurement," *Psychological Review, 35: page 196. reprinted by permission.)*

22. F.L. Goodenough,"The Measurement of Mental Growth in Childhood," in L. Carmichael (ed), *Manual of Child Psychology* (New York: John Wiley & Sons, Inc., 1946).

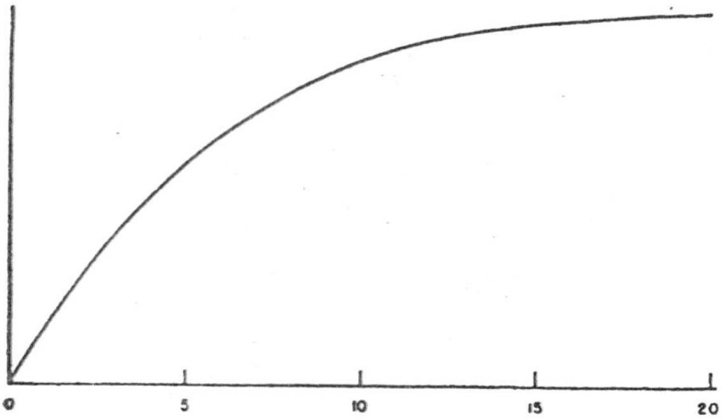

Fig.2.5 The general nature of the relation of attitude of intelligence to age in years, 0 to 20. *(From Thorndike, E.L., The Measurement of Intelligence, page 466. By permission of the Bureau of Publications, Teachers College, Columbia University, publishers.)*

Educational significance of early rapid development: It is clear that many functions develop concurrently in the individual. As we have said above, the child does not maiure in the ability to memorize before he develops any ability to solve problems. One sometimes hears it said that the purpose of the high school is to teach facts, whereas the purpose of the college is to teach how to think about facts. No such notion of serial development seems to be supported by the evidence. Therefore, the school should stimulate, or at least provide the opportunity or setting for simultaneous development in earlier years by providing a rich environment, and encouraging the fullest utilization of the child's capacities as the foundation for later accomplishment.

Basic trends in emotional and social adjustment may be established in the early, plastic years. However, the fixity of emotional conditioning before the age of five or six has probably been overemphasized, perhaps under the influence of Freudian theory. At any rate, recent studies of Vassar students have revealed that personality may change during college years. The senior investigator at Vassar has stated that, in comparison with freshmen, seniors exhibit the following qualities:

> Seniors have more cultivated tastes, broader interests, greater attachment to things of the mind. They are less authoritarian, less

conventional and conforming, less fundamentalist in religions outlook; they show awareness and appreciation of the diversity of viewpoints and standards adopted by others, are more liberal in their views on interpersonal relationships.... They are well ahead of the freshmen in flexibility of thinking, capacity to suspend judgment, tolerance of ambiguity, skepticism, criticalness, realism."[23]

Nevertheless, the seniors seemed to be more uncertain, somewhat confused about their future role, more unstable in the sense that they had throw off traditional values without having established new ones of their own. However, this uncertainty and confusion created heightened educability—an opportunity for further growth that perhaps should have arisen earlier in the students' careers.

Although it does appear that significant changes in personality may occur during the college years, the possibilities of development at this time are by no means independent of the social and emotional characteristics the student has acquired earlier. It is conceivable that more appropriate preparation would enable the college student to take better advantage of the opportunities for fuller development that college should provide.

"Patterns of behaviour in all species tend to follow an orderly genetic sequence in their emergence:" This generalization is quoted from Gesell and means that the order in which various developmental traits appear varies but little from one organism to another of the same species.[24] Gesell believes that "this genetic sequence is itself an expression of elaborate pattern—a pattern whose basic outline is the product of evolution and is under the influence of maturational factors." In other words, he believes the developmental order to be due primarily to hereditary growth factors. This orderliness of growth in large part makes mental testing possible, since it greatly reduces the necessary extent of sampling. In other words, if a child cannot perform one task of a known developmental series,

23. N. Sanford,unpublished paper. For a preliminary account of the Vassar studies edited by Dr. Sanford, see "Personality Development in the College Years," *The Journal of Social Issues*, XII, No.4 (1956)
24. A. Cesell, "Maturation and the Patterning of Behaviour," in C. Murchison (ed.), *Handbook of Child Psychology* (rev. ed.; Wercester,Mass.: Clark University Press, 1933).

it is unlikely that he will be able to do one that regularly develops later. For instance, a child can copy a square (years 5 in the recent revision of the Stanford Binet scale) Before he can reproduce a diamond (year 7); and if he cannot do the former, it is rather certain that he cannot do the latter. The items that make up the Stanford-Binet scale represent a fairly orderly development sequence. Gesell has provided normative schedules of development in many aspects of infant behaviour.[25] The following is a synopsis of reactions to a pellet placed before the infants.[26]

12 weeks	Transient regard for pellet (rarely).
16 weeks	More prolonged regard, usually delayed.
20 weeks	Immediate, definite regard, sometimes with increased handarm activity.
24 weeks	Approaches pellet with pronate hand; contacts pellet with little or no finger adjustment.
28 weeks	Approaches pellet with raking flexion of fingers, without thumb opposition; occasional delayed plamar prehension.
32 weeks	Approaches pellet with raking flexion but with increased thumb participation and digital prehension.
36 weeks	Approaches and contacts with simultaneous flexion of fingers; prehends with defined thumb and index opposition.
40 weeks	Approaches with all fingers extended; contacts with index finger and later by prehends by drawing index finger against thumb.
44 weeks	Promptly prehends with index and thumb and with increased obliquity of hand attitude.
48 weeks	Approaches with index finger extended and lateral digits flexed; prehends with delimited plucking by index and thumb.
52 weeks	Approaches and plucks pincer-wise increased deftness.

Relative developmental rates of individuals tend to remain constant from infancy to maturity: Individuals differ at birth, and the relative position of a given number of them not only tends to remain the same throughout the developmental period, but the absolute differences increase with age. The short

25. A. Gesell and H. Thompson, *Infant Behaviour: Its Genesis and Growth* (New York: McGraw-Hill Book Company, Inc., 1934.

26. *Ibid.*, p. 310; a fuller account of Gesell's point of views with an exposition of several "Principles" of development may be found in "The Ontogenesis of Infant Behaviour," in Carmichael (ed), *op. cit.*, pp. 355-373.

of stature remain short, and the dull of intellect remain dull. Gifted children tend to maintain their superior status into maturity. Studies have shown that there is a positive relationship between level of intelligence in adulthood and in childhood.

The fact that the relative rates of development that may be determined for different individuals in infancy and early childhood tend to be maintained until maturity is of great importance in educational guidance. Since not only the individual's rate but also the ultimate altitude, of his mental development may be estimated earlier, it is possible to estimate in advance approximately the amount and general type of education that will be best fitted to the individual. Here as elsewhere in interpreting human behaviour, the teacher must remember that there may be individual exceptions to the general rule, and that it is undesirable to make prognoses from a single administration of a mental test, or, in the case of group examinations, from a single test, or from mental tests given at too early an age.

Development is a process both of differentiation and of integration: *Differentiation in behaviour:* Although they used different kinds of units, most of the older psychologies described the formation of complex behaviour patterns as the synthesis, or integration, of smaller elements. The structuralist, for instance, considered the elements out of which complex mental processes were compounded to be sensations, images, and simple feelings. The behaviourist's units were simple reflexes. Recent experimentation in biology and psychology has shown, however, that the reflexes that the behaviourist compounded were often earlier derived from larger, less particularized, and less localized patterns of behaviour. This process of emergence of localized behaviour has become better known as the process of differentiation . Thus, Coghill has developed the thesis that "smaller or partial patterns arise by a process of individuation or analysis within a larger pattern, and that the primary pattern is a total reaction which normally expands from the first as an integrated process."[27]

Illustrations of differentiation: This process of individuation of localized reflexes from organismic patterns has been

27. G.E .Coghill, "Individuation versus Integration in the Development of Behaviour," *Journal of Genetic Psychology*, III (1930), 431-435

proceeding in the prenatal period, so that certain of these specific reactions are functional at birth. Nevertheless, Irwin has characterized the typical behaviour of the newborn infant as "mass activity," in which the body as a whole seems to participate,[28] and has described the course of development as one from generalized to specific responses. This process can be observed in many aspects of behaviour. The use of the fingers in grasping is a late stage of differentiation that extends from the shoulder and upper arm to the elbow, forearm, wrist, hand, and digits. Irwin believes that crying in newborn infants is a component of mass activity, and that the first differentiation is the hunger cry.[29] Language development shows the same phenomenon. The child may first use the word "daddy" in greeting many men; later application to one person only is the result of a differentiation process. Children's drawings show progressive development from gross outlines to recognition and use of more and more detail. Word recognition, at first the result of perception of general form or dominant striking detail, finally depends upon perception of minute details.

Development through integration: Carmichael, long a student of the earliest manifestations of behaviour, has said that as a very broad generalization, "...an excellent case can be made out for the view that *individuation* is the pattern of all development, including all learning, but certainly in the experimental situation the concept of the *integration* or the combination of responses also provides, at times, a convenient working hypothesis."[30] Although specific responses may arise out of less differentiated behaviour, they can be integrated to form new and more complex patterns.

McGraw, as the result of the careful observation of development of many types of behaviour in very young children—

---

28. O.C. Irwin, "Amount and Nature of Activities of Newborn Infants Under Constant Stimulating Conditions During the first Ten Days of Life," *Genetic Psychology Monographs*, VIII. No. 1 (Worcester, Mass.: Clark University Press, 1930).
29. O.C. Irwin, "Differentiation of Human Behaviour," *Psychological Review*, XXXIX. No. 4. (July, 1932), 390.
30. L. Carmichael," The Onset and Early Development of Behaviour," in Carmichael. (ed.), *op. cit.*, pp. 60-185.

swimming, ascending and descending inclines, roller skating, and so on—describes the process of integration as follows:

> ...development in behaviour embraces both a process of narrowing down the activity to minimum essentials and a process of knitting together or integrating two or more aspects of a particular behaviour pattern... During the early stages of development the most obvious process appears to be from the general to the specific, but once an aspect of a pattern has attained a certain degree of determinateness, then the process of development becomes essentially one of integration.[31]

Many of our acts of skill involve the selection of already formed reactions and their reorganization, perhaps with other responses, into a new pattern. The development of concepts, or meanings, is a process of refinement that includes, on the one hand, a restriction of particulars to which the class name applies, and, on the other, an inclusion of more concrete items. Thus, development may appear at times to be primarily a process of emergence of specific behaviour from more generalized types of response. At other times it may seem to be mainly a matter of building up larger processes from smaller ones. Actually, development is probably a process in which both differentiation and integration play a parallel, though not always a coordinate, role.

The effect of a specific training varies with the stage of maturation reached by the organism: *Meaning of maturation:* Are there not some forms of behaviour, such as walking and stair-climbing, that develop primarily as an inner growth process, and take form largely without specific training? Some psychologists believe so. Gesell, for instance, wrote: "The nervous system grows according to its own intrinsic pattern and thereby establishes the primary forms of behaviour. These forms are not determined by stimulation from the outside world. Experience has nothing specifically to do with them...."[32]

More recently Gesell has written: "The so-called environment, whether internal or external, does not generate the progressions of development. Environmental factors support, inflect, and specify; but they do not engender the basis forms

31. McGraw, *op.cit.*, p.190.
32. A. Gesell, "Maturation and the Pattering of Behaviour," in Carmichael (ed)., *op. cit.*

and sequences of ontogenesis."[33] Gesell calls this intrinsic growth "maturation." But it is clear that stimulation of some sort is necessary for every form of growth. Therefore, Stoddard and Wellman offer a better definition of maturation as "the expected growth and development of an organism under nutritive and *stimulatory conditions within the normal range.*"[34] (Italics mine) Maturation, then, from the present writer's point of view, is development that will proceed fairly even in the face rather wide variations in environmental conditions.

Maturation versus specific training: Several experiments have been performed that purport to show the relative influence of maturation and specific training in acquisition of behaviour. Gesell and Thompson gave Twin T of an identical pair "daily training" in stair-climbing for six weeks, beginning at the age of forty-six weeks. During this time, Twin C was deprived of specific training in the function. At fifty-two weeks, Twin T climbed the stairs in twenty-six seconds. "Twin C, at the age of fifty-three weeks, without any previous training, climbed the same staircase unaided in forty-five seconds. After two weeks of training...Twin C climbed the stairs in ten seconds. The climbing performance of Twin C at fifty-five weeks was far superior to the climbing performance of Twin T at fifty-two weeks, even though Twin T had been trained seven weeks earlier and three times longer. The maturity advantage of three weeks of age must account for this superiority."[35]

There is no space for summarizing other such studies, but the conclusions of most of them have been criticized on one or both of the following grounds: (1) Training was confused with mere repetition or practice; (2) the controls, although not specifically trained, may have been acquiring other reactions easily transferred to the experimental situation.

There is still a widespread belief, however, that an underlying process of growth, with no more than incidental

33. A. Gesell, "The Ontogenesis of Infant Behaviour," in Carmichael (ed), *op. cit.*, pp. 335-373.
34. G.D. Stoddard and B.L. Wellman, *Child Psychology* (New York: The Macmillan Company, 1934), pp. 194 ff.
35. A. Gesell, in Murchison (ed.), *op.cit.*

experience, at least, is responsible for the emergence of certain aspects of behaviour, or that such an underlying process must occur before special training or practice or stimulation is likely to be productive. Gesell has stated that, "The role of maturation is most conspicuous in the fetus and infant, but it persists throughout the life cycle until the growth potential completely subsides."[36]

Dependence of training on maturation: Astute training given at the right level of maturation might lead to astonishing acquisition of skill by very young children. McGraw has reported that one of the twins with whom she experimented was introduced to roller skates at the age of 350 days and acquired, at the age of 694 days, or less than two years, reactions that "consisted primarily of the broad, rhythmical body sway which is characteristic of a professional skater." McGraw points out that specific training may be given too early or too late in terms of the maturational pattern. She discovered, for instance, that the most economical time to learn skating is when the baby is just beginning to gain equilibratory control.[37]

Little is known about the placement of educational activities in relation to level of maturation and amount and character of previous experience, but it constitutes one of the most important problems of educational research.

Although preliminary research indicated that a mental age of six years and six months was necessary for economical learning in reading, later evidence has shown that children with mental ages below that point can learn to read successfully if appropriate methods are used and adapted to the backgrounds of individual children.

In recent years, there has been a tendency to move the grade placement of arithmetic processes upward, presumably deferring them until pupils are more "ready" to learn them or more capable of understanding them. This may have been desirable, to a degree, but it also may well have gone too far. This is suggested, at least, by a recent comparison of the

36. A. Gesell, "The Ontogenesis of Infant Behaviour," in Carmichael (ed.), *op. cit.*, pp. 335-373.
37. McGraw, *op. cit.*, p. 241.

achievement of eleven-year-old pupils in England and California. A test given to pupils in a stratified random sample of English schools was adapted to American use, and given to pupils in a stratified random sample of urban and rural schools in central California. The average scores on a 70-item test of computation and verbal problem-solving were 29.1 for the English pupils and 12.1 for those in California.

An analysis of the placement of the topics of the test in the arithmetic curriculum revealed that many of them appeared at an earlier level in the English schools. Other factors also might have accounted for a part of the difference in achievement, such as the much greater mobility of the California school population; the fact that English schools admit pupils at age five, whereas those in California admit children to the first grade at age six (kindergarten at age five); and so on. But the difference in the age at which children study certain arithmetical processes is undoubtedly one of the principal reasons for the difference found.[38]

Readiness to learn any task is a complex of many factors, the relative importance of which may be different at different stages. These factors include such things as anatomical structure, physiological development, interest and motivation, preparatory learning, richness of previous experience, extent of language development, adequacy of fundamental concepts and meanings, and the setting in which learning takes place. Although it is obvious that there is probably an optimum placement of learning tasks for a given person, it is very difficult to determine the best order. Important as it is, relatively little is known about the problem of curricular sequence in relation to development. The problem is complicated enormously by the fact of great individual differences in rate of development.

There are wide individual differences in development patterns: That development is a highly individual matter is illustrated by Fig. 2.6, which shows contrasting patterns of development in reading ability for two girls of equal mental

38. G.T. Buswell, "A Comparison of Achievement in Arithmetic in England and Central California," *The Arithmetic Teacher*, V (Feb., 1958), 1-9.

ability. Although between the ages of ten and eleven the two girls had attained about the same reading age ("A" reached a higher level later), the curves from six on were quite different. Whereas "A" showed rapid improvement from the beginning, "B" got a slow start, and then, at age nine, began to progress rapidly and maintained the sport until she overtook "A" one and one-half years later. The authors who reported these data also stated that among 56 individual developmental curves in reading, they did not find one of the shape that would be indicated by average values or norms.[39]

Individual differences in rate and pattern of growth make it clear that uniform treatment of childern at any level or in any subject is unsound. The same learning activities, the same subject

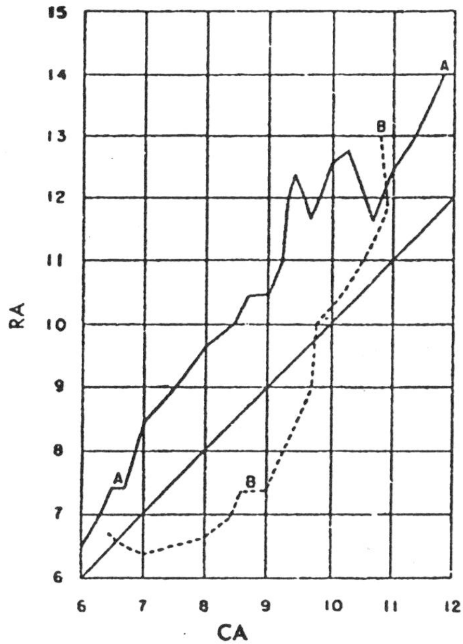

Fig. 2.6 Contrasted patterns of growth in reading in two girls of equal mental ability but unequal total maturity. *(Reproduced by the permission of the Michigan Education Association.)*

39. W.C. Olson and B.O. Hughes, "Concepts of Growth—Their Significance to Teachers," *Childhood Education*, XXX (Oct., 1944), 53-63.

matter, or the same teaching methods will not evoke the same responses or achievement from different children at a given time. Furthermore children are never passive recipients in relation to their environment. They tend to seek out experiences or to reject some forms of stimulation, including teaching. He is a skilful teacher who can adjust curriculum and methods to the particular growth characteristics of individual children.

A review of the nature of development shows the inappropriateness and ineffectiveness of grade classification and of the practice of grouping children in terms of general ability. Children grouped on the basis of mental age may differ widely in reading age. Likewise, children grouped somewhat homogeneously on the basis of reading age may differ widely in their arithmetical achievement. If the teacher resorts to "ability grouping," he will have to classify pupils in one way for one purpose and in different ways for other purposes. Even then, differences in developmental pattern may make common treatment ineffective.

The range of individual differences in a single grade is very great—variations of from six to ten years in reading age in sixth grades have been found, for example. A "strict" promotion standard in which pupils who do not meet a given level of achievement are not promoted does not materially decrease the variability within grade groups. The teacher still has to struggle with the same range of individual differences, and emotional and social problems may be created by children who fall far behind their age group. Neither strict promotion standards nor one or another kind of grouping will eliminate the need for individual treatment.[40]

Finally, it is obvious from developmental data that uniform standards of accomplishment should not be established for all children. Since potentialities differ greatly, the ultimate levels that children may reach will vary accordingly. And since those who finally reach approximately the same level of development may approach it by different patterns, it is unwise to expect all of them

40. W.W. Cook, *Grouping and Promition in the Elementary School*, (Minneapoils: University of Minnesota Press, 1941).

to progress uniformly. All children are capable of certain kinds and certain degrees of development, however, and individual achievement should not be measured in terms of common standards, but in relation to individual possibilities and patterns.

The child tends to use his abilities spontaneously: Jersild has written that as the child's "...capacities for doing, thinking, and feeling emerge in the process of growth he has an impulse to put them to use." He calls this the principle of *indigenous motivation*, and takes issue with the essentially negative view that motivation is to be interpreted merely as an effort to escape from, or to overcome, irritants and obstacles. Jersild believes, on the contrary, that

> ...living involves a positive striving...According to this view, it is natural to seek, to strive, to struggle toward a kind of self-fulfillment.... The healthy child, like the healthy youth and oldster, is constantly involved in a process of self-realization. This does not mean that he does not deal with irritants and cope with frustrations...The main point is that there is a forward impetus to growth; a growing child seeks to be himself, to discover himself to realize his resources. for standing independently on his own feet, and also for being deeply involved in interpersonal relations with others. In this process he must risk and venture, and this may mean failure as well as success, painful consequences as well as pleasant rewards.[41]

Instead of simply waiting for what comes, so to speak, the child tends to search, to explore, to seek out new stimuli. In the earlier years of schooling, this eager, often creative, behaviour is especially prominent. Many observers, however, have noted that this active interest, this creativity, often wanes as the child reaches the upper grades and the high school. It is doubtful that this change is an inherent aspect of development. It is likely that the school fails to give opportunity for seeking behaviour, or fails to reward it, or actually, in some instances, punishes and blunts it. If so, the school checks the impetus to development of the individual's potentialities.

EDUCATION AS CAPACITY FOR FUTURE DEVELOPMENT

How during the plastic years, under the guidance of educative procedures, may the individual attain a power of

41. Jersild, *op. cit.*, pp. 23, 24.

intelligent self-direction that will lead to progressive adaptation to the changing conditions of adult life?

Continued development may be made possible by the acquisition of certain controls of conduct, among which the following would seem to be of paramount importance: (1) permanent interests and attainable, but not too immediate, goals and purposes; (2) economical techniques of learning and unlearning: (3) competence in problem-solving; (4) self-dependence and emotional maturity; (5) attitudes of tolerance of change, of self-criticism, and of open-mindedness; and (6) a mature concept of the self and its possibilities of accomplishment.

The thesis of this chapter is that outcomes such as these are acquired through a process of development. The intrinsic factors in the process are laid down in inheritance, but many of the external factors that will determine the extent to which potentialities will be realized are under the control of teachers and school administrators.

DECLINE OF ABILITIES

It is desirable for man to continue learning throughout adulthood, but is it possible? This question suggests others of importance: At what age do increments in ability of various sorts cease? How rapidly so various abilities of man decline? Is the decline of ability due more to inherent deterioration than to the deleterious effects of undesirable habits, loss of interest, unfortunate attitudes, and the like, acquired by the individual? There is opportunity here merely to outline briefly, and in many instances tentatively, the results of research undertaken to provide answers to the foregoing questions.

Terman originally estimated that, in the average person, mental development as measured by the Stanford revision of the Binet scale ceases at age sixteen, and subsequently concluded that the peak is reached even earlier. Other evidence indicates, however, that when a test capable of revealing increments at the upper levels is used, the peak is more nearly attained somewhere near twenty, or even beyond; a recent investigation indicated a peak of thirty on a verbal, and twenty to twenty-four on a performance measure. The developmental curve of learning capacity plotted by Thorndike (see Fig.2.7) shows a maximum between the twentieth and twenty-fifth years, and declines thereafter very slowly to age forty-five.

The peak of development and rate of decline probably vary considerably for different abilities. (Some abilities, such as knowledge of vocabulary, may show no decline for a long period.) Thorndike concluded after conducting many experiments on adult learning that the general tendency was a decline of about fifteen per cent between the ages of twenty-two and fory-two.[42] It was estimated that the ability to learn school subjects between the ages of twenty-one and forty-one declined about one-half of one per cent per year. Declines seem to be greater in the kinds of learning done in school, and less in learning situations and activities more characteristic of adult experience. Remoteness in time from formal schooling also affects the results, and timed tests indicate more deterioration than power tests. Such findings suggest that decline in learning ability in adults is due less to loss in sheer capacity than to other factors.[43]

Thorndike declares that "unless" it is counterbalanced by factors acting in the opposite direction, *inner growth* gives the person from twenty-five to forty-five as good an ability to learn as he had from twenty to twenty-five, a better ability than he

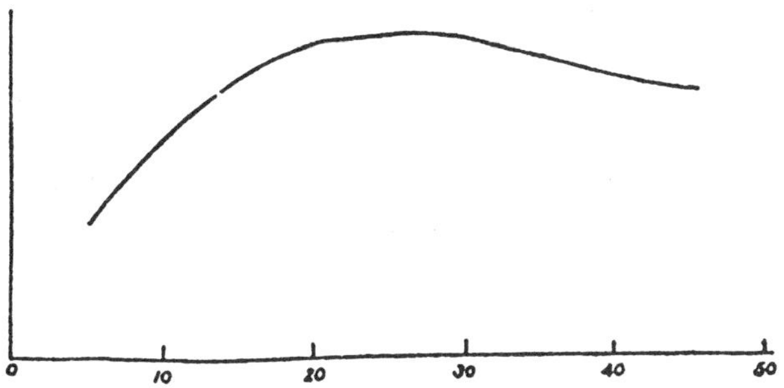

Fig. 2.7 The general form of the curve of ability to learn in relation to age. (*From Thorndike, E.L., Adult Learning, page 127. By permission of The Macmillan Company, publishers.)*

42. E.L. Thorndike, *et.al.*, *Adult Learning* (New York: The Macmillan Company, 1928).
43. I. Lorge and F. Ruch, "Adult Intelligence," *Encyclopedia of Educational Research* (New York: The Macmillan Company, 1950), pp. 32-35.

had from fifteen to twenty, and a much better ability than he had from five to fifteen." He ascribes the reduction in learning by adults primarily to abatement of interest in new adjustments rather than to deterioration in sheer ability.

The relative effect of inner change and that of habits, sets, and attitudes in accounting for the decline of abilities is not quantitatively known. It is evident, however, that lack of desire to learn, inadequate methods of learning, and interference of old habits and ideas often have, in fact, much to do with the inferiority of adult learning.

Decline appears earlier and more regularly in the more purely anatomical and physiological functions, such as sensory acuity. and is less evident in those predominantly "intellectual." Deterioration shows up more prominently in tasks where speed is an important factor. The old have great difficulty in learning that conflicts with well-established habits or that demands a complex reorganization of them. Memory shows much greater deterioration than imagination and judgment. Furthermore, tests have shown that older persons possess more information, and have a more extensive vocabulary than younger persons. These assets may offset, for some time, the gradual but slow deterioration of sheer learning ability.

The peak of development, and the onset and rate of decline, seem to differ, not only with the type of ability measured, but also with the level of ability of the subjects. Several studies have shown that average intelligence test scores of college students increase over the four-year period. A recent investigation showed that verbal ability may continue to increase well beyond college age in gifted individuals. Some 954 subjects involved in Terman's studies of the gifted—422 men and 346 women—were given the *Concept Mastery Test,* a difficult verbal test, first at averages age twenty-nine and one half and again at forty-one and one half. The average scores of both men and women were consistently higher on the second administration, both on the total test, and on the subsections composed of analogies and of synonyms and antonyms. Furthermore, average increases occurred in all the occupations represented (all these occupations were at the professional level) and in all the educational levels (no one of which was below high-school graduation or equivalent), and in all age groups (through fifty).[44]

Another question of general interest is the age at which the most creative work is done. The evidence has been summarized as follows:

> Data regarding notable achievements show that the best creative work tends to be done early in the prime—in the twenties and thirties—with remarkable poetry and musical compositions appearing sometimes in the teens. In general, creative workers tend to be precocious; and though they often continue productivity into old age, later work is likely to be less brilliant than that produced earlier. Also, those who produce most usually begin earlier...Somewhat in contrast, great leadership comes at later ages—military leadership most often appearing in the forties and political and business leadership in the fifties and sixties. And leadership is now tending to come even later—perhaps because of longer life, seniority rules, and the like. Development and change in the nature of abilities through adult life seem clearly suggested. And favouring or handicapping factors in the environment are also shown to be increasingly important.[45]

The aging process has become in recent years a subject of increasing interest and investigation. We are certain to learn much more about the differential development and decline of human abilities. But we already know enough to realize that if they desire to do so, and if they enjoy appropriate opportunities, individuals may continue to perform acceptably in a wide range of abilities and activities into later years, often beyond retirement. One of education's tasks is to provide stimuli to accomplishment throughout the life span.

—*T.R. McConnell*

Questions and Exercises (for discussion and study)

1. Make a study of the ways in which the individual acquires a self-concept.

---

44. N. Bayley and M.H. Oden, "The Maintenance of Intellectual Ability in Gifted Adults," *Journal of Gerontology*, X (1955), 91-107.
45. S.L. Pressey and R.G. Kuhlen, *Psychological Development Through the Life Span* (New York: Harper & Brothers, 1957), p. 161.

2. Criticize the concept of "development tasks." Is "tasks" an appropriate term? How have the "tasks" of any period of development been determined? Is the method valid?
3. If development is not unitary, can some of the phases of development, social and emotional, for example, nevertheless be interdependent?
4. Discuss the significance of this quotation: "...for most adolescents or young adults, self-actualization involves a real problem of renunciation of parts of the self that can never come to fruition." (L.E. Tyler, op.cit.)
5. What are some of thc far-reaching choices to be made by the individual in the course of his education, and at what points are these choices to be made?
6 Argue the case for or against annual promotion.
7 Design a study to compare changes in intelligence test scores of students who continue their formal education beyond the high school and those who do not.
8. Make a study of the relationship of "social class" and intelligence. What problem do differences in cultural and social status create in intelligence testing?
9. What phases of school organization and management make it difficult to base the pupil's progress on his development?
10. How would you define giftedness? How may giftedness (as you define it) be identified? What educational adaptations for the gifted would you propose?
11. Assume that substantial changes in personality characteristics are found to have occurred among a group of college students between freshman and senior years. Can the changes be ascribed to the college environment?
12. It has been customary to determine entrance to the English grammar school, which (with exceptions that need not be noted here) is the only avenue to the English university, on the basis of an examination at age 11-plus. Evaluate this procedure.

References

American Educational Research Association, "Growth, Development, and Learning," *Review of Educational Research* (Washington, D. C.), XXV No. 5 (Dec., 1995).

Carmichael, L. (ed.), *Manual of Child Psychology*. New York: John Wiley & Sons, Inc., 1954.

Gesell, A., F.L. Ilg, L.B. Ames, and G.E. Bulles, *The Child from Five to Ten*. New York: Harper & Brothers, 1946.

Havighurst, R.J., *Human Development and Education*. New York: Longmans, Green, & Co., Inc., 1953.

Jersild, A. T., *Child Psychology*, 4th ed. Englewood Cliffs, N.J.: Prentice Hall, Inc.,; 1954.

——. *The Psychology of Adolescence*. New York: The Macmillian Company, 1957.

Merry, F.K., and R.V.Merry. *The First Two Decades of Life*. New York: Harper & Brothers, 1958.

3

Mental Growth and Development

There are available many studies bearing on the nature of mental growth and intelligence. However, mental processes are so complex that it has been difficult to determine their functional potentialities. In a broad sense, mental development includes the abilities in memory, imagination, language, percepts, concepts, and problem-solving ability. Intelligence tests were developed in the early part of the present century in an effort to measure more accurately the mental abilities and potentialities of children. A vast amount of research has been conducted on the development and use of these instruments. The complexity of mental development makes the task of measuring intellectual development a very difficult one. A study of the identifiable factors related to mental growth and development should be useful to the teacher and others, for a better understanding of the mental development of children at different age levels. The materials of this chapter will be especially concerned with the following aspects of mental growth and development:

1. The growth of intelligence
2. Language development
3. The development of concepts
4. The growth of problem-solving ability

GROWTH OF INTELLIGENCE

Nature of Intelligence: Following the development of intelligence tests near the beginning of this century, many studies were conducted in an effort to measure intelligence. The nature of intelligence has challenged the thinking of many investigators. Binet, one of the earliest investigators, described intelligence as directness of thought, capacity for making adaptations, and auto-criticism. Others described intelligence as the ability to adapt to new problems or situations. Terman has defined intelligence in terms of the ability to carry on abstract thinking. Based on results from more recent research studies, a large number of investigators have challenged these definitions.

To arrive at a more accurate notion of the nature of intelligence, we should first distinguish between intelligence as an inherited potential ability and intelligence as measured by intelligence test. Actually, the only intelligence we know anything about is that manifested in some performance or on some intelligence test. Intelligence as an inborn capacity is to a large degree an abstraction, and is not subject to direct measurement. It might be more accurate to refer to a child's intelligence test score than to his intelligence. Intelligence as used in the subsequent discussions refers to that which is determined from intelligence test scores. Careful studies of the results of repeated tests on the same subject have furnished useful data about the growth of intelligence.

Mental growth curves: The data available about mental growth are based on results of intelligence test scores secured from the same individuals repeatedly for a number of years. Freeman reported results from a study in which tests were administered over a period of years.[1] The average mental growth curves for three groups of children who had different degrees of mental ability to start with are presented in Fig. 3.1. These curves show that each group retains its relative position from one age to another. There are, however, wide individual variations in the rate of mental growth.

It will be noted from a study of Fig.3.1 that the group of children superior at an earlier age remained superior throughout the years of this study, which comprised the school years. One must be careful in generalizing too freely from these data. It was pointed out that children differ in their rate of growth. Because a child develops slowly, it must not be concluded that he is

1. F. N. Freeman, "Intellectual Growth of Children as indicated by Repeated Tests," *Psychological Monographs*, XLVII, No. 212 (1936), 20-34.

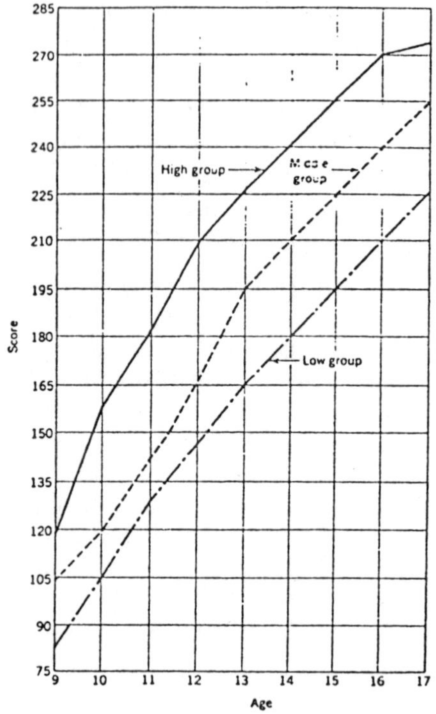

Fig. 3.1 Mean scores for three groups of pupils from eleven to sixteen with consecutive tests. (After Freeman.)

mentally inferior. Neither should it be assumed that if he develops rapidly he is mentally superior. The rate of mental growth of a particular child will depend upon a number of factors, some of which are: 1. the child's pattern of development, 2. environmental conditions, 3. psychological and social forces in his environment, and 4. the nature of the test used in evaluating mental growth.

Consistency of intelligence test scores: The problem of the consistency of intelligence test from year to year has been given considerable attention by educational psychologists. This issue has been referred to as "the constancy of the intelligence quotient (IQ)." The central problem involved is whether an adverse environment will lower the IQ or whether a superior environment will raise the IQ.

The concept one has of "intelligence" has an important bearing on the problem of the stability of the IQ. Certainly we cannot hope to raise the level of one's inherited potentialities. Furthermore, it is not possible to measure inborn capacity. However, intelligence test scores may be obtained on individuals based upon the number of exercises or problems they are able to complete in a given period of time. Long-term growth curves of children and adolescents, based on intelligence test scores, show that although there is a relatively high degree of consistency in intelligence test ratings from year to year at the school age for most individuals, significant changes or fluctuations may be observed frequently. The scores of subject number 1541 of Fig.3.2 illustrate a gradual and stable increase, whereas the scores of subject number 1130 illustrate an irregular increase. Many factors have been assigned to account for these variations. It appears, however, that an explanation must be sought primarily in the nature of the individuals concerned and

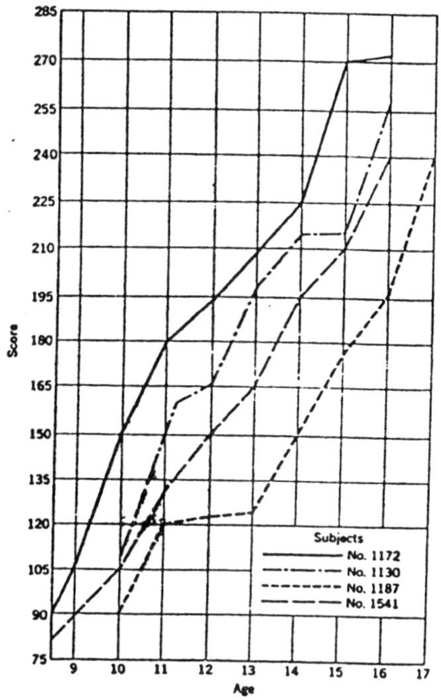

Fig. 3.2 Selected individual mental growth curves. (After Freeman)

in the various forces that have affected them in the past and may be currently affecting them.

MENTAL GROWTH OF DIFFERENT FUNCTIONS

Although most of us think of mental growth in terms of general capacity to adjust, to learn, or to solve problems of increasing complexity, psycologists have also found it worthwhile to consider the growth of different mental functions or processes. Studies show that the pattern of development of these different functions is not uniform. The curves of growth of four of the eleven tests of the *Wechsler Intelligence Scale for Children,* presented in Fig. 3.3, show the general trend and pattern of mental growth processes during the elementary school years[2]. These curves show roughly the proportion of fifteen-year mental maturity attained at the different age levels. The early rate of mental growth for digit span is faster than that for the other processes, since by seven and one-half years a level of maturity is reached that is not reached in the other mental processes until the age of ten and one-half years.

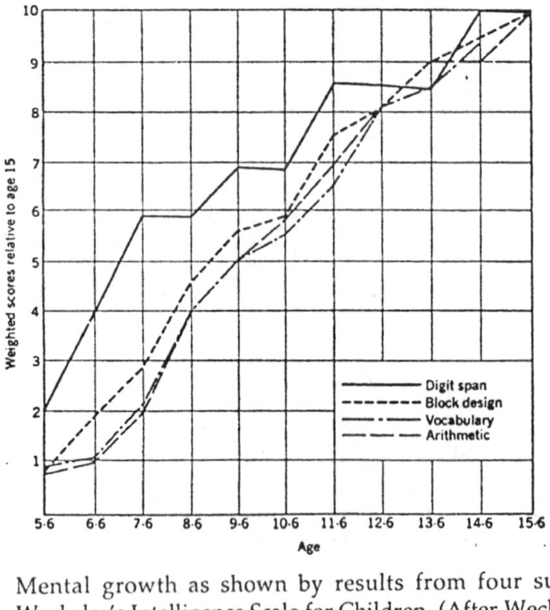

Fig. 3.3 Mental growth as shown by results from four subtests of Wechsler's Intelligence Scale for Children. (After Wechsler)

2. D. Wechsler, "Intellectual Development and Psychological Maturity," *Child Development*, XXI (1950), 45-50.

Age of cessation of mental growth: When individual tests are repeated from year to year, an increase in ability is usually found. The question may be raised: At what age does this increase in intelligence test scores cease? It was pointed out earlier that the pattern of mental growth is not identical for all individuals. Neither is the pattern the same for all mental functions. Thus, the age of cessation of mental growth will vary with different individuals and with different mental functions.

The age at which individuals cease to grow in intelligence has been estimated from thirteen and one-half years to some time in the twenties or even much later. These differences, obtained by different investigators of this problem, may be accounted for by the differences in mental functions being measured by the tests used for evaluating intelligence. Where *speed* is an important factor, the older or more mature person appears to be at a disadvantage. Where *information* or *logical thinking* is an important function being measured, the older or more mature person may be at an advantage. Freeman and Flory[3] reported results from the Chicago Growth Study in which tests were administered to several hundred at the age of seventeen or eighteen years. Some of these were later tested in college. A composite of four standardized tests consisting of 1. vocabulary, 2. analogies, 3. completion, and 4. opposites was used. The growth curves drawn from the raw scores showed that mental development continues well beyond the age of seventeen or eighteen years. There was also some evidence from these data that the children of average ability might continue intellectual growth to a somewhat later age than the brighter pupils. This, however, is in all likelihood a result of the failure of the average environment to present opportunities for stimulation in such a way as to continue an accelerated rate of mental growth on the part of the bright pupil.

The results of the study reported by Freeman and Flory are substantiated by data reported by Bayley.[4] Thirty-three subjects

3. F. N. Freeman and C.D. Flory, "Growth in Intellectual Ability as Measured by Repeated Tests," *Monographs of the Society for Research in Child Development*, II (1937), 116.
4. N. Bayley, "Data on the Growth of Intelligence between 16 and 21 Years as Measured by the Wechsler-Bellevue Scale," *Journal of Genetic Psychology*, XC (1957), 3-15.

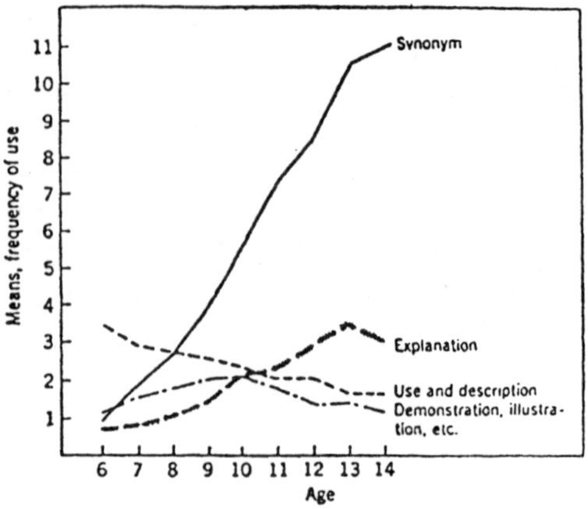

Fig. 3.4 Mean frequency of use of qualitative language categories by age. (After Feifil and Lorge.)

of the Berkeley Growth Study took the *Wechsler-Bellevue Intelligence Scale* at sixteen, eighteen, and twenty-one years of age. The results indicate that intellectual functions continue to improve through twenty-one years and probably beyond. The gains occur at all levels of intelligence found in the sample tested. However, there are indications that some individuals reach their top capacity by sixteen to eighteen years. Whereas others may still be growing at the age of twenty-one.

DEVELOPMENT OF LANGUAGE

Language development on the part of the preschool child furnishes the most interesting and one of the best indices to his intellectual development. The development of language follows the principles characteristic of other aspects of development. It emerges as a result of both maturation and learning and involves both the acquisition of new responses and the refinement of responses already acquired.

Development of comprehensible speech: The development of comprehensible speech takes place during the second and third years of life and reaches a plateau at a relatively early age. Thus, when the child enters kindergarten or the first grade, his comprehensible speech is well established. In studies at the preschool level, it has been noted that there is a relationship between children's language and the socio-economic status of the home. Rosenthal[5] noted that children of high sociometric status tend toward language characterized by meaningful communication. Their communication is in longer units, with a greater variety of words. No differences were observed in the total number of words used and the relative variability in length of communication units. A number of factors may account for this superiority of the privileged child, one of which is the greater amount of time and guidance given to children by parents in higher socio-economic and educational status. Also, there is evidence that children who associate mainly with adults are more precocious in their language development than are children who associate mainly with other children.[6]

Vocabulary growth: Studies by Terman, Thorndike, and many other investigators have shown that there is a continuous increase in the size of one's vocabulary during childhood. The investigation of children's vocabularies by Seashore[7] furnishes useful information about vocabulary growth during the preschool and early school years. He suggests that a time estimate of a child's vocabulary can only be secured by giving the child an opportunity to display all he has learned from his varied experiences. A new test, consisting of 89 items, developed under his direction, employed the pictorial principle. This was administered individually to 117 children ranging in age from four to ten. Based on the results of this test, the following list of estimated vocabulary sizes was compiled:

Age 4	5,600	basic words
Age 5	9,600	basic words
Age 6	14,700	basic words
Age 7	21,200	basic words
Age 8	26,300	basic words
Age 10	34,300	basic words

5. F. Rosenthal, "Some Relationships between Sociometric Position and Language Structure of Young Children," *Journal of Educational Psychology*, XLVIII (1957), 483-497.
6. A.J. Brodbeck and O.C. Irwin, "The Speech Behaviour of Infants without Families," *Child Development*, XVII (1946), 145-156.
7. R. Seashore, "A New Light on Children's Vocabularies," *School and Society*, LXVI (1947), 163-164.

Studies of the qualitative aspects of the vocabulary of children at different age levels reveal also a growth in the character of the word definitions. Feifel and Lorge[8] studied the general quality and completeness of word definitions given by children of different ages. The subjects tested consisted of 900 children ranging in age from six through fourteen. The children were slightly above the average in intelligence except for the fourteen-year age level. The vocabulary test of Form L of the *Stanford Revision of the Binet Test* was administered, and the definitions given were studied for their completeness and qualitative nature. The results are presented in graphic form in Fig. 3-4.

The children six and seven years of age gave the use and descriptive type of response most often. For example, a response to the word "orange" would be "something to eat." The explanation type of response is used very little at this age, but appears to grow slowly and continuously in use until the twelve-year age level. The synonym type of response, although used very little by the six and seven-year-olds, grows rapidly in use throughout the following years. The decline in the demonstrational and illustrative type of responses during the twelve, thirteen, and fourteen year age levels may be attributed to the growth in size of the vocabulary and the ability to symbolize things and events in terms of opposites and similarities.

Growth in length of responses: There is not only an increase in the size and quality of the child's vocabulary with age; there are also pronounced changes in the length of each response. The one-word response characterizes the early language behaviour. This grows so that by the age of six the individual child is using a large variety of words and almost every form of sentence structure. This development is noteworthy when we consider that it has occurred in such a relatively short period of time.

There is evidence from many sources that growth in language is more rapid on the average for girls than for boys. The data presented in Table 3.1, from a study reported by Heider and Heider,[9] indicate that there is a gradual and continuous growth in the number of words per sentence during the

8. H. Feifel and L. Lorge, "Qualitative Differences in the Vocabulary Responses of Children," *Journal of Educational Psychology*, XLI (1950), 1-18.
9. F.K. Heider and G.M. Heider, "Studies in the Psychology of the Deaf," *Psychological Monographs*, LII, No. 1 (1940), 42-103.

elementary-school years. A further analysis of the data shows that the average length of sentences is longer for girls than for boys. The superiority of girls may also be observed in the clarity of enunciation and in freedom from speech defects.

Table 3.1 Mean Number of words per sentence in written composition

Age	*Grade*	*Words per sentence*
8	3	10.2
9	4	10.9
10	5	11.1
11	6	11.1
12	7	12.8
13	8	13.7
14	9	13.9

Source: Heider and Heider, *op. cit.*

DEVELOPMENT OF CONCEPTS

An important aspect of the child's mental growth involves the acquisition of concepts. In the development of a concept, it is first necessary for the learner to recognize the essential feature. For example, in the acquisition of the concept of "mountain" the child learns from observing a number of mountains that contain the feature of being higher than the surrounding areas. It is also necessary to vary the concomitants such that special features found in only a particular mountain or group of mountains are eliminated from the emerging concept. A child living near Atlanta had seen Stone Mountain many times. The great mass of exposed granite stood out in his concept of a mountain, since he had no experiences with other mountains. The features common to all mountains must, through a wide range of experiences, be recognized as the quality that characterizes mountains, whereas those features common to particular mountains must be recognized only as special types.

A child normally acquires a number of concepts before entering school. These are, however, rather broad in nature, including such things as automobiles, books, doctors, and schools, without a refinement of these into subclasses. The first-grade teacher takes it for granted that the child has acquired many gross concepts. If the child has not acquired a concept of a particular word, it will be difficult for him to learn the word and he will be unable to grasp the full meaning of a sentence in which the word is used.

The importance of experience: It has been already suggested that a wide range of experience is essential for the formulation of concepts. The results of scientific studies bearing on this problem indicate clearly that actual experience on the part of the preschool and elementary-school child is the most important factor in concept development. However, vicarious experiences are useful at all stages in concept formation. This is borne out by the results of a study by Osburn and others[10] of the concepts of kindergarten children based upon vicarious experiences. The importance of pictures, illustrations, models, and the like, in making more concrete relationships implied in language, is revealed by this study. Children do not readily acquire concepts by merely meeting words in context. Rather, it appears that at all age levels the building of concepts necessitates a certain amount of actual experience.

When concepts are inadequate or inaccurate, they have an adverse effect upon the child's interpretation of reading materials. This may be noted in connection with a story about fishing. In such a case, the words *perch, cast, line, rod,* and *hook* were used. To children unfamiliar with fishing terminology, these words have entirely different meanings from those implied in the story. *Perch,* which was used as a noun in the story, to such children may be a verb. The word *cast* to these children may mean a group in a play. *Line* to these children is what you draw on a piece of paper to indicate direction or distance, whereas *rod* is a mathematical term. The word *hook* may be interpreted as a verb rather than the object to which a fish becomes attached.

The development of concepts requires a sort of pacing or "seasoning." In order to grasp certain concepts or meanings, it

---

10. W. J. Osburn, M. Huntington, and V. Meeks, "The Language of Relativity as Related to Reading Readiness," *Journal of Educational Research*, XXXIX (1948), 583-601.

becomes necessary for the child to have an accumulation of experiences distributed over a period of his growth and development. This is quite noticeable in the development of concepts of space, distance, and time. It is also observable in the development of social science concepts, such as the community, cooperation, and political activity.

Perception of space and distance: The perception of space and distance is such a commonplace feature of everyday life that adults are inclined to look upon this as an outgrowth of maturation alone, with little consideration of the importance of experience. Studies show that binocular vision is poorly developed in preschool children. This contributes to their inadequacy in depth perception. To the preschool child, the train, when viewed from a distance, may appear as a toy train. It is through experiences with standard objects in the distance that he comes to learn that objects appear much smaller when they are far away.

The perception for depth is poorly developed in the six-year-old when he enters school. The immature child may be observed placing his cup very close to the edge of the table. He incorrectly estimates the height of things. This may account for a certain amount of awkwardness in handling things.

There is a constant and continuous increase in the verbalized manifestations of the sense of space by children. By the time they arrive at school, they have developed an understanding of the ordinary space and distance words. *In, on, up, at,* and *down* are space words frequently used. Thus, he is able to understand directions on the part of the teacher or others in which space words are used. The statement. "Place the ball on the lower shelf," has meaning for the six- or seven-year-old. However, his perception of space and distance is almost completely limited to his concrete experiences. A more abstract concept of space, such as that used in studies involving maps, the globe, or reading matter, develops slowly during the elementary-school years.

Time concepts: A study by Bradley dealt with the growth of the ability of elementary-school children to understand ordinary time words and the development of a concept of the universal and continuous nature of the time scheme. Four tests were administered to a group of urban school children aged five to thirteen years. The purpose of the first test was to trace the growth of an understanding of ordinary time words used in everyday life, whereas that of the other three tests was to explore the grasp of the child's time scheme extending into the past and the future. In the first test, 30 questions were asked of each child, such as: What is your age? Is it afternoon or morning now? What season is it?

The results shown in Fig. 3.5 indicate a gradual and continuous growth in understanding of time words throughout the elementary-school period.[11] By the age of five years, distinctions between the present, past, and future seem to have been established. The first of the time words used after this stage were those referring to natural phenomena and personal activities. In general, the ability to understand the conventional time scheme and to use particular time words appeared later

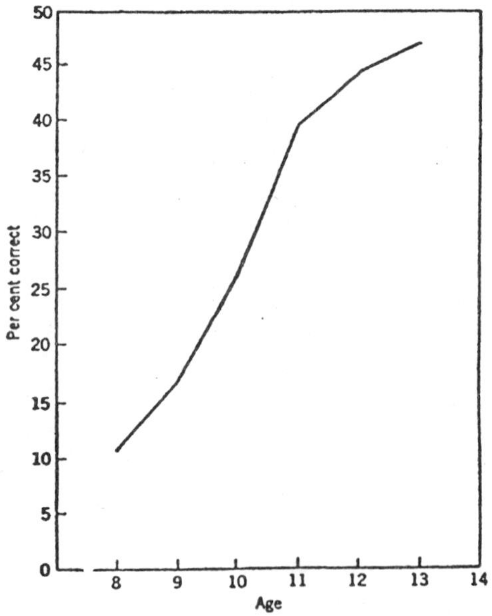

Fig. 3.5 The percentage of correct responses made by different age groups on the temporal absurdity test. (Afer Bradley)

11. N.C. Bradley, "The Growth of the Knowledge of Time in Children of School-age," *British Journal of Psychology*, XXXVIII (1947), 67-78.

than was generally believed. Nine- and ten-year-olds were able to comprehend a long period of years. Twelve- and thirteen-year-olds could answer questions that were mainly concerned with duration. The principle of a sequential order of the acquisition of time knowledge was apparent in this study.

Studies and observations of the time concepts of elementary-school children suggest that their background of time concepts is developed largely outside of the organized classroom instruction. Adequate time and space concepts are essential, however, for the acquisition and understanding of social science materials. A sound educational programme will take into consideration the nature and extent of the development of these concepts at the different age periods.

Growth in number concepts: One of the contributions of the nursery school and kindergarten is to furnish children with many favourable opportunities for the development of number concept. Through being with other children and working with different things where numerical terms are used, meanings are gradually developed and become a part of the total self. Many opportunities are available for stimulating the growth and clarification of number concepts. The children working at a particular table or on a special problem are counted, glasses for orange juice are counted, the number of chairs needed to seat some visitors are estimated or counted, the number who brushed their teeth are counted, and many other situations appear that call for number combinations. Growth in memory ability, experiences with numerical situations, and opportunities for a variety of experiences with numerical problems provide for growth in the child's numerical concepts.

Brotherton, Read, and Pratt[12] studied children's knowledge of indeterminate number concepts through their application of such terms as *hardly, few, some, several,* and *many* to actual groups of symbols. Children were tested at three grade levels: second and third, sixth and seventh, and tenth and eleventh. A reliable increase was noted in precision in the use of these

---

12. D.A. Brotherton, J.M. Read, and K.C. Pratt, "Indeterminate Number Concepts #II. Application by Children to Determine Number Concepts," *Journal of Genetic Psychology*, LXXIII (1948), 209-236.

concepts from grades two and three to grades six and seven. However, there was little increase noted from grades six and seven to grades ten and eleven, indicating that these concepts are established with a relatively high degree of precision at the sixth- and seventh-grade levels.

Development of concepts of causal relations: An important aspect of children's thinking is that of the development of their concepts of causal relations. Concepts of causal relationships appear as an aspect of the development of scientific concepts. However, scientific concepts go beyond explanations of causes to a consideration of the nature of proof, a differentiation of facts and opinions, and an understanding of scientific laws.

Two types of analysis of children's causal thinking were made by Deutsche—quantitative and qualitative.[13] Questions of causality were selected and tried out with children. Quantitative scores were obtained from the adequacy of the answer, as an explanation of the phenomenon, to such questions as:

What makes the wind blow?

What makes the frost on the window pane?

What makes water boil?

The mean quantified score increased for each of the questions asked throughout the age range studied—eight through fifteen. However, the increase was greater for some of the questions than for others. These differences were no doubt related to the difficulty of the different questions. Also, individual differences within each age group were very pronounced. Such differences would normally be greater for the more complex questions than for the simple ones. A qualified analysis of the answers revealed important differences. There was a growth with age in the use of logical deductions, and a decline in explanations in terms of the phenomenon itself.

Children's concepts in relation to instruction: It was pointed out in Chap. 2 that learning must be geared to the child's

13. J.M. Deutsche, *The Development of Children's Concepts of Causal Relations* (Minneapolis: University of Minnesota Press, 1937).

maturational level. Teachers often fail to realize the range and limitation of a child's understanding. Part of this stems from the fact that concepts develop gradually. The child's grasp of many topics encountered at school is often quite incomplete. He may use words in proper context without understanding their complete meaning. Causal relations are frequently misunderstood. This was illustrated several years ago when the writer asked an eight-year-old girl where she obtained so many pretty flowers on the same day. The little girl answered by pointing out that her mother planted all the flowers on the same day. The same child may be well informed on some topics and poorly informed on others. Maturation and experience operate together at all stages in the child's development. This notion must constantly be recognized in the evaluation of mental growth of children.

A failure on the part of teachers and others to appreciate a child's lack of understanding can frequently be observed in the teaching and learning of social studies materials. The results of studies by Eaton[14] suggest that the amount of understanding and information sixth-grade children have on many topics commonly studied in the social studies classes is not directly related to the amount of time devoted to such topics at school. The learning of many concepts are vague, because they have been presented before the child has had adequate experience to understand them. Concepts of an abstract nature develop slowly. They can only be understood when they are taught in such a manner that the child can interpret them in terms of his everyday experiences.

GROWTH IN PROBLEM-SOLVING BEHAVIOUR

Although problem-solving will be discussed more fully, it is presented here in relation to mental growth during childhood and adolescence. Problem-solving behaviour is here regarded as those activities involved in trying to reach a goal or solution to a problem situation. The problem situation may vary in complexity from that of the child trying to stack two or three blocks to a situation involving space and time relationships.

14. M.T. Eaton, *A Survey of the Achievement in Social Studies of 10,220 Sixth Grade Pupils in 464 Schools in Indiana* (Bulletin 20, No. 3, School of Education, University of Indiana, 1944).

Differences in the complexity of problem situations have contributed to different explanations of the nature of problem-solving behaviour. Robert L. Thorndike has suggested that problems may be divided into two main categories: (1) practical problems, or the need to achieve something, and (2) intellectual problems, or the need for understanding.[15]

Problem-solving of the pre-school child: Students of child development have noted that reasoning occurs as early as two and one-half or three years. However, reasoning at this age is confined to concrete and personal things from the child's immediate environment. This is shown in an investigation by Guanella[16] of the development of block building from two to six years of age, under conditions where there were plenty of blocks and a minimum of adult teaching and interference. Guanella noted that block-building begins around the age of two years, with the "arch" and "representative building" appearing around three years. At first the child names the structure after it is constructed; later he may state what he is going to build before he begins building. Thus we note that at first the child deals with single blocks, piling one on top of the other one; later he works with block combinations in "representative building; still later, he makes use of blocks in dramatic play, announcing his intentions before beginning the construction.

Some investigators have attempted to explain problem-solving of preschool children as trial-and-error behaviour. Such an explanation may be an outgrowth of the puzzle-like nature of problems used in studying problem-solving behaviour of preschool children. It should be noted, however, that children actually show a wide range of behaviour in dealing with problem situations, the type of behaviour depending in a large measure upon the nature of the problem. Concerning this, Anderson states: "Studies of the behaviour of children in problem-solving situations reveal a complete range of behaviour from random

15. R.L. Thorndike, *How Children Learn the Principles and Techniques of Problem-Solving*, Forty-ninth Yearbook of the National Society for the Study of Education, Part I (Chicago: University of Chicago Press, 1950), pp. 192-216.
16. F.M. Guanella, "Block Building Activities of Young Children," *Archives of Psychology*, XXVI, No. 174 (1934).

activity through to the immediate solution with ability to state the principle."[17]

Problem-solving of school-age children: Concrete, direct experiences are important to the school-age child's problem-solving activities. However, as he grows older there is a significant increase in his ability to state a problem in words and to verbalize its solution. An important difference in the problem-solving behaviour of younger and older children is that the older children recognize the problem as a problem, whereas the younger children tend to emphasize the objects used in the problem rather than the problem situation. This was apparent in a study reported by Heidbreder[18] in which the problem was to find a small celluloid doll concealed in one of two boxes. The children were to solve the problem by responding to different clues presented, such as the design at the top of the box. Heidbreder noted that three-year-olds were concerned only with obtaining the doll from the box, that some four-year-olds appeared to react to the problem as such, and that children six to ten years of age definitely responded to the problem as a problem.

Problem-solving behaviour of primary-grade children should not be limited to things about them in their physical environment. There is plenty of evidence from observations of elementary-school children that they are capable of solving problems in the realm of people and human relations. However, the ability to generalize the solution to a problem increases with age and a wider range of experiences. The seven-year-old who is concerned with fair play in games with other children of his block, may, at the age of fifteen, be concerned with fair play of a much larger scale and involving a greater range of activities. It appears, however, that the same mechanisms of problem-solving are to be found at the different age levels. Trial and error, imitation, following directions, logical deductions, and insight appear among preschool, elementary-school, and high-school children and adolescents.

17. J.E. Anderson, *Psychology of Development and Personal Adjustment* (New York: Henry Holt & Company, Inc., 1949), p. 190.
18. E. Heidbreder, "Problem Solving in Children and Adults," *Journal of Genetic Psychology*, XXXV (1928), 522-545.

Problem-solving ability improves with age in terms of both speed and accuracy. Ausupel and Schiff [19] found significant and progressive increases with age in the ability to learn a relevant causal sequence and to inhibit the learning of an irrelevant causal sequence in a teeter-totter problem. The authors concluded that the ability to learn a relevant causal relationship (namely, that the side of the teeter-totter which is farthest from the fulcrum will fall) is a function of age in children. This was a challenging problem for kindergarten and third-grade children. However, sixth-grade children were able to master it directly without an error. Parallel results were obtained with respect to the ability to resist the learning of an irrelevant causal relationship.

SUMMARY

The vast amount of research conducted during the past several decades on the development and use of the intelligence tests has yielded valuable information about the mental growth of children and adolescents. Data secured from repeated measurements of the same individuals over a period of years show wide variations in the rate on mental growth throughout the period of childhood. These variations may best be accounted for by 1. individual differences in pattern of development, 2. environmental differences, 3. psychological and social forces, 4. the nature of the tests used in evaluating intelligence.

Studies of the pattern of development of different mental functions show that these are far from uniform. Where information or logical thinking is involved, the older or more mature person is at an advantage. However, some individuals appear to reach their top capacity on the different test items at an earlier age than others. Language development during the preschool and early school years furnishes one of the best indices of a child's intellectual development. There is, however, a relationship between children's language and the socio-economic status of the home. Significant changes take place in the completeness and qualitative nature of the child's vocabulary from age six through age fourteen.

19. D.P. Ausupel and H.M. Schiff, "The Effect of Incidental and Experimentally Induced Experience in Learning of Relevant and Irrelevant Causal Relations by Children," *Journal of Genetic Psychology*, LXXXIV (1954), 109-123.

The child normally acquires a number of rather broad concepts before entering school. The exact nature of these concepts will depend largely upon the nature of experiences he has encountered. Concepts of space, distance, and time develop gradually through everyday experiences at home, on the playground, and at school. Growth in memory ability, experiences with numerical situations, and opportunities for a variety of experiences with numerical problems provide for growth in numerical concepts during the kindergarten and early school years. There is a continuous increase in precision in the use of these concepts to grades six and seven. Concepts of causal relations undergo important changes with age, with a pronounced growth in the use of logical deductions and a decline in explanations in terms of the phenomenon itself.

Although reasoning and problem-solving behaviour appears at an early age, during the early period reasoning is confined to concrete and personal things from the child's immediate environment. As the child grows older, there is a significant increase in his ability to state a problem in words and to verbalize its solution. Also, older children are significantly better at recognizing the problem as a problem. Elementary-school children are capable of solving problems involving human relations, provided such problems appear as an important aspect of their immediate environment. At all stages in his growth, the child needs guidance in the development of better methods of solving problems.

—*Karl C. Garrison*

Questions and Exercises (for Discussion and Study)

1. Look up several recent definitions of intelligence. What similarities do you note in the definitions? What differences?
2. How do normal children differ in mental growth and development? What are some factors that may account for such differences?
3. List four or five important generalizations based upon studies of the constancy of the IQ.

4. If you have the opportunity to study a child, evaluate his or her language ability in relation to his chronological age. Evaluate his language development in relation to his environment.
5. What is meant by comprehensible speech? Trace the growth of comprehensible speech.
6. How are reasoning and problem-solving related to language ability? What other factors affect the nature of the school-age child's ability to reason?
7. How can the teacher help the child acquire number concepts? What cautions should be considered?
8. Show how a child's lack of understanding of a particular situation may be a result of lack of experience with the situation.
9. Show how a child's concept of a word tends to grow as a result of a wide range of experiences with the word.

References

Breckenridge, M. E., and V.E. Lee, *Child Development*, 3rd ed. Philadelphia; W.B. Saunders Company, 1955, chap. 11.

Forest, I., *Child Development*. New York; McGraw-Hill Book Company, Inc., 1954, chaps. 7 and 8.

Frandsen, A.N., *How Children Learn: An Educational Psychology*. New York: McGraw-Hill Book Company, Inc., 1957.

Garrison, K.C., *Growth and Development*, rev. ed. New York: Longmans, Green & Co., Inc., 1959, chaps. 8-10.

Goodenough, F. L., "The Measurement of Mental Growth in Childhood," chap. 8 in L. Carmichael (ed.), *Manual of Child Psychology*, 2nd ed. New York: John Wiley & Sons, Inc., 1954.

Jersild, A.T., *Child Psychology* 4th ed. Englewood Cliffs, N.J.: Prentice-Hall, Inc., 1954, chaps. 12 and 13.

McCarthy, D., "Language Development in Children," chap 9 in L. Carmichael (ed.), *Manual of Child Psychology*, 2nd ed. New York: John Wiley & Sons, Inc., 1954.

Millard, C.V., *Child Growth and Development in the Elementary School Years*, rev. ed. Boston: D.C. Heath & Company, 1958, chaps. 6 and 7.

Thorpe, L.P., *Child Psychology* and *Development*, 2nd ed. New York: The Ronald Press Company, 1955, chaps. 6 and 7.

4

Emotional Development

A study of the earlier investigations and books of child psychology will reveal the belief that there are three basic emotional states experienced by the child. These primary emotions are said to be fear, rage and love. According to this theory when the support from under the infant is withdrawn and he is faced with the danger of falling he experiences fear. When his movements are restricted and he is inhibited in his activities he goes through another emotional state that can be called rage and again when the infant is hugged, fondled and held close to the mother's body he experiences the emotion of love.

This theory was in currency till some of the investigators took up the challenge and put this thesis to test through investigations conducted with infants as well as adults. These empirical studies failed to prove the existence of three basic emotions in the infant. On the other hand these researches came out with the finding that any form of sudden stimulation like dropping the infant, loud noise, restraint, pain, etc, produces, in the young infant, a kind of aimless activity of most of the musculature, accompanied by crying.

It is further claimed by these research workers that the earlier psychologists tend to read different emotions into this aimless activity according to their own experience. They interpret the infant behaviour according to as they themselves would feel when support is suddenly removed or a sudden noise is made or if their actions were restricted through outside barriers. It has become apparent from the subsequent research that emotional behaviour of the new born fails to show clear-cut patterns to which definite labels such as fear, rage, and love can be attached. It is gradually, through the developmental period, that the child starts showing more differentiated emotion which can be labelled with definite names. Psychologists today do not give any precise number of emotions experienced during early childhood but they do agree that as the child grows older, an increasing number of emotions becomes apparent.

Bridges[1] has done extensive work in the field of emotional development of children. The growth pattern of emotional behaviour she represents in a diagramatic form according to the specific age levels at which the specific development stage is reached.

Table 4.1

(Approximate ages of Differentiation of Emotion in Early Childhood)

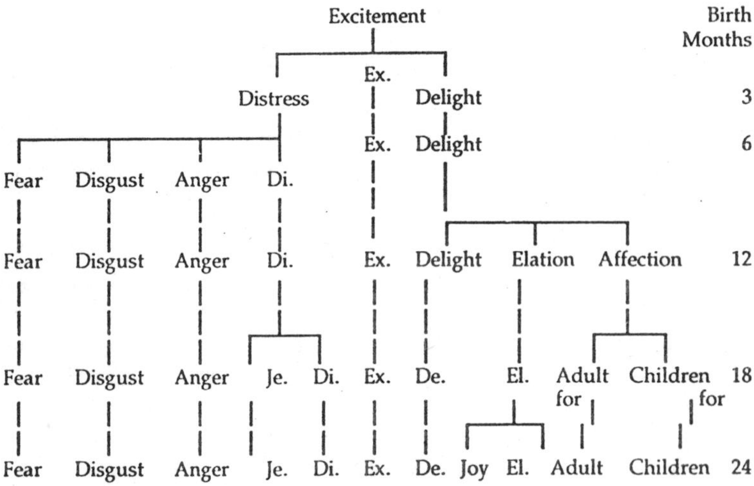

Bridges based her findings on a study conducted with a large number of babies ranging in age from birth to two years. Among this sample the investigator could discern only a state of general excitement. At the age of three months this general state spilt into distinct states of distress and delight. So that at this age together with general excitement two distinct emotions

1. Bridges, K.M.B., "Emotional Development in Early Infancy", Child Development, 1932, 3; 340.

of distress and delight were also discernible. During the next three months of the child's life distress differentiates into fear, disgust, anger and distress. State of general excitement stays as it was before and so does delight. At 12months of age delight also differentiates and shows three distinct emotional states of delight, elation, and affection. By the age of eighteen months jealousy appears as differentiation of disgust and affection differentiates into affection for adults and affection for children. At the age of two years joy is added as a differentiation of delight and so by the age of two years we find the emotional life of the child quite well differentiated showing eleven distinct emotional states. If we accept these research findings then we do not find any room for the older theory according to which three basic emotions exit at birth.

This theory, in all probability, is based on general observations of the children. This would amount to judging the emotional state by the facial expression of the subject. Today psychologists have come to the conclusion that judgements of emotions based on the mere facial expression are inadequate and unreliable. This finding came as a result of a research study done on a number of medical students. They were shown a number of photographs representing the facial expressions during various emotional states. They were asked to look at the photographs and name the specific emotion that the individual must have experienced. The labels given to these photographs by different students showed a lot of variation and overlapping . For the same picture many would give different possible emotions and for different photographs many of them gave the same label. Besides other things this study clearly proved that one could not rely only on the facial expression for determining the emotion undergone.

On the basis of the findings of the this study, we can safely conclude that giving names of basis emotions in the child by mere observation of his facial expression is misleading. Subsequent workers have studied the changes in the body and organs of the child as well and have concluded that the State resultant of all these changes is nothing else but a state of general excitability. It is much later that the differentiation is so clear that different specific emotions can be discerned.

Here we may pose a question, are emotions a function of maturation or are they an entirely learnt phenomenon? The most suitable answer to this question is that both maturation and learning play their respective roles in the display of emotions. In certain situations their respective roles are clear and distinct so that we can mark them out while in others they are so interwoven that the differentiation between the two is difficult.

An evidence for the maturation and the role that it plays in the development of emotions is clear from the fact that all children learn to smile, laugh, cry, (with tears) and display other elementary emotions at distinct age level irrespective of the variations in stimulation given to them. These emotions have appeared at precisely the same age level even when children have been restrained from witnessing this behaviour in others around them. People attending to these children under experimental conditions have been instructed not to show any emotions through their behaviour while attending to these children; even then the emotions have been discerned in the subjects. It is enough evidence of the part that maturation plays in the development of emotions.

Similarly another piece of evidence is the fact that blind and deaf people also exhibit emotional behaviour inspite of the fact that the blind has never seen people smiling, the deaf has never heard the sound of laughter and does not know how it is produced; still those who are born blind or deaf exhibit some sort of emotional behaviour. Considering that they do not have the opportunity to learn these through imitation the only method left for them to learn is through touch it has been observed that are even when they are not given any tactual experiences they display emotions which are very much like those displayed by normal people. Learning having been eliminated from such cases the only factor that plays the determining role is maturation.

The role of learning in development of emotions becomes obvious when we examine the entirely different expressions that are given to the same emotion by individuals belonging to different countries. A Chinese, for example, shows surprise by chewing on the index finger or putting the index finger on the cheek and leaving the mouth half open. The same emotion of surprise is expressed by the Western people by raising the eyebrows. This shows how people under different conditions have learnt to express the same emotion in an absolutely different fashion.

Another evidence of learning in emotional behaviour is that children at a young age do not show fear from the objects which ordinarily frighten the adults in the same surroundings. The example can be that of snakes and other poisonous animals. It is found that before the children are taught to be afraid of a snake they do not display the emotion when put in touch with the reptile. Similarly fire does not frighten them, it rather attracts them with its colourful beauty. Moreover, studies in fears of children have brought out the fact that children resemble their parents to a great extent in the kind of fears that they display. This leads to the conclusion that parents unconsciously pass on their fears to the children and children learn to experience the same fears as the parents suffer from.

Control of Emotional Responses

Together with the differentiation of emotional expression, the child shows a decrease in expression of emotions as he grows up in age. While previously the child has given a completely unrestrained outburst of emotion now his expression is less frequent and more restrained in nature. He gives expressions to his emotions in a more subtle way as he grows up in age and maturity. This is an indication of the emotional development as the appropriate control of emotions is one of the criteria for judging the emotional stability of the child.

This aspect of emotional development is determined by many factors working in the life of the individual. Development of language helps him to express his emotions in a more subtle way than an outright physical outburst. Responses from his environment help him to learn that many of his problems do not find a solution by resorting to open physical expression of emotion.

Social factors play their role in development of emotional control. The group expects him to act as a big boy. To achieve the status of a grown-up he is expected to show a certain amount of maturity and control in his emotional expression. Thus, the control comes as a social pressure in exchange for 'grown-up' status. The social groups encourage inhibition of emotions because free and outright expression can create a chaos in life. However, it is in place here to point out that undue inhibition can be a source of trouble as well.

Many problems could have been easily solved if people expressed their emotions in a free and uninhibited manner. Pressure against express of emotions leads to suppression and we know how harmful suppression can prove for the mental health of the individual. Inhibition is specially harmful when the individuals begin to have a false impression about themselves.

Control of expression of emotions refers to social settings only, in personal life the individual seeks free expression. In case the controls are so rigid that even this is not permitted then the individuals are known to seek expression through mental disturbances and symptoms.

Change in Emotion Arousing Stimuli

As the individual grows older there is an obvious shift in the emotion arousing stimuli. In early infancy the child reacts to stimuli which directly impringe upon him. As he grows older there is an increase in his activities and the environment. He has a wider range of experiences, he remembers and draws from his past experiences and he plans for his future. Thus the stimuli which arouse him now cover a wider range and exercise a long range influence on him. His emotional reactions are now determined by the nature of happening i.e. the stimulus and his inner State at the moment. His interests, urges, needs and motivation at the moment determine his emotional reaction. An identical happening may cause joy to one child, distress to another and disappointment to still another depending upon how he views the happening as a gain or loss, how much he expects from himself and how much does he think others expect from him.

In view of the above discussion it can be said here that the understanding of the child's emotional behaviour depends on the understanding of the child as a whole. A teacher has to understand his needs, urges, motivation and the entire background in order to understand why the specific emotional response. An objective view of a particular stimulus may make it look like a very simple and ordinary situation but the emotional reaction of the child is not an objective, one to one reaction. It is a result of many forces—personal and social—which act in the life of the individual.

A teacher must understand the bases of the emotional expression of a child in order to adapt and modify his teaching and discipline of his pupils. In an attempt to understand these bases the teacher must remember that the feelings of the child are more important than the objective truth.

Summary

The theory of three basic emotions has been discussed and evaluated. Subsequent research evidence has disproved the theory and the research conducted by Bridges has brought out the fact that the emotional development is a continuous process. Beginning with the state of general excitement it completes by the age of 24 months when the child gives expression to eleven distinct emotions.

Emotional development is a function of an interaction between maturation and learning on the part of the child. Control of emotions is an aspect of development and a criterion of emotional maturity. Development also shows a change in the stimuli which arouse emotions at advanced stages of development.

Emotional reactions of children are determined by the situation as such and the child's mental make-up at the moment. This is entirely a subjective response which a teacher must remember in order to understand the emotional behaviour of his pupils.

Questions for the Students

1. Discuss the theory of basic emotions. Quote research evidence in favour and against it.
2. What is the contribution of K.M. Bridges to the study of emotional development of children?

3. Discuss some of the factors which bring about control of emotions.
4. How does the personality of an individual determine his emotional reactions?

References

1. Garrison, Karl C., *Growth and Development*. Longmans Green & Co., New York. 1952.
2. Garrison, Karl C. and Gray, J. Stanley, *Educational Psychology*. Appleton Century-Crofts, Inc., New York; 1955.
3. Gates, A.I. *et. al. Educational Psychology*. The Macmillan Co, New York. 1948.
4. Hurlock, Elizabeth B., *Child Development*, McGraw-Hill Book Co., New York. 1950.

5

Intellectual Development of the Child

Having observed children of various age levels in their usual free play activities, psychologists have arrived at the conclusion that as the children grow older they are able to perform acts that are difficult in nature and also they are able to do more difficult tasks at a faster speed. The result of this is that as the children go through higher age levels the index of their intelligence also increases. We can further conclude from this that there is a relationship between the chronological age and the mental age of the child. What the precise nature of this relationship is we have yet to find. Some of the other questions that perplex us today are: Does the mental age of ten for a boy aged nine mean the same as the mental age of twelve for the boy with a chronological age of eleven? If we accept the idea that the mental age of an individual goes on increasing with the chronological age then we are faced with the question as to when does this increase stop? Psychologists have been concerned about all these questions from the very early days and have attempted a reply to most of them by working out theories about the intellectual growth of the child.

With the measurement of intelligence made possible through the introduction of intelligence tests we have found that the ages and the scores achieved in these tests can be scaled along the two axes and a curve of intelligence at different age levels can be drawn. These test scores have also been helpful in screening out the children with different intelligence levels. Psychologists have been separating the dull from the borderline cases and the super or from the average children basing their judgements on the scores achieved by them. Thus the index of intelligence has been converted to numerical terms and the difference between the dull and the bright child has been proved to be that of quantity rather than quality.

Typical curves traced on the basis of these conclusions have recorded a steep rise in the intelligence upto a certain age after which the increase stops resulting in a flat top in the curve till the age from where a definite decline is obvious. A typical mental growth curve world look somewhat like the one given in Fig.5.1

The curves are determined by the standardization data collected for different intelligence tests. So it has been found that every test gives a different chronological age at which the rise in the growth turns to a decline. In the first revision of Binet Scale that Terman completed he found that the mental age did not increase after sixteen years of chronological age. Therefore he suggested that at sixteen and after, the denominator for the calculation of I.Q. should remain the same and sixteen.

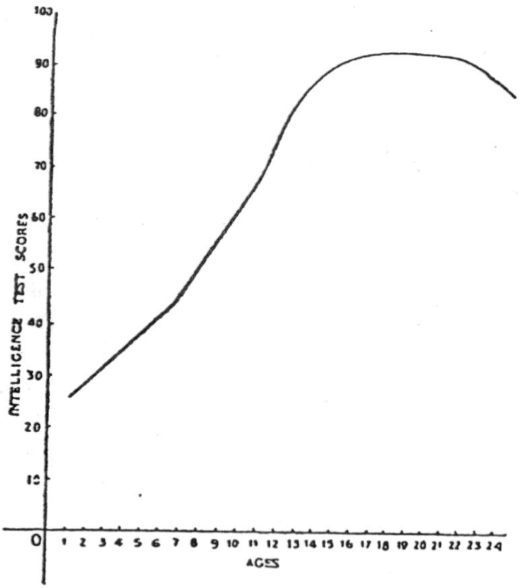

Fig. 5.1 The curve shows the growth in intellectual ability when age is represented along X-axis. The characteristic feature of the curve is the sharp rise upto the ages of 14, 15 and 16 years. A gradual decline follows a plateau which shows the levelling of the growth rate.

Working on the data for his second revision he came out with the conclusion that this rise stops at the chronological age of fifteen so thereafter, the denominator for the calculation of I.Q. has been set at 15 for the subjects who were of the chronological age of fifteen and older. On the other hand the standardization data collected by Wechsler points out very clearly that there is an abrupt deceleration at about the age of thirteen. Considering this difference of opinion about the chronological age at which the decline in mental growth begins, Wechsler started the procedure of standardization within the age groups.

So far we have been talking of intellectual development in quantitative terms. We have talked of the amount of development from time to time and the curves which can be drawn on the measures so obtained. There is another aspect of intellectual development which can be rightly called the qualitative aspect. How is the development measured? It is measured from the type of tasks which the individual is capable of attempting and how fast he can do so. Observation and experiments with the type of tasks which the children can do at different age levels have revealed that the intellectual tasks move from mere understanding to description and then to interpretation.

At very early stages the children show a mere understanding of a phenomenon. When shown a kettle, a very young child will just say out the word kettle. In absence of it he will not be able to describe it nor will he be able to give the functions of it and the uses to which it can be put. A little later the description is possible. The child can describe the phenomena, whether present or not. Finally he comes to the stage where he can interpret the phenomena and understand its implications. At this stage he realizes that kettle can be used to heat water and that while boiling it can be dangerous to touch, etc.

These stages are evident even before the use of languages appears. Through gestures the child can convey his recognition, description as well as the interpretation of various phenomena. Use of language is an important correlation of intelligence. The correlation between language and intelligence scores has often been dismissed with the argument that it is a result of the verbal loading in an intelligence test. Still one cannot underestimate the symbolic nature of language. The use of language is, perhaps, the most difficult and complicated abstract function which an individual is called upon to perform together with its abstract and symbolic nature, the individual has to maintain a very high speed. Communciation is face to face interaction. It does not give time for preparation or thinking. Thus, it may be considered an index of a fairly high intellectual level. Individual with low intelligence finds verbal communciation difficult.

The language development itself proceeds from mere naming to the use of other types of words. For a long time the child uses only nouns in his communication. At older ages also the analysis of vocabulary shows the largest count of nouns. Descriptive words like adjectives and adverbs show a lesser count and appear at later stages than the names. This pattern has been the same in studies of English and the one made of Hindi vocabulary.[3] Studies of sentence construction reveal the same pattern viz. the development proceeds from small enumerative sentences to descritive and interpretative sentence structures. Descriptive clauses are added to the sentence much later in the developmental continuum.

Intelligence and the Physical Growth

Children differ in their intellegence, so that the psychologists have often asked the question as to what makes this difference? They often wonder if the children who have good physique also possess higher intelligence. Are children who grow faster in physique also expected to grow faster in intelligence? What is the relationship between the size of the head and the level of intelligence exhibited by children? Also the psychologists have been pretty occupied considering the part that maturation or heredity plays in the development of intelligence as compared with that played by environment.

Various researches that have been planned to answer some of these questions have led to the conclusions that, in general the physical growth is related with the intellectual level. In other words the children who maintain a faster rate growth along the physical characteristics also develop faster along the intelligence. However this is a mere correlation. It has not been conclusively proved that the one is the cause of the other. Most of the psychologists agree that a correlation is shown between these two aspects of growth because both of these variables indicate the kind of general organism that an individual is. An all round healthy child will have good physique and so will he have a good intelligence and if he is studied along other growth aspects he will show a similar superiority there as well. Though it has not been proved finally that a good physique causes good intelligence yet it has been found that a good intelligence usually goes with good physical growth.

As far as the size of the head is concerned the research evidence has proved that with the normal range of intelligence the size of the head is not a correlate of intelligence. Beyond the normal range, however, an exceptionally small head does mean a kind of mental deficiency—microcephaly. Similarly an exceptionally large head is also an indication of brain disturbance known as macrocephaly. By studying the X-ray photographs of different aspects of body build the psychologists have arrived at the conclusion that general characteristics like gross weight and height etc. may show a correlation with the intellectual growth but when we go into a study of the detailed indices of body-build we find the correlation missing. The two become independent variables.

In a longitudinal study planned by Abernethy[1] similar conclusions were arrived at. For this study the Stanford Binet Test and a large battery of tests for measurment of physical growth were administered to a large number of children at various age levels. The comparisons showed a low correlation between these two types of growth among the sample. There was a general trend of decrease in these correlations after the age of fourteen or fiftten. So that ultimately for the higher age levels the correlations between the physical and mental growth were negligible. On the basis of these results most of the psychologists today agree that the attempt to correlate mental growth with the gross physical growth will yield little fruitful results. A more useful field for investigation would be the correlation betweeen the activity of the central nervous system and the mental growth.

Intelligence and the Cultural Conditions

Intelligence has always been operationally defined by different psychologists as such it has no definite meaning attached to it. When we define a construct operationally one point that has to be kept in view is the culture to which the individual psychologist belongs and for which the definition is being framed. It has been found, through various researches designed by psychologists that the value judgement of a particular culture, the activities favoured by the culture and also the specific meaning of intelligence as it is understood by that particular culture are well reflected in the intelligence tests constructed for that specific culture. Psychologists, today are aware of the fact that any intelligence test has a bias towards one group or the other for which it might be designed. A test designed for urban children is very rarely applicable to the rural ones and similarly the urban children cannot be expected to do well on the tests meant for the rural children.

It is argued by the psychologists that the usual tests that are most popularly used in the testing in schools, favour the children of the professional groups. This is done because the psychologists themselves belong to this class within the culture. The result being that their idea of the activities and the skills that a child of a particular age group possesses is based with the skills that their own children exhibit. It is further argued, therefore, that a test which is framed with one particular cultural group in mind should not be considered fit for another no matter how slight the difference between these cultures may obviously seem to be.

Following this argument we find that in Indian set up we are handicapped for the use of test materials. So far the materials available are mostly framed for the cultures other than India—American or English. The application of the same for our children, without modification, does not give us very dependable findings. Realization of this fact and as a result the paucity of test materials have brought in the wave of test construction that we observe in our educational and research institues. In intelligence testing we are all the time testing abilities that are influenced by different factors that are in turn determined by the culture. Some of those factors we will consider in more detail here.

Within a specific culture the socio-economic status of parents makes a difference in the level of intelligence of the child as reflected in a Intelligence Test. In a democratic set up, where no other bias exists, we find that the superior individuals achieve higher level of socio-ecomomic status than the one achieved by those who are less superior in intelligence. These superior parents pass the characteristics of superior intelligence on to their children through heredity. An added advantage they have is that these intellectually superior parents provide superior environment for their children. They have better facilities for education, better play materials and many other aids to education; which the children from lower level homes cannot afford to have. An intelligence test is usually based on the activities which are followed by the children who have more chances to indulge in those activities during their play will naturally score better than the ones who do not have such opportunities. Therefore, a positive correlation is always shown between the intellectual level of the child and the socio-economic status enjoyed by his family.

In order to find out the precise relationship between the environmental factors and the intelligence level Bayley and Jones[2] conducted a longitudinal study of fifty-nine families. Through a period of six years they have been able to prove that the intellectual status of a child becomes more and more closely related with the various environmental factors particularly the eduactional and economic conditions of the family. This finding brings out on one hand the increasing influence of the environment on the child as he grows older and on the other it shows the environmental bias which our intelligence tests have. A child's environment is always influencing him through his socialization and so the child is learning to act in a particular way, behave in a particular fashion so much so that he learns to develop particular attitudes towards the games he plays and the way he plays them. Naturally a child brought up in the environment where he has facilities, materials and everything else provided for him makes an adjustment to these things. In a test situation when he is required to make an adjustment to these and similar facilities and educational materials he finds himself at home with them and scores higher on the intelligence test. Many psychologists argue on this score by saying that this is a correlation due to the bias in intelligence tests and that it does not prove that the good environment, higher education of parents and a higher economic level of family cause a rise in the intelligence level.

From the above point psychologists often get into discussing the role that is played by heredity and environment in determination of the intellectual level of a child. If according to the researches we argue that the environment are not causal factors in the raising of intelligence level then shall we claim that heredity is a causal factor? Psychological opinion is divided on this score. There are psychologists who believe that the development of intelligence may be affected by the environment but the potential intelligence that an individual child is born with cannot be affected. So they conclude that the level of intelligence of a child is determined by the potential intelligence. However, we have a lot of researches done which go to prove the effect of environment on the developmental improvement or deterioration of intelligence. Thus we cannot exclude environment from the factors that influence the level of intelligence. Considering that the potential intelligence cannot be modified or improved due to humanitarian and other reasons, environmental factors are the ones that can be improved if we expect to bring about an improvement in the intelligence of a child. That is the reason why so many educational programmes are organized with the hope of helping children who are not quite upto the mark as far as their level of intelligence is concerned.

The importance of environmental factors is also proved through the data collected on extremely impoverished children. Very often through accidents, it so happens that children get cut-off from the cultural suroundings and have to live a life completely different from the one they would have led under normal conditions. Subsequent studies of these cases have shown the extreme deterioration that their intelligence has suffered. On the other hand experiments are known in which psychologists have taken such children and put some of them under average environment and others under specially enriched environment. After a certain period of time, the ones brought up under enriched environment have shown a definite improvement over the others.

From this data the inference has been often drawn that children with average intelligence, if they were enabled to attend nursery schools that had enriched programmes would show an improvement in their intelligence as well. Wellman[8] has emphasised that attendance of a stimulating nursery school helps to raise the I.Q. of a child at pre-school age. To prove this she[7] summarized a number of studies that has been conducted in the United States on the effect of pre-school experience on the I.Q. changes. The conclusions drawn from these studies indicated that the children attending a pre-school nursery showed an increase of five to six I.Q. points against a very negligible increase that was recorded by the children who were not attending any nursery school.

Longitudinal studies done on adopted children by Skodak and Skeels[4,5,6], followed such children through thirteen years and came out with the findings that, even though the true mothers of these children had a very low intelligence level, these children if placed in the adopted homes earlier than the age of six months, showed above average intellectual growth. This again supported the earlier findings that favourable surroundings accelerate the rate of intellectual growth.

We may conclude from these findings that a child with average level of intelligence can gain a great deal if he is provided with environment that stimulate the individual and which have provisions for enriching experiences for the child. In conclusion we may sum up that the average normal child follows a somewhat normal curve of growth which shows a rise in the earlier part of his life and a stationary trend towards the later part of his adolescence. This curve maintains the same shape but if the child is provided with good and enriched surroundings this earlier rise is more obvious and he achieves a comparatively higher intellectual level than what he would have achieved under ordinary circumstances.

Summary

An evidence of intellectual development can be derived from the fact that the child is capable of handling more difficult tasks at faster speed as he gains in age. The growth curve of intelligence takes the shape of a more or less normal curve. It registers a steep rise leading to a plateau and terminating in a definite decline. Qualitatively intellectual development progresses from understanding to description and to interpretation. Intellectual development shows a close positive relationship with the physical growth and the cultural conditions under which the individual lives. It is difficult to separate heredity from environment, but given an average intelligence, individuals have shown a definite gain when kept under rich environment.

Questions for the Student

1. Discuss the rationale for use of a constant denominator, after a certain chronological age, in calculation of the I.Q.
2. Give your comments on the statement, "All men are born equal, environment makes the difference in their adult intellectual status."
3. Is higher intellectual level the cause of good language? Discuss.
4. Do children attending nusery school show any superiority of intelligence over the ones who do not attend school? Quote research in support of your answer.

References

1. Abernethy, E.M; *Relationships Between Mental and Physical Growth.* Monogr. Soc. Res. Child Development, 1936, 1; No. 7.
2. Bayley N. and Jones, H.E; *Environmental Correlations of Mental and Motor Development:* A Cumulative Study from Infancy to Six Years. Child Development, 1957, 8; 329-41.
3. Pasricha, P. and Das, Sudhir K., *A Study of the Written Vocabulary of the Sixth Class Children in Delhi Schools.* Central Institute of Education publication No. 24, 1959.
4. Skodak, M. and Skeels, H.M; *A Final Follow-up Study of One Hundred Adopted Children.* Jr. of Genet. Psychol. 1949, 75, 85-125.
5. Skodak, M. and Skeels, H.M; *A Follow-up study of Children in Adopted Homes,* Jr. of Genet. Psychol. 1945,66: 21-58.
6. Skodak, M. Children in Foster Homes. *A Study of Mental Development.* Univ. Iowa Stud. Child Welfare,1936, 16; No.1.
7. Wellman, B.L; I.Q. *Changes of Pre-school and Non-pre-school Group during the Pre-school years:* A Summary of the Literature. Jr. of Psychol. 1945, 20; 347-368.
8. Wellman, B.L. The Effect of Pre-school Attendance Upon the I.Q., Jr. of Exper. Edu., 1932-33, 1; 48-69.

6

Development of Social Behaviour

Development of social behaviour follows the same pattern as is followed by development in other aspects and is closely related with the development in other areas. It is difficult to separate social development from intellectual when the question of recognition of different faces or use of language is discussed. Language is an instrument of social communication and at the same time is closely related with the intellectual status of the individual. Similarly discrimination of different faces has social implications but is a function of intelligence as well.

Social behaviour of a child begins with non-discriminative responses, passes through differentiation and leads the organism to make discriminated social responses. Social behaviour of an individual and its development follows a specific pattern and is the result of many factors and forces acting on him. This chapter plans to discuss this pattern and some of the factors which influence social behaviour.

Social Development During Early Childhood

The child's very first social responses are with adults and are self-centered in nature. His primary consideration being fulfilment of his basic needs, soon he acquires the skill of attracting adults and making them fulfil his needs. It is comparatively later that he starts taking note of other children. At six months of age some children show this tendency but it is a stage of just taking note of other children. There is no interaction so to say. In some studies conducted to explore children's interactions, it was found that upto nine months of age children showed very little awareness of other children around them. Between nine and fourteen months children continued to give more attention to their surroundings and play-materials than other children around them. Between fourteen and eighteen months the emphasis started shifting, now more attention was given to the children rather than playthings and the surroundings. Children now resented being excluded from the group and also showed their preferences for one child over another.

The play and social interactions of children have been further studied by Parten[6] who has found out that the degree of social participation of children ranges from unoccupied behaviour to co-operative and organized supplementary play. On the very elementary levels the child is usually found in an unoccupied state. He is obviously not doing anything except watching other children who are playing around and happen to catch his attention for the moment. He would aimlessly follow the teacher and sit on the floor just looking around. A stage later than this is what Parten calls the solitary play, where the child plays by himself with the toys that are different from those occupying other children. He is obviously unaware of other children playing around him. In this type of play the child does not show any desire to get close to or speak to other children.

A stage further and the child spends most of his time in onlooker behaviour. He is attracted by others' play, watches it and talks to the children engaged in play. At this stage his social participation is different in nature inasmuchas other children and makes an attempt at social communication with them. He is no more unoccupied and moving aimlessly. He gives more evidence of social tendencies in onlooker behaviour than he gave in unoccupied state.

A little later we find him indulging in Parallel play. This type of play differs from solitary kind in the sense that now the child uses identical toys with those being used by others but through his play he does not make any attempt to influence the play of others nor does he try to change his own play. In other words, at this stage he plays beside other children rather than with them.

Associative play is still an advanced stage when the child plays with others. He borrows toys and lends his own play-materials. They run after each other with toys in their hands. Still there is no division of labour or actual co-operation in this type of play. Each child acts as he likes, nobody is interested in co-ordination and the sameness of goal in their play.

Co-operative and organized play is the highest form of social participation shown by the pre-school children. In this there is borrowing and lending together with specific roles assigned to each child and the play has one single aim for all the participants e.g. if they are building a castle there are some children who are carrying bricks, there are others who are pulling the trolley for reloading. Still others are busy constructing the castle. Thus all activity is coordinated towards the making of the castle which is a common goal for the moment.

The above-mentioned types of social participation are witnessed among children according to their age. The sequence appears as it has been given; the younger children indulge more in unoccupied, onlooker and parallel play comes next, and as they grow older the play takes over the form of associative and co-operative play.

Besides the type of social participation psychologists have also attempted to study the size of the group in which a child participates as he grows up in age. Green[3] through her study with pre-school children came to the conclusion that along with the increase in age of the child there is an increase in the size of the group in which a child participates. She also concluded that the duration of group activity goes through an increase with the increase in age. Older children participate in bigger groups and in activities that occupy the group for a much longer time. Older children are often found to prefer the company of much younger children rather than indulge in solitary play or an onlooker behaviour.

As the children grow older they develop the ability to identify themselves with the group goals. If the group is building a castle, a particular child belonging to the group considers it his castle and associates with it as if it was his personal project.

Together with the increase in social participation of the child we find an increase in conflicts and quarrels among children. The child gets into a group and tries to acquire a position for him .elf among his peers. This he tries to achieve by participation in different types of activities. While pushing himself in he often comes into conflict with the desires of his peers or their play so that a quarrel or a fight ensues. According to Green[3] the quarrels are correlated with the number of activities that the child participates in. It is a logical conclusion from the above reasoning, because by participating in more activities the child is edging in more often and as such is exposing himself to conflicting situation more often.

Very often a quarrel is not over a possession. Though a toy may be an obvious object of conflict yet behind this obvious trifle is the deeper motive of over-powering the peer. Self-assertion is at work here and that is the reason why high stakes are put on a small thing like a tiny box or a toy. This point is often missed by the adults when they intervene in the quarrels. They decide the issue in favour of one or the other party but in doing so hurt the vanity of others. Adults often attempt to prevent fights and quarrels, this does not necessarily help the children in learning socially approved ways of getting along with one another. Also these fights are often interpreted as an indication of dislike among children and so are discouraged. In reality studies have proved that quarrels are more frequent and seemingly more violent among children who are more friendly and close to each other. Close friends fight oftener and more violently. With age and learning of socially approved ways, children tend to engage less frequently in quarrels.

In due course the child learns to appreciate social position of other children as well as his own. This is the first time that he realizes that others have status and so has he himself, that others enjoy certain social rights and so does he and that inter-personal interference in such rights leads to unpleasant experiences and frustration. This is commonly called the learning of 'give and take'. The child now starts realizing his qualities as well as drawbacks and that is what enables him to indulge in self-criticism and self-evaluation.

Social participation leads to another aspect here. When the child starts building self image, the kind of self image that a child holds is very much dependent on the type of social participation he indulges in and the type of response he gets from his peers. Whether he is accepted by them or not, whether he is popular and sought after or he is rejected and unwanted member of the group, whether he is quarrelsome and as such shunned by others or is friendly with the other children and a sought for companion goes a long way to influence his ideas about his own self. A rejected and unwanted child often lacks confidence, suffers from inferiority feelings and confines to himself. The attitude of group members towards him is rejected in many ways during his subsequent behaviour towards others.

In his relationship with adults, the child at this stage begins to resist and contradict other's ideas. This, in a way, is an outcome of his growing self. When he has gathered that the ideas or wishes of others clash with his own he naturally responds with resistance. Usually resistive behaviour on the part of a child is interpreted as opposition to adult authority, disobedience and revolt against adult wishes but in reality the initial resistive behaviour of the child is a mere attempt at achieving self-help and independence. It is only the chance which makes it directed against others. Appropriate handling is important for the subsequent behaviour of the child. Often wrong handling at this stage gives rise to further negative reactions and in due course these reactions become purposive and directed against the authority of the person responsible for wrong handling at the first instance.

In most of the children resistance in relationship with others becomes most noticeable at the age of eighteen months with a peak at three years and a conspicuous decline by four years of age. This is precisely the period when children are exercising their will and are going through a period of self assertion.

From the point of view of adults this behaviour often takes over an alarming interpretation. It is an inconvenient nuisance and a rebellion against adult authority. Often it is a threat to the adult self-esteem and that is when the conflict starts. However, such resistive behaviour is short lived. As the child grows older he understands the social implications of negativism and resistance and so automatically a decline in such behaviour sets in. This decline is also a function of the understanding that adults have gradually acquired of the child's problems and the methods of handling them. The pattern of such a decline differs with different children and so does the age at which different children may shed this type of behaviour.

Certain conditions in the home tend to accentuate resistive behaviour on part of the child. Parents when they check the child on everything he wants to do provoke this kind of behaviour. His actions are often interfered with, he is coerced into doing things that are against his wishes and often he is teased needlessly. All these types of behaviour lead him to resist and revolt against this handling.

Sometimes parents try to stimulate and coax the child into doing things which are beyond his limited capacity. Examples can be when the child has just started talking, we often find parents who repeatedly ask the child to say out new words. This kind of behaviour proves tiring for the child and as a result he behaves in a negative fashion. Excessive nagging, coercion and teasing often leave their mark on the personality of the child so that even long after the period of childhood is past we see signs of resistant behaviour in an individual which is very much like that of a child.

Sympathy

Sympathy is one of the more advanced types of social participation, it is a much later development during childhood. It has been noticed that children show signs of sympathy round about two or three years of age, but actual appreciation of the good or bad of others is shown much later. In a study conducted on nursery school children Murphy[4] found that younger children do not show sympathy to black and blue bruises. Their sympathy is more obvious to bandages, crying, restriction of activities of children. It is with age that the child starts showing sympathy towards bruises, blood flowing, discomforts of illness or a swelling. These findings obviously go to prove that younger children have not yet acquired the discrimination and the power to perceive these phenomena as signs of distress. Distress for them should be an obvious distress and not expressed in subtle ways. She also found that the same phenomena shown under one type of situation brought out a sympathetic response but if shown under a different situation would fail to do so. Children were found to sympathize with others when their wishes were thwarted but if those wishes contradicted with their own then they failed to elicit any sympathy. Again if the child's initial effort to sympathize was rebuffed he would fail to show sympathy in a subsequent situation.

Competitiveness is also a function of age. Jealousy, though very close to competition, appears much earlier in the life of a child. He is jealous of parents' affection for each other, he is jealous of the possessions of other children in the group. Jealousy is witnessed very early and by two it is quite obvious. At this age the child does not show much competition but gradually as he advances in age signs of competition appear. It has been found to exist among children between the ages of two to six. The motives and causes of competition seem to differ from child to child and the degree of competitiveness in a child varies from situation to situation.

Competition, specially in class-room situation, is considered to be a healthy sign for improvement and as such is encouraged by the teachers. These teachers often forget some of the harmful effects of competition when this is carried on unchecked. Competition often gives rise to some callousness. A child is often respected by the teacher as well as his peers for he does better than others and not because he is a child. This leads to another situation when very little attention is paid to the child who does not excel.

Competitiveness has another distasteful effect that it takes enjoyment out of the task. In competition the work in hand loses its beauty and interest for the child. It is done because another child is doing it and not because the child is interested in it. Again it is done well in an attempt to do better than somebody else and not because the child has a desire to acquire skill. Competition when carried too far is often interpreted as a sign of underlying fear and insecurity on the part of the competing individual. A child when not helped to control this tendency often misses the fun in doing things and becomes a liability to the society at large with his attitude of self-protection and insecurity.

Leadership

As the child is developing through different stages of social participation, we see signs of leadership developing in his behaviour patterns. During their play in groups children take over the roles of leader and follower. Some of them possess qualities that enable them to make a forward move before the other members can. They take the role of indicating the right direction for the group activity. Obviously only a few children possess these qualities and so there are only a few leaders. Rest of the children take over the role of followers. Often during group play, it has been observed that different children act as leaders during different types of activities. A leader in the class is not necessarily a leader during games and vice-versa. For each situation the leader child has to have certain qualities which are essential for leadership. Some of these qualities are resourcefulness, intelligence and a number of new ideas. Often it has been observed that a child leader is not necessarily an aggressive child. Often a docile, quiet and unamusing child directs the activities of the group by throwing ideas which catch the fancy of more aggressive group members and as such are explored.

Leadership among children is not a one-sided affair. A child with all the positive qualities is not necessarily a leader. A child in order to fill the role of a leader has to be chosen a leader by other children. He has to be accepted in that role. In other words, he has to have an appeal, and has to fulfil some need in the activities of the group. Once the roles are taken they stay more or less constant. This is the reason why it is hard for a new child to get into the centre when the group is already set. Once a child has won a particular position in a group he is not very easily thrown out. Because of this very often there are cases of maladjustment in social relationship. Children who need to shift into the group cannot do so and as such suffer from certain difficulties. These are the situations when adult's help is needed. It is not always the case that the maladjusted child is at fault. Very often the group is so definite an hostile that the child is rendered helpless, in such situations an adult intervention can always help his acceptance in the group. Newly admitted children very often are put in this situation, other children in the class have already formed their groups and cliques. So that the new child is left alone to find a place for himself. An understanding teacher at this stage can easily come to his help in finding him a place.

Every child has a very strong need and desire to belong to a group. This desire urges him to be like other children, like them in the minutest detail of dress, hair-style and the way of talking. This identity helps him to feel one with others and get lost in the group and thus feel that he belongs to the group. Acceptance of the child in a group adds a great deal to his security, confidence and thus to the kind of personality that he develops.

The craving for social contact is apparent very early in the life of a child. For a healthy growth it is very essential that he gets an opportunity to move with other children, strive for his social position and succesfully occupy it. Considering the dangers involved in undirected participation, a little adult guidance and help can assure adjustment with least painful experiences and lesser waste of energy. A well-trained teacher understands the needs of children and also knows the ways to satisfy those needs. She acts as a common link between the members of that group and in a skillful manner she can help them to establish social ties among themselves.

Besides this guided help in social relationship the teacher can also help children in mastering certain skill—motor skills, artistic skills and again social skills. Any skill that the child has mastered is a help to him in his social relations with other children. A child who is good at drawing and painting has an instrument in his hand to attract other children around him. Similarly a child who can tell a story well or sing well has the beginning stage set for further social interaction with other members of the group. A well-trained teacher helps children gain these skills that are advantageous for their further growth as well as social behaviour.

The beginning made in social relations is very important for later development. Thus the importance of the kind of education, help and guidance which he receives during his first experiences in the group.

Social Behaviour from Childhood to Maturity

The instable and loosely organized social behaviour of early childhood takes on a stable and definite form during later childhood and adolescence. Older children make lasting associations and participate in definite groups. They start making definite appointments with each other and their meetings acquire a definite purpose. Groups are now formed around interests, hobbies and common personality characteristics. The group shows an obvious increase during adolescence.

Group ties are very strong during this period and the appreciation from group members means a great deal to the child. He spends most of his time in groups but goes back to the family for basic love and affection. On the provision of this security depends the nature of effect which the group will have on his behaviour. A secure, accepted and loved child seeks groups for enjoyment of sports, friendship and companionship while a starved and unaccepted child runs the risk of joining anti-social gangs and finding satisfaction in anti-social acts. During pre-adolescence the sexes show a complete separation in group life i.e., boys mix with boys and the girls with girls.

Adolescence is marked with sexual development and the accompanying attraction for the opposite sex. There is a tendency on our part to think that this mutual interaction is characteristic of Western culture alone. Practical work with Indian youth, however, has pointed out that this attraction is as natural with them as with any other group. Moreover it is complicated by the repressive controls and the inhibitions put on him. The recognition of this fact brings out the need of proper sex education for the adolescents.

The changes during adolescence are responsible for many new needs and problems. The adolescent, therefore, makes friendships because of these needs and problems. Those who fail to satisfy such needs are often replaced by others who would be capable of satisfying such needs. Once a social bond is established between the children the subsequent duration and frequency of social interactions depends upon the common interests, hobbies and skills or the satisfaction of mutual needs of the two. This explains the phenomenon of cliques and gangs.

The importance of these groups has been discussed in detail in the chapter seven on 'Psychology of Adolescence'. Some common trends found in friendships during adolescence are:

1. While the childhood friendships depend upon the same neighbourhood or class, in the adolescent friendship propinquity loses importance. Other factors come to determine the choice of friends;
2. Pre-adolescents and adolescents tend to choose friends of their own age and mental status;
3. Adolescents tend to choose friends from the same socio-economic status as their own family belongs to;
4. Friendhip being based on interests, goals and needs, tends to last longer than the friendships made in early childhood.

Social Maturity

Just as physical and emotional development aim at adult status and maturity so does the social development aim to achieve a mature adult status. The child moves from a completely dependent and self-centred existence to independent and socially mature behaviour. The question now can be raised as to what is socially mature behaviour? Certain criteria derived from the social roles and expectations have been established to determine the social maturity of an individual. A discussion of these characteristics is in place here.

1. A socially mature individual is expected to make judgements, decisions and take appropriate action in face of problems and crucial issues. The judgements and decisions are expected to be independent in nature and considerate of the rights and opinions of others. In other words he should be capable of recognizing individual problems and social roles of others.
2. He is expected to participate in co-operative activities without conflict with others. This can be possible if he knows the rules of fair give and take in social situations. He needs to recognize others' rights as well as his own.

3. A socially mature individual is capable of taking responsibility for his own actions. He ought to understand the significance and the implications of his actions. Also, his development should be secure enough to help him shoulder the responsibility of his behaviour.
4. Socially mature individual is capable of making and keeping a large number of friendships. Making friends and maintaining them over long period of time is an indication of his temperamental stability and the skill at avoiding conflict with others.
5. A socially mature individual is expected to have a well-balanced and objective estimate of himself. His attitude towards self and others depends upon the right estimate of his position in the group. A correct estimate of his assets and liabilities is helpful in the social interactions.
6. He is able to adjust to different situations. He finds it easy to assume different roles in view of the immediate situation. Temporary upheavals do not disturb him.
7. He is not self-centred but keeps the group welfare as his goal. He is capable of identification with the group and thus putting the benefits before his own gains.

Factors Affecting Social Development

Hereditary factors have often been mentioned as determinants of social development. However, there is very little conclusive evidence to establish that it is the action of heredity and not individual differences or early learning. The heredity is decided upon as a factor from studies conducted on infants in which they have shown significant differences in social behaviour. Another evidence in favour of heredity is the fact that children from the same family show different patterns of social behaviour. The former of these can easily be marked as a case of individual differences while the latter as differential family status or treatment. It is difficult to separate heredity from environmental or learning. The same difficulty persists in case of determining the role of heredity in social development.

Family provides the most important environment and learning ground. The influence of family is a continuous one and lasts over the entire life span. Family is a closely knit unit where members are closely associated and bear emotional ties with each other. Social reactions in this set-up get easily emotionalized and thus exercise a lasting influence on the individual.

The treatment given to children in the family is another factor influencing their social behaviour. Secure, self-confident, independent and accepted individual shows a different pattern of social interaction from the one shown by an insecure, dependent, helpless and unaccepted individual. A great deal of implicit learning takes place through imitation in family which is proved by the family habits and manners. The social status of the family determines the neighbourhood and the type of social associations which the child is going to enjoy. The frustrations from socially low homes is of a great social significance.

School also plays an important role in the social development of the child. The school programme, its activities, opportunties for healthy social communication and the guidance from his teachers are important factors in his social development. The type of discipline exercised is another factor which determines the social development of the child. One of the conclusions of this study pointed out that the social reactions in the democratic groups were characterized by friendliness and mutual understanding while those in an autocratic group indicated attempts at mutual domination. From these researches it can be concluded that the type of discipline exercised at home and school affects the social behaviour of children.

Measurement of Social Behaviour

Social behaviour and its various aspects have been studied through various techniques employed by the scientists. Through repeated and careful use these techniques have been improved and refined so as to give accurate and reliable results. An understanding and application of these techniques is essential for a student of educational psychology.

Rating scales have been widely used in the study of social behaviour. Under this method people familiar with the subjects are asked to assess them and assign a numeral to their behaviour on a given continuum. These scales are usually arranged along a certain number. We have five-point scales, seven-point scales and some of the psychologists have gone as far as to use an eleven-point scale for their studies.

In other words, we can have a rating scale spread over a number of points according to the degree of refinement which we seek in the ratings. The more extensive the continuum of a rating scale the finer and more delicate the discrimination is. At the same time we have to remember that too extensive a scale may lead to inaccuracy because of extreme refinement. A usual scale spreads over five or seven points. Besides being useful with adult subjects, rating scales have proved useful for children as well. In case of children usually teachers are asked to give their ratings on the characteristics under study.

The difficulty encountered with such rating scales is the subjectivity element. An individual who knows the child well also has the danger of knowing him too well and so being biased for or against him. To avoid this bias, scientists have used many refined techniques. They have used more than one observer and then compared the ratings of these raters amongst themselves. In one of the well controlled studies designed by Goodenough and Leahy the raters' agreement ranged between .84 and .97. Another check often applied on the reliability of ratings is their comparison with the observations recorded under standardized and well controlled methods. Considering the amount of work and refinement brought about in the rating techniques we have the assurance today that the rating scales can serve as a very reliable method of exploring the social behaviour of children.

Experimental method has been extensively used for the study of overt social behaviour. Under this method laboratory conditions are created and the child is put under these conditions and studied for his social behaviour. Studies are well known in which experimental play situations were created and then children were put under those conditions for study. Examples of experiments are available wherein emotions have been aroused under experimental condition and studied with minute accuracy. As reliability measure the experimental method has been compared with other methods and has now been established as a reliable method for psychological studies.

Sociometric Techniques: The study of the social interactions of a particular individual with every other member of the group is made possible through the use of sociometric technique. While using this technique the children are asked different questions and their responses to these questions are considered as their choices for companionship. Questions like "Who would you like to play with", "Who would you like to study with", "Who would you like to spend your leisure time with", etc. are asked. Children give their responses without suspecting the purpose of these queries. These choices are mapped in form of charts so that we can clearly see the children who are most popular in the group and the ones who are left alone and not very much associated with. This device shows us the social reaction of the entire group at a glance.

Besides asking questions sociometric techniques have often involved rating scales. Children in a group are often asked to rate each other along a scale and their preferences are thus determined. "Very often paired comparisons are used to determine the choices of children in a group. This is a very elaborate and extensive technique because in this case each child in the group has to be paired with every other so that the particular child can make definite choices regarding his social preferences. This is a technique which is rarely used when compared with other techniques, sociometry being the most extensively used.

Together with these techniques, observations have been an old standby. From the very early days of psychology, observation has been a tool in the hands of psychologists, and through its extensive use they have tried to make it as scientific as possible. Starting with completely uncontrolled running accounts in the diary records we have today come to the well-controlled and systematized technique of time sampling, which assures us the maximum amount of objectivity and least bias.

Time sampling can be defined as a technique for the study of behaviour in which repeated samples of observation of a standard duration are collected at periodic intervals. As a technique it owes its development and its considerable popularity to a series of related studies made at the University of Minnesota, in the United States during 1926 to 1928 and to sociological research programme in the Columbia Child Development Institute during 1929-1930.

Olson[5] originally developed this technique in 1926-27, for measuring the incidence of nervous habits in groups of children and the amount of these habits in each individual. Parten[6] took up the technique and introduced certain methodological refinements to it. For a good record of time sampling we need well defined variables that are to be studied and also we need to determine the length of a time interval during which the record is to be kept. Observations are taken during these units of time on each one of the variables observed, for instance if we are observing quarrels then they will be observed and marked in the respective cell during the Ist, 2nd, 3rd.... minutes of the observation interval. With the well defined variables, investigators claim, there is very little scope for subjective bias. The observer has no more to do than to put a tick mark whenever that particular behaviour pattern is encountered.

Inter-observer reliability was calculated as a check on the objectivity of the method. This method helps to limit the variables for observation and also facilitates scoring. Unlike other observational techniques it affords numerical data which can be transformed into quantitative analysis rather than qualitative and a descriptive treatment.

Summary

Social behaviour of a child begins with non-discriminative responses and after differentiation leads him to discriminated social responses. Early social interactions of the child are with the adults. It is much later that he starts communication with other children. His social behaviour ranges from unoccupied behaviour to co-operative supplementary play. The development along this range is a function of age. The size of group also increases with age, sympathy, competition and leadership are still later developments.

Social behaviour is more stable and meaningful during later childhood and adolescence. Adolescence also brings in the phenomena of intersex attraction. Social maturity is the ultimate goal of social development. Heredity, family, treatment at home, school and the kind of discipline exercised are some of the factors affecting social development. Rating scales, experiments, sociometric techniques and observations are some of the techniques used to study social behaviour.

Questions for the Student

1. Trace the relationship between social participation and group size and the age of the child.
2. What is the pattern of social interaction during adolescence? How does it compare with the early childhood pattern?
3. Discuss the criteria of social maturity.
4. Which is the best technique to measure social behaviour?

References

1. Gates, Arthur I *et.al. Educational Psychology*. The Macmillan., New York; 1948
2. Garrison, Karl C. & Gray, J. Stanley; *Educational Psychology*, Appleton Century Crofts, Inc., New York; 1955.
3. Green, E.H. *Group Play and Quarrelling Among Preschool Children*, Child Development 1933. 4; 302-307
4. Murphy, Lois B. *Social Behaviour and Child Personality*. Columbia University Press, New York; 1937.
5. Olson, Willard C. *The Measurement of Nervous Habits in Normal Children*. University of Minnesota Press, Minneapolis; 1929.
6. Parten, M.B. *Social Participation Among Pre-School Children*. Jr. of Abn. Soc. Psy., 1932, 27; 243-269.
7. Sargent, S. Stansfeld and Williamson, Robert C; *Social Psychology: An Introduction to the Study of Human Relations*. The Ronald Press Co., New York 1958.
8. Thompson, George G., Gardner, Eric F. & Vesta, Francis J; *Educational Psychology*. Appleton Century Crofts, Inc., New York; 1959.

7

Psychology of Adolescence

Adolescence implies the period of developmental sequence during which the individual is making a transition from childhood of full- fledged adulthood. it is difficult and erroneous to assign definite years to it because they will differ from country to country and from individual to individual. Surveys conducted on the age of maturity show that nutrition is closely related with the age of maturity. Children getting nutritious food mature earlier than others. The age of maturity also varies from individual to individual. Some children mature earlier than the others called 'early maturers'. There are others who mature obviously later than the average population and are popularly labelled 'late maturers'. However, a rough estimate is usually placed at eleven years of age to the early twenties. During this period the individual completes the process of maturity and achieves the status of a mature adult member of his society. Maturity, as the term is used here, does not mean mere physical maturity, it also implies mental, emotional and social maturity. Adolescence is the period when it is expected that the individual will show at least average intelligence, expected of an adult, as measured with intelligence tests. It is also expected that instead of giving immature uninhibited emotional responses an adolescent should be able to give mature and socially acceptable responses to emotional situations. He is also expected to respond to social situations in a way expected of adult maturity.

As the adolescent is going through this stage of development the rate and the type of changes which take place become conspicuous. The adolescent achieves physical maturity, which means changes in his body; from the child physique he acquires an adult appearance. With the physical maturity comes the sexual maturity and the obvious physical changes accompanying it viz. the growth of breasts in the female and the appearance of the hair on the face of male. Because of the changes along so many dimensions and at a conspicuously rapid rate, adolescence has been labelled by the older psychologists and educationists as a 'period of stress and strain'. Hall[4] has emphasized and so have other American and European psychologists that adolescence is inevitably and necessarily a period of tremendous rapid change. Change at such a speed that it involves a great strain for the adolescent to go through this stage. Because of this emphasis, the period of adolescence used to be given expressive names like 'rebirth' or 'renaissance'of which strain and stress form a prominent component.

In more recent times, however, psychologists and educators have been trying to gather experimental evidence in favour of the above beliefs. Objective research in this line has brought out the fact that adolescence does not necessarily and inevitably have to be the period of strain and subsequent frustration. Contrary to the origin all belief, it could be proved that the stress is not a natural part of adolescence instead it is the result of inhibitions, restrictions and limitations imposed by the culture on its adolescent members. Work of sociologists and anthropologists has pointed out that in cultures which impose comparatively fewer restriction and taboos the adolescents find it easier to achieve adult status and can successfully avoid the strains considered to be natural with these restrictions.

An added factor which contributes to the strain and the stress on the adolescent, is the lack of any proper recognition of this transition that the individual has gone through. Most of the so-called advanced cultures have no marked ceremony which marks the completion of this transition. The achievement of adult status is not marked in any way but is implicitly implied. This is, in a way, a reflection of the attitude of the social set-up towards their adolescent members. They are not given a definite status, their position is shaky and undefined. The parents, teachers and other elders can treat them as children or adults as may be convenient at the moment. Contrary to this position certain primitive cultures have definite rites which are performed during this period and publicly marked the recognition of an individual as a adult member of society. These societies impose lesser restriction and social pressures so that the adolescent grows up without facing much of conflict or strain. Mead in her studies of the primitive culture has clearly brought out the fact that adolescents from Samoa find adolescence far from being a period of stress and strain. On the other hand it is an easy transition from childhood to adulthood, relatively free from conflict, revolt against parents and consequent neurosis.

Most of the primitive groups have specific public ceremonies which are impressive and dramatic in nature and marked out an achievement of adult status by the individual. Tests are set for the prospective adult and only after going through successfully he is given this status. Therefore, these ceremonies are not a mere public announcement of their achievement but they serve the function of assuring them of their ability and making them feel proud of their achievement. After going through the set test they can confidently say that they have earned adult status through their own ability and potentiality. This helps a great deal in the formation of their self image. A comparative study of the adolescents coming from these cultures and the ones coming from advance cultures gives a very amusing picture. The primitive cultures bring forth confident, happy, well adjusted adolescents while the adolescent from the advance culture is shaky, insecure, not so confident of himself and is awkward.

The above discussion highlights the role played by the customs, ceremonies and restrictions of a culture on the development of an adolescent of the group. Reviewing the rites of our own culture we find that in certain sections of Hindu community a young man enjoys a special privilege as compared with a young girl of the same community. There is the 'thread ceremony ' arranged for him which usually comes during the late adolescent years. It is the symbolic ceremony when one tries to analyse the subsequent rights, which he gets. Only a man wearing the sacred thread can perform all poojas or perform the last rites of a dead ancestor etc. So, one could conclude that after the' thread ceremony ' a man enjoys all rights of an adult member of the society. In effect therefore, the ceremony is a declaration of the achievement of maturity by the adolescent. Compared with this the girl grows to womanhood unrecognized without obvious acceptance and recognition being given to her. Anthropologists and sociologists have dwelt at length on the problems of adjustment which the young boys and girls, brought up according to different standards, have to face when joined in wedlock. No doubt, our young men and women face some of these problems when the male is made so secure in his development without much attention being paid to the female.

The influence of repressive cultural customs and conventions has been dealt with in detail here in order to emphasize the importance of help needed by the young in tiding over this period as smoothly as possible. The logical sequence is restrictions, repression, conflict and frustration and the resultant revolt or the symptom. Young people revolting against the authority, running away from home and getting involved in delinquent acts are common occurrences of our times. All these acts are, in one way or another, the result of a revolt against the social restrictions, taboos, and inhibitions. These incidents are not only problems for the adults but involve a tremendous amount of waste of energy and time on the part of the youth. While torn with conflicts he is not able to make the contribution to society, which is commensurate with his potentiality. Compared to the future gains of the society the effort involved is very little. A social set up which can offer responsible and functioning role to its adolescents has made a good contribution to facilitate this transition of the adolescent.

Significance of Physical Change

A reference has been made to the quick and sudden changes that take place during adolescent period. It has also been brought out that these changes affect the personality of the adolescent in the sense that they make him shaky, uncertain and lacking in confidence. It seems in place here to consider how and why these changes lead to insecurity, lack of confidence and the awkwardness well associated with this period of life.

It was brought out that the formation of the self-image starts as early as the age of 2-3 years. From the process of this development, it is clear that like development along any other aspect this is also a process which continues throughout the life span of the individual. An adolescent is also adjusting himself to a self-image, which is in the process of development. Sudden bodily changes take sometime for him to adjust to. Specially so in view of the fact that the most parents show a surprise and unfortunately often tend to laugh at the awkward physical changes that the youth goes through. His own embarrassment about the fast growing limbs, and different parts of the body coupled with the laughing attitudes of others cause a particular disturbance in the ideas which he is forming about his identity. Rapidity of the change affects his appearance almost everyday, as a result his image of himself becomes highly unstable, which in turn makes him insecure and lacking in confidence.

One should not conclude, from the above that an adolescent desires to stay young or resents growth. On the contrary, he is keen to complete this period of growth as rapidly as possible and achieve adult status. The conflict comes when in spite of this desire he fails to accept the reality. He craves to grow old but when he does look grown up he needs to adjust to the amusing remarks and attitudes reflected by the people around him. Physical self of an individual is an important factor in the self-concept and if this very factor becomes an object of ridicule then it is but natural for the person to get disturbed about it.

Besides the effect on the development of self-concept, these changes are responsible for changes in other aspects as well. Among the physical changes the most important change is the sexual development. With the sexual maturity comes a change in the physical appearance as well as coming into activity of the endocrines, which mark the beginning of sexual arousal and the need to seek satisfaction for the same. The adolescent has already been made conscious of the changes in his body. He keeps preoccupied with these changes and the possible causes of the same. He feels awkward because the changes are too obvious. Embarrassment about his own physical self makes him conscious about other's physique as well. He starts observing others and the changes that his peers have gone through. Arousal of sexual urge coupled with this awareness about the growth in physical self attracts him to the opposite sex. His interest becomes heterosexual so that he passes through a period of conflicting desires. He wants to look attractive and appealing especially to the opposite sex and still has his own embarrassment to fight back.

Added to the already mentioned effects which culture exercises on the adolescent this becomes another aspect which gets affected by the conventions of the society. Sex carries the largest number of taboos and restrictions in most of the cultures. An adolescent with growing urges is clamped down with all the restrictions, inhibitions, and taboos. The frustration becomes greater in view of the fact that these restrictions come on without proper explanation of the phenomenon or the sex education imparted to them. The latter situation is peculiar of the Indian society.

It is also a common occurrence that the adolescents are brought to the clinics for guidance or therapy for personal problems. Enquiries regarding sex education given to these children reveal the obvious embarrassment of the parents. They are reluctant to impart sex education to their children and pass on responsibility to the clinician as if it is an undesirable task. In absence of parent education our teachers are also not trained along this line. They are not equipped with techniques of imparting this education simply because the training colleges do not consider imparting of sex education as a duty of the teacher. With complete deficiency along this line the adolescent is left with no alternative but to solve his queries regarding sex, all by himself. He often seeks the help of his peer group the members of which are no better equipped with the knowledge than he himself is. A counsellor or a therapist commonly deals with adolescents completely confused and shaken up by the scattered and unauthentic knowledge given to them by their fellow adolescents.

Attraction for the opposite sex, at this time, is a common phenomenon but the taboos forbid our adolescents all communication. Masturbation is a common phenomenon at this age loading the adolescent with a tremendous sense of guilt. Almost all the cases who come with problems consider masturbation as a source of physical weakness or a sinful thing to do or they express the opinion that by acquiring the habit of masturbation they have ruined their life and they will be rendered unfit for any future sexual life. In our educational system there is no provision to help this young members of the society to make an adjustment to the urges and cravings which are a natural outcome of sexual maturity. The problems of adjustment to sexual maturity are identical with boys and girls. Whatever difference exists is that of degree only, boys may find the adjustment slightly easier than the girls.

Menstruation and ejaculation through natural occurrences at puberty come as a shock to most of the adolescents. They need to be prepared for the change so that the shock associated with the sudden physical and other changes is warded off. In the absence of such preparation there is every danger of an adolescent developing personal and emotional problems. Against the background of complete unpreparedness when the phenomenon like menstruation occurs the child suffers a natural dread. Inhibitions on any reference to sex forbid her from talking about it to anyone capable of giving an explanation. Thus an adolescent is virtually driven to the life of dread, frustration, sense of guilt etc. depending completely on her own personal resources to fight these complexes back. No doubt, we find her awkward, unnerved and insecure.

Adolescence as a Period of Psychological Weaning

With maturity the individual gains an adult status. During adolescence, though he may have achieved maturity yet his adult status is not so secure. It can be argued that an individual can be either called a child or an adult but adolescent is going through a stage when sometimes and in certain situations he is called a child while in others he is counted as an adult. The self in the adolescent is well developed and the individual is constantly struggling to exert this self. There is a perpetual struggle in the adolescent to be independent, on his own and experience the delight of expressing his opinion or will or making his own decisions. This involves establishing himself as an individual besides the family. It is common in most cultures and specially so in our own that the parents and elders are constantly counselling the adolescent advising him and making decisions for him. With a turmoil to get emancipated from these psychological bonds he has two alternatives—either to continue with this struggle for emancipation and achieve it or tó take the easier path of postponing the psychological weaning and abide by the counsel of the parents and other elders.

The postponement often leads to further complications in case of marriage of the young adult. With the new member coming into the family and finding her mate completely dependent on the elders for any significant decision threatens the marital harmony of the new couple. Understanding the necessity to make independent decisions and leading an independent life can contribute a great deal to the attitudes of the parents towards their adolescent children. Parents can facilitate the growth of independence and this emancipation if they understood that this was the first step towards maturity.

The difficulty in the way of weaning comes from the fact that the adolescent who seeks it has still habits and ways, which are completely childish in nature. Conflicts between their urge for independence and their actual behaviour sets the parents against independence. Instead of encouraging the child to grow out of the childish way he is often held back from seeking independence. Often enough it causes a great deal of frustration and interest among the adolescent.

Psychological Functions at Home

For the adolescent, home is the primary social set up which performs two most important functions for him. The first one of these has already been dealt with in the previous discussion viz. defining the specific roles for the youth and assigning him social status. First and foremost, it is the family that recognizes the adolescent as an adult, entrusts him with responsibility and participation in decision-making for the family. A family may perform this function smoothly and thus help the unnoticed transition of the adolescent into adulthood and a family may fail to do so and thus cause conflict, strain and stress for the growing youth. The second function of vital importance that the home performs in the life of an adolescent is that of giving him opportunity of new experiences. The more extensive, educative, liberal and varied experiences he gains in the home the better adjusted and informed an individual he grows into.

The breadth and variety of experience is not the only consideration here. The quality of experiences influences his future responses, reactions and adjustment to life. The experience which he has of the parental attitudes towards him, whether he is wanted by the parents or not, whether he is accepted by them or not etc. bear a mark on his future role as a parent. A child growing up in a home predominated with conflicts and frequent encounters between parents finds it hard to develop feelings of security and confidence. Social climate of the house is another important factor, which may influence the development of an adolescent. How much a dominance is exercised in the house and how much submission is accepted from him influences his behaviour. Indulgence on the part of parents is another phenomenon, which affects the personality of an adolescent. Over-protected children grow into timid, dependent and helpless adults.

A peculiar type of experience in parent-child relationship is being experienced as a result of the peculiar family structure, which is coming to our society. The root cause of his peculiarity is the economic pressure in the fast industrialization. The necessity of both the parents working and staying away from home for long hours affects the growing child. He may develop the feelings of being neglected and not wanted by the parents when in reality that may not be the case. In such cases the parents do not get opportunity to act as ideals for the adolescents, they fail to set examples of expected behaviour due to sheer lack of time. A home with poor economic condition provides a completely different experience to the child. Due to lack of privacy, such homes give experience of witnessing all the processes of life as bare as they can be. Thus we see that the type of experiences which the adolescent gets depend very much on the type of homes he lives in. Type of social atmosphere which prevails in the home and the type of attitudes which his parents hold towards him.

A proverbially good home may be defined as one which can reassure and encourage the adolescent through the feeling of being loved, wanted and accepted. Side by side with this an ideal home should be able to help the adolescent towards maturity by encouraging his participation in family activities and decision making. In such a home an adolescent should feel welcome to bring his friends and associates who are accepted by the parents. The members of this family know how to have enjoyable time in the house and outside. Parents do not show anxiety, neglect or undue fussing over their children and each member feels free to express his emotions and feelings towards each other. A family, which satisfies all these conditions, is the one, which can help adolescent to achieve mature adult status in society without much tension, anxiety or strain.

It must be remembered here that the above description is that of an ideal home. All homes cannot be expected to satisfy all these conditions. As a matter of fact very few will satisfy even most of these conditions. There is, however, no harm in keeping an ideal in view and make efforts to achieve it. The young parents can hope to imbibe some of these qualities into their homes. The importance of the role played by home surroundings in the life of an adolescent cannot be over-estimated in view of the fact that most of the conflict and distress experienced by the adolescent is due to the pressures of life at home rather than due to their inherent nature.

Social Adjustment of the Adolescent

As a child the individual is a highly ego-centric organism. He starts his life as a center of the world, every activity, feeling and response is directed at his needs and their satisfaction. He views others around him as mere means of his gratification. He gradually grows out of his attitude. As he grows up he finds that the mother does not always run to him at the slightest noise that he makes, his demands are often overlooked and the world tends to acquire a different meaning than it used to. People start existing for other purpose besides the satisfaction of his needs and this marks the beginning of his social contacts and sociability. He begins recognizing others around him. To begin with he takes note of adults alone and gradually the recognition of other children comes in and responses are made towards them.

The early contacts of the child are very few and limited, the area of his contacts is in the family or just around it in the nearby neighbourhood. Researchers have shown a high positive correlation between age on one hand and the sociability on the other. It has been proved that as the child grows older he associates with more children, in larger groups and spread over larger distance. This increase in social contacts, group size and the distance in residence continues throughout the period of adolescence. Adolescence is the period of increased sociability with social contacts covering a large variety of interest groups. In the early adolescence, a child is found to idealize physique so that he has more fascination for adults than for his own age group but gradually his fascination wears away. He feels less closely related to the adult group and more to his own age group.

Besides an increase in sociability, age also witnesses increased differentiation in sociability. During childhood the physical presence of a individual child gives him membership of the group. Even during the co-operative play he just participates in the group play, he does not yet play a specific role. Adolescence marks the period of specific roles in the group and adolescence talks of playing the goalkeeper while an eight year old will talk of playing hockey. At this stage the nature of participation also goes through a change. Previously it used to be passive while now it has to be essentially active in nature. It is no more enough that the child is there but he must play a role and a specific role. A further complication is added to the situation by the fact that the group is no more passing and accepting, as was the case during childhood. On the contrary, an adolescent group is highly critical and trying. The member who is seeking acceptance from the group must go through trials set by himself or by the group. His acceptance depends on whether he can successfully pass through those trials or not. No acceptance is unconditional during adolescence and in adolescent groups.

When there is so much premium placed on the group acceptance, opinion of the peer group on various phenomenon acquires great importance. Acceptance is largely determined by these opinions and so the individual develops a peculiar loyalty to these opinions, which is generalized to the group as such. In this respect boys and girls show no marked difference. The group loyalty is as important to the boy as to girls. The group loyalty and the need for good opinion of the peer group is at the root of many conflicts between a teenager and his parents. The conflict between the mother and the daughter on account of hairstyle or the type of clothes, which she should wear, is too common in our home. It is a well-known fact that in these conflicts the mothers have always been the loser for generations. Why? The answer is simple, the opinion of the contemporaries carries more weight. On their opinion depends his acceptance in the group and at this age feeling of belongingness is even more basic than it was during childhood. At this stage it helps the awkwardness, insecurity and the developing lack of confidence. If only the mothers knew how much security it means to the adolescent to be like others, the minor conflicts could be avoided. A great deal of unconscious damage is done by a mother when she insists on how the daughter should dress up without reference to the styles of the age group. Nothing seems to disturb the emotional balance of an adolescent more than the realization that he is different from others in the group. Allowing a margin for individual differences, any adolescent deviating to a marked degree from the social peer norms should be a signal of potential maladjustment.

Parents and teachers often raise the question of harmful effects, which the peer group may cause. Peer group can cause unnecessary accelerated weaning from the family or pass on sketchy information about vital problems—specially sex in our social setup. It may also be a carrier of undesirable habits for the growing individual. On the other hand advantages of peer group participation have already been brought out earlier. The doubts can be partly removed if the parents and youth organizations take over the task of educating the youth in the community. If each adolescent is helped to acquire correct knowledge of the facts which is going to encounter as a result of the onset of adolescence than the adolescent groups are well equipped with authentic knowledge and do not run the risk of gathering sketchy knowledge.

Social and Moral Values During Adolescence

The child, to start with, is neither moral nor immoral, his activities can be best considered as a-moral. He acts as a result of the action and reaction of forces working around him. His conduct is a result of simple forces, which have played a part in conditioning his behaviour during early childhood. This is no more true of the adolescent. The child in the meantime has developed attitudes, ideals and established norms. Now onwards he is thinking and reacting in terms of ideals, which are taking their place in the individual personality. At this stage a large amount of his newly acquired abilities are used towards interests and problems, which are far reaching in nature and involve common ideals.

In western culture, an important role is assigned to the church as regards the development of moral values, character and personality. Situation in our own country is quite different. Temples are not the places where sermons are delivered or confessions made. They are merely places of worship where worship is highly individualized. Mores and attitudes towards religion and character are passed on to children in this country but the source of transfer is usually the parents and the family. The home and family are still the primary agents in the development of the moral valucs and character. Standards of moral behaviour are passed on the child almost unobserved and unnoticed by the parents.

Though it is the most important source of transmission of moral values yet home and family are not the only source. There is other agencies also at work in the development of moral values and character. Next in importance to home comes the school. The school should not be considered a direct source of character development but indirectly it influences the values that a child develops and the standards of moral conduct which he sets up. A school should normally aim at programmes fitting with the abilities of the majority of its students, if not all. A school which fails to do that is running the risk of students losing interest in school and finding ways and means of escaping the uninteresting school for some more exciting occupation. The activities indulged in for purposes of excitement are usually anti-social and non-conforming in nature. This is a first step towards retardation or a deviation in the character development of an adolescent.

A school needs to have staff available to the students. Not only that but the staff with proper understanding of the youth should be at hand. The teachers need to understand the needs of the growing individual. They need to understand his problems and be able to help him with these problems. A programme which is not conducive to motivation coupled with lack of understanding on the part of the teacher is a clear road to indiscipline and delinquent behaviour. The school can make its teaching really effective by making its programme well integrated with the life of the community. A programme which is set apart from the everyday community life is hardly effective in the development of moral values or character.

Neighbourhood and the community come next in the role, which they play in the development of values of the adolescent. The child usually selects friends and playmates from his immediate neighbourhood. Not only that but the values prevalent in the neighbourhood are easily picked up by the youth. It is the well-established fact by now that social and moral values differ with the group of reference. Delinquency is a praiseworthy quality in the society of thieves, middle class group is known for its rigidity apart the moral values while the slum dwellers and aristocrats alike are known for their laxity about the same.

Last but not least in importance comes recreation as a factor in character development. All children look for excitement, recreation and fruitful utilisation of their time and energy. When properly planned programmes are lacking the adolescent continues with his search for recreation and excitement. Very often, under the above circumstances, he finds this excitement in the delinquent behaviour and trespassing of certain social and moral standards.

Summing up the above discussion we can conclude that with his transition from childhood to adolescence the individual has learned the meaning of morality and has formed certain attitudes towards morality and social values. His development along this line is based on pure learning. He learns his attitudes and values through everyday experience in his family, school and neighbourhood. Thus, the major responsibility of value development of the adolescent lies with these institutions.

Intellectual and Religious Curiosity

Having gone through the complete sequence of intellectual, social and emotional development the adolescent makes his presence felt by questions and arguments. The newly acquired adult status needs assurance and acceptance, this is tested by the adolescent curiosity and by challenging the existing beliefs. On the intellectual side the adolescent asks innumerable questions about the phenomenon which previously he used to take for granted. The development in thinking and reasoning leads him to seek logical explanations of every concept.

Intense adolescent curiosity often becomes embarrassing for parents and teachers; specially so if the child is exceptionally intelligent and ask questions which they cannot answer. Often this questioning is interpreted as an obstinate act and revolt of the adolescent. Initially such questions are a mere desire to satisfy his intellectual curiosity. He does not mean to test the knowledge of the teachers or parents neither does he want to tease them but later when the adults do get teased and assigned motives to his innocent curiosity, the adolescent may indulge in purposeful teasing and testing the knowledge of adults.

At this stage for the first time he feels the impact of the religion and religious practices. The concept of God becomes a reality for him and again his curiosity leads him to the questions about God, religion and relationship between God and religion. Curiosity combined with the need for independence often gives us adolescents proclaiming themselves atheists. This challenge to the existence of a spiritual power is positively related with the individual's needs to exert his independence and the adult status. Insecure adolescents who come for help to the clinics are often the ones who proclaim atheism the loudest. The basic insecurity and the need for acceptance overcompensate by challenging the universal belief in God. Questions regarding religion are usually an expression of his intellectual curiosity discussed earlier.

Vocational Choice and Related Difficulties for the Adolescent

As already mentioned adolescence is the period of decision making. At this time the individual has to take a decision about his vocation as well. It does not mean that the choice comes all of a sudden at this time, it is a gradual process rooted in the experiences of early childhood. Yet the final choice does take place during this period. Importance of the choice is enhanced in view of the various fields open to him for choice and lack of proper scientific help in making the choice. Here the lack of proper guidance facilities is being pointed out. Vocational decision is an important decision for the adolescent and he often finds himself not quite up to the mark in making a right choice. His confidence in the choice is further shaken due to the fact that at this age he has started expanding his interests. He discovers new interests, abilities and attitudes. He desires to experiment with them and very often discards the ones which he does not find interesting after the preliminary experimentation. In other words his interests are not definitely marked yet, they are still flexible and waxing and waning in nature. This uncertainty about interests and abilities makes it rather difficult for the adolescent to make the final vocational choice. His task would be easier if the school system was to provide him with well qualified guidance workers and counsellors so that he could be helped in making this choice in his life.

A certain amount of experimentation is possible for the adolescent under a system of education like the United States of America have. Children are allowed larger mobility from course to course without binding them down to the final choice. This gives them an opportunity to explore their interests, know more about the nature of work involved and the qualities necessary for doing the job successfully. In case the career does not suit his interests and qualities he has the alternative of going to another field and experimenting there. This gives him an opportunity for knowing a vocation before he finally takes to it. On the other hand our educational system does not permit an adolescent any experimentation without paying a penalty for it—in the form of failing in the examinations. The choice, therefore, becomes more grave in nature than it is for the youth of other countries. Alternatively, the youth should have all information about different lines and the job opportunities, which also is not provided to our adolescents in the absence of guidance programmes.

Educational and vocational problems added to the existing personal problems make the burden of an adolescent heavier. He is left to struggle with their solution without any help from a sympathetic individual who may have the skills to help him with a possible solution. Guidance workers who are making pioneer attempts in organizing guidance and counselling work with adolescents witness great relief and happiness on the part of the adolescents when they realize that they have found a sympathetic listener who is willing to offer help with the solution of their problems.

Summary

Adolescence is defined as the period of transition from childhood to adulthood. Older psychologists considered it a period of stress and strain almost implying that the stress and strain were inherent in the period and that they were a part of it. Later work and experimentation has brought the evidence to prove that the stress and strain are not inherent in the period as such but that certain factors in the environment and cultural conditions' make this period acquire a certain amount of stress and strain commonly associated with adolescence. Knowledge of these factors together with the skill to control them can go a great length to avoid or lessen the amount of tension and frustrations.

Factors which are of vital importance to the adjustment of an adolescent are: (1) The changes which take place in his physical build and the coming into activity of certain glands and organs. There are rapid and sudden changes so that the adolescent has to make an adjustment to them as well as to the attitude of others towards these changes. (2) The natural growth of an urge for independence in the adolescence. The process of so-called psychological weaning from the home begins at this age and the youth struggles for it against heavy resistance on the part of parents and the family. Home during this period performs the function of helping the individual acquire adult status without much friction. This can be done by recognizing the status of the growing adolescent, assigning him proper roles and responsibilities and by giving him ample opportunity for experience along different lines. (3) Increased sociability and the adjustment involved come as an other factor to influence the adolescent experiences. The adolescent is going out of the family fold and acquiring contacts outside the family. The period is marked with intellectual curiosity and questions regarding religion and God. (4) With the physical and sexual maturity comes the time when an adolescent is acquiring certain social and moral values. He is also forming certain attitudes towards these values, which exercise great influence on his character as an adult member of the society. (5) Over and above all these comes the factor of a vocational choice which he is called upon to make at this moment. He needs help and guidance in making this choice and he needs a sympathetic individual to listen to his problems and difficulties. The community will be taking sound steps in providing a school programme, which may be challenging, satisfying and recreational for the adolescent. The community will render a still greater service to its youth if it provides him with adequate guidance and counselling facilities.

Questions for the Student

1. Why is adolescence considered to be a period of great stress and strain? Can the stress be minimized in any way?
2. How does culture influence the development of an adolescent?
3. Describe an ideal home for an adolescent. What is meant by psychological weaning from the home?
4. Discuss some of the special aspects of social adjustments of the adolescent.
5. Discuss factors which influence acquisition of social and moral values of the youth.
6. Describe the role of a guidance worker in development of adolescents.

References

1. Cole, Luella; *Psychology of Adolescence*, Rinehart and Co. Inc., New York; 1959.
2. Fleming, C.H; *Adolescence: Its Social Psychology*. Routeledge & Kegan Paul Ltd., London; 1949.

3. Garrison, Karl C; *Psychology of Adolescence*, Prentice-Hall Inc., New Jersey; 1956.

4. Hall, G. Stanley; *Adolescence*, Vols. I and II. Appleton, New York; 1911.

5. Horrocks, John E; *The Psychology of Adolescence: Behaviour and Development*. Houghton Mifflin Co., New York; 1951.

8

Basic Learning Theory for Teachers

Introduction

What is learning? How do we learn? What do we learn? These are questions to which almost anyone can give offhand answers. But to the psychologist and educator such answers are generally not good enough. The psychologist, as a scientist, wants and works to get verifiable, explicit, and detailed facts of the condition and circumstances under which learning takes place. He formulates a careful definition of what it is he is gathering facts about. He then organizes these facts into generalizations, principles, theories, and even laws that become a scientific description or explanation of learning. He wants to know all of this as a scientist.

The educator wants the same thing, because his fundamental task is to guide or direct the learning of others so that educational goals or purposes are accomplished. The educator is, in effect, an applied scientist who, on the basis of his knowledge and understanding of learning, can set the conditions and can guide the activities of others so that learning which is contributory to educational goals is most likely to take place.

In this chapter we will approach learning in terms of some of the more fundamental considerations. We will outline and examine some of the theories that have been developed as to what learning is and how it occurs.

Broad Groups of Learning Theories

Theories of learning can be classified into two broad groups:

connectionist, or stimulus-response theories, and field theories. Field theories of learning are also sometimes called Gestalt theories, organismic theories, or cognitive theories. The meanings of these terms will be discussed later. There is also what is called a functionalist theory of learning. Functionalism can scarcely be considered a third broad group, because it stands more or less alone.

Connectionist theories: Practically every beginning student of psychology understands the paradigm, S→R, which is assumed under connectionist theories of learning. The symbols S→R mean stimulus is connected with or leads to response. We know that the environment contains sources of energy that impinge on the sense organs of living creatures. We call these impingements of energy, stimuli. Light waves impinge upon the eye and we see sound waves upon the ear and we hear, chemicals upon the taste buds and we taste, and so on. Under appropriate circumstances of such stimulation, the creature—and in educational psychology we are almost totally concerned with human beings—responds or reacts. His muscles contract or his glands secrete. Certain responses seem automatically to follow certain stimulation. We typically call these "unlearned responses." But in learning, responses or reactions that do not normally follow certain stimulation do become connected with these stimuli. The circumstances under which this comes about is what interests the learning psychologist. When these circumstances are studied and are brought together in some logical, coherent pattern, we have a theory. When these circumstances are brought together as items of data, generalizations, principles, and laws, and have as their central focus the relationships between and among stimuli and responses, and how the two are connected, we have theories of learning that are then classified as connectionist or stimulus-response theories.

The simple analogy is often repeated that connections are made in this nervous system between stimuli and responses as connections are made on the telephone lines and the telephone switchboard between the persons making and receiving a telephone call. The nervous system is universally assumed to be the instrument of the human being through which this connecting occurs. In succeeding parts of this chapter we will list and describe in more detail the essential elements of this group of theories.

Field theories: The idea of field theories of learning is perhaps best comprehended by starting with an analogy. We have used the commonplace one of the telephone system with its switchboard to help us comprehend the concept of connectionist learning theories. Hilgard[1] once used the analogies of the soap bubble and the whirlpool as descriptive of field theories. These analogies are probably too simple to be particularly meaningful or enlightening. Perhaps a better analogy is an electronic vacuum tube, or even better, a battery-powered transistor radio. With such a radio we know the radio waves strike a particular part of the apparatus and sound (organized so that it is music or speech) comes to us from the loudspeaker. The radio has a connecting system of electrical circuits, but the important part of the apparatus is in the transistors-tiny bits of a particular metal in and through which energy gets reorganized to take a different form so that the instrument "behaves" by transmitting sound. The essential difference in the analogies lies in the relatively static concept of establishing connections in the telephone system and the dynamic energy transformations in the radio receiver.

Field theories of learning are focused in their concepts on "processes which intervene"[2] between stimuli on the one hand and responses on the other. What is meant by the phrase: "processes which intervene"? Although field theorists have done as much of their research as have other psychologists on rats or other animals, a discussion of the theory that uses terms that are a part of our language in referring to humans and their mental processes is perhaps more useful at this point. The human being is believed intuitively by all of us to have a mind that is controlling to some degree at least, as we act or react. We know; we think; we are conscious; we have purposes; we anticipate; we believe. The field theorist does not ignore these concepts but believes it is necessary to come to grips with them in collecting

1. E.R. Hilgard, *Theories of Learning* (New York: Appleton-Century-Crofts, Inc., 1948), p.14.
2. Hilgard, *op. cit.* (2nd ed.; 1956), p. 187.

his data, formulating and testing his hypotheses, and in organizing his material into a learning theory.

In a word, field theories are basically cognitive. By cognitive we mean that insofar as the human learner is concerned, there is an organization of his perceptions.[3] Stimuli from the environment are not discrete and independent each from the other. And, as the stimuli impinge, we are aware of the fact that we are seeing, hearing, and so forth. These awarenesses are related to previous awarenesses, so that we know for example that we are eating the same food (or almost the same food) or hearing the same music (different music but almost the same music) as on a previous occasion. Likewise, we can anticipate; we can know what is going to follow after. We relate events (stimuli and reactions) in time. We hypothesize means-to-end relationships. We do something because we want something. The word "cognitive" connotes a type of activity in the mind (brain) that correlates with these concepts. The field theorist makes cognition a significant aspect of his theory.

The field theorist looks upon the learner as a dynamic energy system set into an environment that is in turn a complex of other dynamic energy systems. The dynamic system that is the learner is in constant interaction with these other systems. Through this interaction there is change, and those changes that are attributable to the interaction are, in part at least, the products of learning. We would wish to emphasize the word *dynamic*, because the learner is not passive. He is undergoing constant change as a natural process of life. The environment is in turn not static but dynamic. The learner, then, as one dynamic system, is part of the larger system (environment), constantly interacting, hence adjusting, adapting, modifying, changing, or, in short, learning. The changes are lawful, that is capable of being accounted for in terms of generalizations or principles. The descriptions of the lawfulness of these interactions and change become the field theories of learning.

---

3. W.S. Verplanck, "A Glossary of Some Terms Used in the Objective Science of Behaviour," supplement to the *Psychological Review*, LXIV, No. 6, Part 2 (Nov., 1957), p. 7.

What is the meaning of the word field as a modifier of theory of learning? Hartmann has explained the term this way:[4]

> The generalized notion of a "field" within which all events occur is a commonplace in modern physics and astronomy. It has been found equally necessary and enlightening in recent biology, psychology, and sociology, considering these disciplines as representative of the whole domain of organized empirical knowledge or "science." All events in nature—and this statement plainly includes psychological and educational phenomena—always occur within some field, big or little, whose properties and structure explain the localized occurrence that it embraces and simultaneously permit increased control over it. The so-called inherent properties of an object are said to be ultimately traceable to forces impinging upon it from the surrounding field which is construed as the effective whole determining the attributes and behaviour of the part or parts coming within its influence.

Functional theory: A "functional" theory of learning would scarcely be called theory at all by some psychologists. In the subsequent chapters of this book that deal with learning, the reader will encounter descriptions of research and principles of learning that are almost entirely a part of the body of learning theory, which, if it is to be called theory, is functional. Perhaps the majority of educational psychologists, if forced to a choice of schools or theories of learning, would identify themselves with the functionalists. These psychologists have conducted their research more frequently with humans—children, college students, and adults—rather than with animals as their subjects. They have not vigorously pursued theoretical issues but have most often concerned themselves with limited problems, for example, forgetting, whole vs. part learning, memory, or transfer of training. They have been eclectic in that they take their clues for research or the data from research as they find them, whether or not they seem to fall into a theoretical structure. Typically, they ask a straightforward psychological question—for example, is it better to learn a poem as a whole or by parts, should addition

4. G.W. Hartmann, "The Field Theory of Learning and Its Educational Consequences," in *The Psychology of Learning*, Forty-first Yearbook of the National Society for the Study of Education, Part II. (Bloomington, Ill.: Public School Publishing Company, 1942), p. 166.

and subtraction be taught together or separately, what is the relation between practice and learning—and they have sought an answer through research. Having gathered their data, they make a generalization about the matter at issue but are not disposed to move much beyond their generalization. The word "functional" itself simply refers to the concept that one set of circumstances is related to another set; that in learning, for example, one set of outcomes has a functional relationship to an antecedent set of conditions. The functional psychologist is interested in knowing this relationship, and, at the moment at least, nothing more.

General Nature of Learning

Before proceeding further it is desirable to state something of the general nature of learning, to state its relation to behaviour in general, and to contrast it with maturation (or growth and development).

Behaviour: All living creatures seem to be continuously responding. Responding is generally described physiologically in terms of the contraction of muscles or the secretion of glands. We move about; we eat; we drink; our heart beats; we do a myriad of things. We call this activity behaviour. Not all behaviour is overt, that is, observable. When we read or listen to music we are also behaving. This behaviour is the basic datum of the psychologist. He wants to understand it. The learning psychologist, however, is interested specifically in *those changes of behaviour that he calls learning.*

Learning and maturation: Changes in the behaviour of the human being are ordinarily described under one of these two terms: maturation and learning.[5] Certain changes in behaviour can also occur as a result of physiological or anatomical changes. Changes may also result from such things as accidents, drugs, and so on, or deterioration of the body. These latter types of changes, however, have limited, although sometimes important, psychological or educational interest. Changes that are associated

5. See the article on "Learning" in the *Encyclopaedia of Educational Research* (New York: The Macmillan Company, 1950).

with certain changes in body physiology following work are said to result from fatigue.

Those changes that are associated with normal growth are called maturation.[6] Such behaviour occurs apart from any specific stimulation from the environment. *Those changes that are associated with specific stimulation are said to be learned.*

In any particular situation, these distinctions are seldom clear-cut. That each child talks, normally saying his first words at eighteen months of age and using phrases by the age of thirty-six months, is generally ascribed to maturation. But the language a child speaks is obviously the result of a specific environment and we say a specific language is learned. Speech is, however, highly complex and complicated behaviour, involving not only words, but articulation, voice quality, accompanying gestures, and other body movements. Other changes can occur in speech that result from anatomical or physiological changes in the individual or from fatigue. But they are apt to be recognized as such.

Distinctions between behaviour that is the result of maturation or of learning might seem to be of only academic or scholarly interest. This is, however, not the case. If the teacher or other applied psychologist understands the complexity of the changes that are occurring as the result of both processes and the interaction between the two, he is not apt to go far astray in his teaching. On the other hand, if he assumes that he can teach something that is actually in large measure the result of maturation he may do actual harm to the individual. Likewise, if he assumes that something cannot be learned because it must wait for maturation when the reverse is the case, he may neglect to teach what should be taught. For example, forcing a child to attempt to learn certain speech patterns before a certain maturation has occurred can disrupt the normal development of speech in the child and do damage. On the other hand, failure at an appropriate time to provide specific training in speech may be a cardinal educational error.

6. Part Three of this book deals with those changes that occur as we mature (grow older) and which are called growth or development.

Factors Associated with Learning

People learn, but they also forget. Learning may or may not be useful in new situations. We are all quite sure that whether we want to learn or need to learn makes a difference in whether we learn or not. Each of these sentences deals with an aspect of learning that is recognized to be important in one way or another. Psychologists have been systematic in their concern with these matters and have had something to say about each. A complete and perfect theory of learning would take each of the many factors associated with learning and deal with it in an explicit and precise way. All do not do so. The major factors are, however, here enumerated so that their relevance to learning and learning theory can be clearly discerned.[7]

Ability or capacity: A description of learning must take into account the difference among human beings in their ability or capacity to learn. The various species of animals have different capacities to learn. This is obvious. Man is known to have greater capacity to learn than other living things. However, man cannot learn to swim as well as the fishes or whales no matter how hard he tries; nor can he fly like the birds. Within the species, there are differences in what can be learned. We know men differ in their abilities to learn. One branch of psychology makes a study of these differences. Predictions of behaviour, including predictions of learning based upon these differences, are an important part of psychology. When we classify children as feeble-minded, normal, or in the genius class, we are classifying them in part in terms of their ability to learn.

Motivation: Motivation is a general term that encompasses those states of the individual under which he attends to certain aspects of his environment. As a result, his behaviour is both initiated and directed. It is said that motives have an energizing function and a directing function. We use such terms as "need," "want," "interest" to indicate certain aspects or conditions of motivation. These terms including the term "motivation" itself, are general and do not have precise definitions. We infer these conditions of motivation in terms of the way an individual is

---

7. The concepts that follow in this section are derived from Hilgard, *op. cit.*, (2nd ed.), pp. 7-8.

reacting. We infer hunger when he eats, or thirst when he drinks. We also infer needs for affection, or interest in science, as a result of individual behaviour. Because all human beings tend to display certain behaviour under certain environmental conditions, we ascribe certain motives to all persons because they are members of the human race. We say such motives are primary. They include such physiological needs as the need for food, water, and sex activity. Other behaviour is more specific and seems to be derived from primary motives. An interest in science, mentioned above, or the love of money would be examples of such motives that are called secondary motives. They are in one sense learned. They are, however, very important in accounting for learning.

How motives are defined and the roles they are presumed to play in human behaviour are very important aspects of learning theory. For example, one theory may hold that learning can occur without motivation, another that all learning is motivated.

Purposes or goals: Just as we infer from behaviour that a state or condition, which we call motivation, exists as an individual responds, we also infer that as he responds he has an end object or state in mind. This object or state is called a goal and he has as his purpose the attainment of the goal. Just as hunger is inferred as a motive, getting and eating food is a goal. As interest in science is an inferred motive, reading or hearing about science is a goal. Goals can be immediate or long-range. They can be objects or states or conditions. They can be simple or complex. The term "incentive," although not synonymous with "goal," is in many respects equivalent. It is ordinarily used to specify a goal-object or state which is somewhat explicit. The accumulation of money may be a goal, whereas a specific sum of money is an incentive that is part of the goal.

A part of the development of learning theory is to formulate ever more explicit and more rigorous definitions of these concepts. A second part of theory is to state the relationships between these concepts of goals or purposes and the learning process.

Rewards or effect: All learning theory must come to grips with this type of question: What are the effects of rewarding or punishing responses? On the one hand, there is the concept that sheer repetition of a response can cause it to become learned; on the other, that some sort of reward is essential if a response is to become established. These concepts become theoretical differences. A special term, "reinforcement," is frequently used in contemporary discussion of learning. It refers to the effect of attaining an object or state (goal) that satisfies a motive (need or want) on the establishment of a response.

Practice: "Practice," "exercise," "repetition," or "drill," terms used in everyday speech, are presumed to have something to do with learning. What is the role of practice in learning? Does practice alone result in learning? Does it take practice plus something else to produce learning? Can we learn without repetition? This concept of practice or repetition should be treated with some precision in any discussion of learning.

Forgetting: That we forget is acknowledged by all. Do we forget simply because of the passage of time? Or, is there something actively going on in the individual that accounts for what is properly called forgetting? This is still another aspect of the totality of learning that a complete theory must reckon with.

Transfer of training: It is a generally accepted assumption that responses learned in one situation may be elicited and be appropriate in a new situation. New learning may also be accomplished with greater ease of efficiency because of previous learning. This condition is called transfer of training. How this is accomplished is an item to be accounted for in a theory of learning.

Why more than one theory of learning?

One can very legitimately ask why there are several theories of learning. Why not one theory? As Hilgard said, "All the theorists accept all the facts."[8] Why, then, should there be differences of opinion among learning psychologists? There are several reasons.

First, there must be agreement that a fact is a fact. As psychologists conduct their research, there is seldom if ever any deliberate distortion of data. But populations on which data are gathered may differ. Data are gathered on children, on college

8. *Ibid.*, p. 9.

students, on adults. Subjects may be dull, average, or bright. Only after findings seem to be established for a variety of populations can we begin to assume that we have a fact of human learning.

Many psychologists work almost entirely with animals. This research is highly useful, and many fundamental principles could only be established by such research. But other psychologists are not certain that findings based on animals research can be held to be valid, in toto, for learning by human beings.

The material learned has significance in determining the nature of the data gathered. It is held by many that learning of nonsense syllables is not the same as learning meaningful material. Learning motor skills may not produce the same kind of data (facts) as learning how to solve a complicated intellectual problem.

Even when facts become firmly established as facts and are accepted by all psychologists, they may be subject to different interpretations. Every person brings his own unique experience to any problem of interpretation. One psychologist will give emphasis to one set of facts, another psychologist will emphasize other data. Perhaps the most important consideration is that not all the facts are in. All of human behaviour is exceedingly complicated, and learning is no exception. It will be a very long time until all the data that are important to understand learning are available to us. One can only speculate about the missing data either as he makes decisions in teaching or as he works out a theory. These speculations will differ from psychologist to psychologist and will cause them to form different conclusions.

McConnell[9] made a detailed analysis as to why different theories have arisen. He concluded that these items were important: (1) the different kinds of tasks learned in observational or experimental situations, (2) the different terminology used, with the connotations that these terms have, and (3) the emphasis placed on certain features of learning to the exclusion of other features.

9. T.R. McConnell, "Reconciliation of Learning Theories," in *The Psychology of Learning, op. cit.*, pp. 243-254.

A few psychologists have attempted to resolve the dilemmas presented by these apparent conflicts by postulating more than one kind of learning. Mowrer is a psychologist who has proposed two kinds of learning.[10] One is a kind of learning dependent upon contiguity (association) alone; the other requires reinforcement (effect). Tolman has suggested "that there are really a number of different kinds of learning." He goes on to say that, "it may turn out that theory and laws appropriate to one kind may well be different from those appropriate to other kinds. Each of the theories of learning now current may, in short, still have validity for some one or more varieties of learning, if not for all."[11]

Origins of Research and Theory

The earliest experiments that began to produce the basic data on which our knowledge and theory of learning rest were conducted by Ebbinghaus in Germany and Bryan and Harter in this country. Ebbinghaus studied the learning of nonsense syllables and drew the first curves of learning and forgetting. Bryan and Harter studied the learning of telegraphic language and identified many of the characteristics of learning curves that are as valid today as they were almost sixty years ago when the studies were made. They identified among other things the irregularity of the learning curves and "plateaus." Also, before the turn of the century, Thorndike, whose work will be discussed in more detail later in this chapter, was doing experimental work on learning with animals as subjects.

Conditioning: It was the work of the Russian physiologist, Pavlov, which has become known as conditioning, that gave the major impetus to theory-building in learning. The essential elements of the classical conditioned-response experiment are well known. A reaction that normally follows a specified stimulus is selected. It is assumed that this stimulus-reaction is a part of original nature or unlearned. A new stimulus is now presented

10. Hilgard, *op cit.* (2nd ed.), pp. 413-414.
11. E.C. Tolman, "There Is More Than One Kind of Learning," *Psychological Review*, LVI (1949), 144-155; reprinted in L.M. Stolurow (ed.), *Readings in Learning* (Englewood Cliffs, N.J.: Prentice-Hall, Inc., 1953), pp. 62-77.

in association with the original stimulus. After a time, when the original stimulus is withdrawn, it is found that the new stimulus now elicits the original response. The response has now become *conditioned* to the new stimulus.

Psychologists have studied the conditioned-response type of learning in great detail.[12] In Pavlov's classic experiment he conditioned the flow of saliva in a dog to the ringing of a bell. Other forms of behaviour that have been conditioned include the knee-jerk reflex, winking, the pupillary reflex, pulse changes, pitch of voice, gastric secretion, and the taking of food in newborn and older children. It has been found that the time relationship between the unconditioned and conditioned stimulus is a critical factor. Ordinarily the conditioned stimulus should precede the unconditioned stimulus. A second important factor is that of reinforcement. After a conditioned sitmulus-response reaction is established, if it is not reinforced with the unconditioned stimulus from time to time, the response will weaken and disappear. It has also been found that new unconditioned stimuli can be conditioned to a conditioned stimulus. That is, if B is conditioned to A, then C can be conditioned to B.

The most important contribution of conditioning has been to give us basic scientific data on which to begin to build a theory of learning. Hull's theory, which will be discussed later, is derived directly from conditioned-response data.

Now let us turn to descriptions of two stimulus-response theories of learning: Thorndike's connectionism and Hull's drive-reduction theory.

Thorndike's Connectionism

Edward Lee Thorndike (1874-1949) is generally considered to have been the foremost educational psychologist not only of the United States but of the world. He contributed to research and theory in the field of learning and to the fields of genetic psychology (individual differences), testing, and social

12. E.R. Hilgard and D.G. Marquis, *Conditioning and Learning* (New York: Appleton-Century-Crofts, Inc., 1940).

psychology. He also made fundamental contributions to the psychology of reading and arithmetic.[13]

Thorndike first stated the elements of his theory of learning in 1913.[14] That connections are formed in the nervous system between stimuli and responses is basic. These connections formed are illustrated by the symbols, *S→R*. Another word used to describe these connections is the word "bonds." Thorndike's theory is sometimes called a bond theory of learning. Thorndike has written, "Learning is connecting. The mind is man's connection system."[15] When and how this is accomplished was stated first in three laws: the laws of readiness, exercise, and effect.[16]

In the law of readiness, Thorndike stated: "When any conduction unit is ready to conduct, for it to do so is satisfying. When any conduction unit is not in readiness to conduct, for it to conduct is annoying. When any conduction unit is in readiness to conduct, for it *not* to do so is annoying."

The laws of use and disuse are subsumed under the law of exercise. The law of use reads: "When a modifiable connection is made between a situation and response, that connection's strength is, other things being equal, increased..." The law of disuse is stated thus: "When a modifiable connection is not made between a situation and a response during a length of time, that connection's strength is decreased."

Thorndike stated his law of effect in these words: "When a modifiable connection between situation and response is made and is accompanied or followed by a satisfying state of affairs, that connection's strength is increased. When made and accompanied or followed by an annoying state of affairs, its strength is decreased."

13. The beginning student in educational psychology should realize that the summaries of the various learning theories presented in this chapter represent in just a few pages what is often the major portion of a man's life work. To know all about a single learning theory would often require the reading of research monographs, dozens of journal articles, and perhaps several books produced by a single man.
14. E.L. Thorndike, *Educational Psychology*, Vol. II: The *Psychology of Learning* (New York: Teachers College, Columbia University, 1913).
15. From *Human Learning*, by Edward L. Thorndike. Copyright, 1931 The Century Co., p. 122.
16. Thorndike, *Educational Psychology*, *op. cit.*, pp. 1-5.

Thorndike modified his position in the early 1930's as a result of research he himself conducted. At this point, he placed much less emphasis on the law of exercise and gave much greater emphasis to the law of effect. Thorndike concluded, as a result of the type of experiment cited in *Human Learning Chapter 1*,[17] that exercise in and of itself did not result in learning. Repetition simply supplies the circumstances under which the law of effect can work.

The law of effect: When a connection in the nervous system between a stimulus and response is followed by a satisfying state of affairs, the connection is strengthened. Thorndike de-emphasized the effect of an annoying state of affairs, saying that annoyers do little or nothing to cause a connection to be weakened or eliminated. The nature of a satisfying state of affairs is an all-important consideration. At one time, satisfaction was associated with pleasure and dissatisfaction with pain, but this relation is not now held by Thorndikian psychologists or others. A satisfying state of affairs has been described as that condition which causes a connection to be formed. This has been called a circular definition in that a satisfier causes a connection to be formed, whereas a satisfier is defined in terms of connections formed. However, the dilemma is solved in another way. The way is to determine by empirical observation or research what it is that serves as rewards or satisfiers and hence are effective in causing connection or bonds to be formed. In this way there is no theorizing but simply empirical testing. For this reason, Thorndike's law of effect has been called *The Empirical Law of Effect*.

The strengthening influence upon a connection is known as a *confirming reaction*. Thorndike did not profess to know the physiological processes or what happened in the neurons as a result of the confirming reaction. He did, however, make this explanation:

> The confirming reaction is independent of sensory pleasures; indeed a pain may set it in action. The confirming reaction, though far from logical or inerrant, is highly selective. It may pick out and act upon the words one is saying, leaving uninfluenced one's posture and gross bodily movements and all that one is

17. E.L. Thorndike, *Human Learning*, pp. 8-15.

> seeing. The confirming reaction seems often to issue from some overhead control in the brain, the neural basis of some want or "drive" or purpose or then active self of the animal. This overhead control may be rather narrow and specific, as when a swallow of liquid satisfies thirst... It may be very broad and general, as when the purpose is to do well and win a game or to pass the time pleasantly... It may be stimulated to send forth its confirming reaction by a rich sensory satisfier, such as freedom, food, and companionship... or by a symbolic satisfier, such as the announcement "Right" in an experiment in learning.[18]

Insofar as education is concerned, there are two irreducible minimums in connectionism. First, the "bonds to be formed" must be identified. Second, the right responses must be elicited and rewarded. Practice under conditions of appropriate reward is the *sine qua non* of learning.

The concept of identification of bonds to be learned has led in education to detailed analysis in the various school subjects of the items (facts) or skills to be learned. In arithmetic, for example, each of the one-hundred addition facts (from 0+0 through 9+9) is to be studied in isolation from all the others, that is, practised and rewarded. The names, dates, events of history are to be identified as such. The 1,000 or 10,000 most frequently used words in reading are identified and then used over and over again in reading material.

For almost half a century, a connectionist psychology has been the dominant one in school practice. It is, however, now being modified and reformed in terms of other theories that have emerged since Thorndike's connectionism. They will now be discussed.

Hull's Theory of Learning

Hull's theory of learning has two highly significant characteristics. First, it is what scientists would call the most "elegant" theory of learning presented to date. Second, it is a "drive-reduction" theory. These characteristics are substantively different, and each will be briefly described.

---

18. E.L. Thorndike, *Human Nature and the Social Order* (New York: The Macmillan Company, 1940), pp. 15-16.

Nature of a theory: Clark L. Hull made a greater attempt than any other psychologist to work out a theory that would meet the tests of criteria that would characterize an ideal theory. In his most important book, *Principles of Behaviour*,[19] Hull's first chapter is titled" The Nature of Scientific Theory."

Hull has stated in this chapter:

> .... a theory is a systematic deductive derivation of the secondary principles of observable phenomena from a relatively small number of primary principles or postulates... In science an observed event is said to be explained when the proposition expressing it has been logically derived from a set of definitions and postulates coupled with certain observed conditions antecedent to the event. This, in brief, is the nature of scientific theory and explanation as generally understood and accepted in the physical sciences after centuries of successful development.[20]

Hull, as does modern science, recognizes two components that make up theory: data acquired by observation and interpretation of data. Data can be gathered by the most casual of observations or with great rigour from the most carefully designed controlled experiment. Science puts a premium on the latter. Interpretation can also be most casual or it can meet the most rigorous tests of logical thought. The latter requires careful definition of terms, stating basic assumptions as postulates, and the derivation of theorems through deductive logic.

Hull's theory conforms to these requirements of science and logic to a greater degree than any other. In this sense his theory has "elegance."

Drive reduction: Hull's theory of learning is a drive-reduction theory. Hull begins with the assumption that as a part of the process of living, the organism finds itself in disequilibrium with its environment, that is, it finds itself deprived of something it needs. This may be, as an example, the physiological need for food. Drive then becomes the "tension state" associated with the need. Drive causes the organism to become active, that is, it is energized. This activity produces its own stimuli and its own

---

19. From *Principles of Behaviour*. Copyright, 1943, D. Applenton-Century Co., Inc., pp. 2-3.
20. *Ibid.*, pp. 2-3.

responding. In the process, an object, state, or condition is attained that reduces the drive by satisfying the need. The word used to define this final process is reinforcement. The reinforcement of a response causes it to be learned.

Elements of Hull's theory: Hull's theory is a stimulus-response theory. Since only the stimuli and response in a situation are observable, Hull postulates what are called intervening variables or symbolic constructs. In its most elementary form the schemata of the total learning situation-process is as follows:

A stimulus (S) impinges on the organism.[21] This results in a neural impulse. If there are two or more stimuli, there will be neural interaction. The neural impulse leads to a reaction *(R)*. For this to occur, however, drive *(D)* is assumed to be present. Drive is a tension state resulting from a need. If the reaction *(R)* reduces the drive *(D)*, we have the condition of reinforcement *(G)*. The reinforcement brings about an organization in the nervous system known as a habit *(sHr)*.

Hull however postulates these additional symbolic constructs. It is assumed that the organism has a potential for reaction (called reaction potential or *sEr*) and that this reaction potential is not a constant but varies from moment to moment (oscillation or *sOr*). This accounts for the fact that a response or reaction to a stimulus is not always forthcoming or that it varies in strength. Likewise, as the organism reacts, work is done. If the reaction is not reinforced, as a result of changes in the organism following work the reaction is inhibited. This is known as experimental extinction and accounts for the dropping out of reactions (no learning).

Two additional considerations of importance are primary and secondary reinforcement. When a response results in the reduction of a need, we have a condition known as primary reinforcement. However, as Hull writes, "Careful observation and experimentation reveal, particularly with the higher

21. This and the succeeding paragraph are derived from Hull's summary of his theory presented in his book, *Principles of Behaviour* (*op. cit.*), pp. 383 ff. It follows, however, the form used by Hull, with the symbols used by him to identify some of his important concepts.

organisms, large numbers of situations in which learning occurs with no associated primary need reducation."[22] We have used food as an example of a reinforcing agent for the hunger drive. Yet it is not until food is eaten and perhaps digested that the need is reduced. It would therefore seem that reinforcement occurs before the hunger is actually satisfied. Or, perhaps better understood, money can be a reinforcing agent although it reduces no primary drive. This is assumed to be the case because money is associated with, among other things, the securing of food. Consequently we accept the concept, which has been experimentally verified, that the reinforcing agent may be a situation "involving a stimulus aggregate or compound which has been closely and consistently associated with the need reduction."[23] This is called secondary reinforcement and is recognized by Hull and others to be of very great importance, particularly in human learning.

Although a stimulus seldom if ever exactly reoccurs, we react as if it did. Hull accounts for this with the principle of stimulus generalization. When a stimulus and a response become connected through reinforcement, the response also becomes connected to other stimuli that lie on a "stimulus continuum." The stimuli that now evoke a learned response belong to the class of the original stimulus either in intensity or quality.

Hull's theory is of the same class as Thorndike's. As has been stated, however, it is more elegant—that is, it is more precise and refined. It would seem to give greater emphasis to motivations, particularly as these are related to basic and acquired needs of the organism. The law of effect, which is simply an empirical law with Thorndike, becomes related to the concept of need and gives to one who would guide or direct learning a rationale for the "rewards" that seem so fundamental in bringing learning about.

Perhaps the greatest contribution that Hull's concepts can make to contemporary education is the rationale it provides for associating classroom activity with the needs of children. The modern school curriculum is presumed to harmonize with human need, and classroom activities find their meaning in their

22. *Ibid.*, p. 387.
23. *Ibid.*, p. 387.

relation to things that children as human beings do. Hull says learning occurs because a need is satisfied either directly or indirectly. Hence, modern education in some respects find in Hull a theoretical base.

But what of meaning in education? Are men simply mechanical robots. Or, do they have purposes? Do they have understanding? Education which is simply training does not seem to be education. Perhaps the educator can find some help on these matters by looking at two representative field theories of learning.

All of field theory is developed on the basic assumption that an organizing principle is at work in governing the behaviour of living organisms. The more detailed nature of field theories will be explored by discussions of classical Gestalt psychology and the congnitive-purposive theory of the American psychologist, Tolman.

Gestalt Psychology

Gestalt psychology began with the work of German psychologists who were studying the nature of perception. Wertheimer is generally considered to be Gestalt psychology's founding father. We are all now well aware that the "moving picture" is not a moving picture at all but is a series of still pictures. The reality of the still pictures as flashed on the "movie screen" becomes our perception of moving pictures. "The focal point of [Werthimer's] theory is the fact that when two optical stimuli are perceived by the human eye in quick succession, the reaction is one of simultaneous patterning. "[24] Wertheimer called this the Phi phenomenon. The authors of this sentence just quoted also write, "Perception now has been demonstrated as being, not a series of optical stimuli, but a process requiring a physiological correlate apparently existing in the cortical process of the brain."[25]

Out of these observations of perception there emerged certain principles that have implications for the general nature of learning. One principle is that the human mind gives an

24. L.P. Thorpe and A.M. Schmuller, *Contemporary Theories of Learning* (New York: The Ronald Press Company, 1954), p. 207.

organization or pattern to the environmental world revealed to the organism through sense perception. The mind is not just a connecting system but a transforming system. Thinking back to our analogy of a transistor radio, it was said the transistors transformed radio waves into something else—sound waves. Without stretching the analogy, it can be said that the mind (nervous system, including the brain) does something to the stimuli from the environment. Responses are not mechanically automatic because connections have been formed but are adaptive and "good" because the mind gives an organization or meaning to the stimuli of the environment.

The German word "Gestalt" has as satisfactory English equivalents the words "pattern" or "configuration." In classical Gestalt psychology, the larger environment, although dynamic, is constantly achieving organization. A living organism, although in a sense self-contained or functioning semi-independently, is able to achieve equilibrium with the larger dynamic environment because the organism has the capacity and the force (by virtue of being a living organism) to accommodate to the environment. In other words, organization and reorganization are constantly occurring in the organism as it interacts with its environment. This activity of organization and reorganization of the organism has as one of its manifestations those changes in its responding that we call learning.

Insight: The word "insight" is used more frequently than any other to describe what is occurring in the organism as it is responding and learning. About the time of World War I, on the island of Tenerife, Köhler, another German Gestalt psychologist, conducted experiments in which apes learned in problem situations.[26] Typically, he would place an ape in a situation where it had to secure a banana (food) by piling boxes to reach the banana or by joining sticks together to reach outside its cage and drag the banana to it. The animal had to select an indirect way to solve a problem or reach a goal when the direct way was barred. Köhler used the term "insight" to describe the learning of his apes. He set up as "the criteria of insight the appearance of a complete solution with reference to the whole

25. *Ibid.*, p. 208.
26. K. Köhler, *The Mentality of Apes* (New York: Harcourt, Brace & Company, 1925).

layout of the field."[27] Köhler found that his apes did solve their problems and that they solved them not through blind trial-and-error but through perceiving the total situation and reacting "insightfully" to it.

In a more technical sense, the criterion of insight is "the sudden grasping of the solution which results in a process that runs its course in accordance with the nature of the situation, so that the complete solution takes place with reference to the configuration of the filed of perceptin."[28]

The whole and its parts: A further concept important in Gestalt psychology is that the whole is greater than the parts. In stimulus-response theories, there is the implicit assumption that both stimuli and responses can be analyzed and reduced to basic elements. In conditioned-response experiments, for example, an unconditioned stimulus is isolated and selected as one with which another isolated stimulus is to be associated. The response that follows the unconditioned stimulus and which is to be attached to the conditioned stimulus is looked upon as a relatively unitary and isolated response. Both stimuli and responses may be linked in chains or may occur simultaneously as a complex, but the assumption is that they are additive. The Gestaltists disagree. Considering largely the complex of stimuli, they hold that they are not additive in that the complex has properties not found in summing the properties of the individual stimuli. The stimuli are patterned or organized, and this organization provides properties of its own. In other words, the whole is greater than its parts.

Gestalt psychology's contribution to education lies in its concepts of the organization of stimuli and of insight. The world of the classroom in which the child is living and learning is not just a body of discrete stimuli, nor are his responses to it those of trial-and-error adaptions. The world is organized; it has meaning. The child can react with understanding; he has insight. Arithmetic is not isolated facts but a system of numbers. History is not names and dates but the sweep of events through time, with one thing leading to or following another. The child can

27. *Ibid.*, p. 198.
28. K. Koffka, *The Growth of the Mind* (New York: Harcourt, Brace & Company. 1928), p. 214.

respond to 3 × 4 because he can add three fours. The senior-high-school student can relate the insecurity of the depression years to the enactment of social security laws. Learning is meaningful. So say the educators, and so says Gestalt psychology.

Tolman's Purposive Psychology

Just as Hull has made more precise the same psychological concepts that are basic to connectionism, Tolman has given greater order and precision to Gestalt concepts. It has been hard for many persons to accept a connectionist or even drive-reduction concept of learning because of its seemingly purely mechanistic character. It appears to leave out that which everyday experience confirms as being most significant about human behaviour; that is, that it has purpose. Tolman has come to grips with this problem and has developed a theory of learning that puts purpose or "striving toward a goal" at the heart of it.[29]

Cognitive structure: In stimulus-response theories it is held that what a learner learns is a series of movements. These movements are connected to stimuli either by association in time and space (contiguity) or by reinforcement. In Tolman's theory, however, it is not a series of movements that are learned but signs or expectations. Movements in successive circumstances can never be assumed to be identical. The learner perceives the nature of the situation and responds in terms of these perceptions. These perceptions are assumed to have their neurological correlations, but their nature is now unknown. However, Tolman and others have a phrase to express the concept that somewhere in the neurological structure there is a correlate to the perception of the signs, expectations, and goals. The phrase, "cognitive structure," is still intangible in that it is not yet explicitly described. It is, however, an inference based on behaviour.

A molar theory: Tolman's theory is molar, in contrast to molecular. By molar, it is simply meant that its concepts are larger and more comprehensive in nature and scope than those of stimulus-response theories, which deal with smaller units. The concept of the atom in physics is molecular; that of the solar

---

29. The basic reference for Tolman's position is: E.C. Tolman, *Purposive Behaviour in Animals and Men* (New York: The Century Company, 1932). A detailed summary can be found in Hilgard, *op. cit.* (2nd ed.).

system, molar. Whereas stimulus-response theorists tend to analyze and reduce behaviour to its minimum elements, Tolman deals with the patterns, the larger masses of behaviour. He states that these larger concepts connote properties of behaviour that will never be revealed by making a molecular approach to behaviour. In this sense, Tolman's concepts are analogous to the Gestalt concept that the whole is more than the sum of its parts.

Sign learning: It may be asked in what respect Tolman's position on purpose differs from Hull's concept that the learner responds to satisfy a need. Both psychologists accepts the view that behaviour occurs as a result of a need; but whereas Hull finds a response being reinforced, hence learned, by need reduction, Tolman finds a response being learned in terms of the learner's perception of the stimuli. For Tolman, the stimuli take on a meaning as the result of their perception by the learner; hence they become a "sign" that behaviour will lead to a goal (satisfy a purpose). But the response is learned in terms of the "sign." Tolman has borrowed from the Gestalt psychologists the concept that the stimuli are patterned or organized. He has consequently used the phrase "Sign-Gestalt learning" to categorize his theory.

Tolman's theory is, like Hull's, a behaviour theory. Although it recognizes purpose, it is not a mental-state theory. Tolman's basic data are responses made by the learner in a stimulating situation. This is why it can be called a theory of behaviour. But Tolman's interpretations are important. The behaviour of those who are learning, according to Tolman, does not show a blind, mechanistic series of movements or other responses but rather that an intelligence is at work. Mechanistic theories would lead to the inference that the learner seemed not to be playing any part in his learning. It might be implied that the learner is simply a victim of his needs and the stimuli that impinge on his sense organs. Tolman would say that the learner is an active participant in the process. Through the processes of his brain, albeit that the nature of these processes are still unknown, the learner organizes the stimuli, attaches meaning to them, and responds accordingly.

Educators have not made a systematic analysis of the applications to their work implied in Tolman's theory. Yet it is obvious that there is a great affinity between Tolman's position and what teachers do. Teachers do not use such phrases as "cognitive structures," "Sign-Gestalts," or "molar behaviour." Yet they operate in complete harmony with the meaning of these concepts. As they teach, they will say, "What does this mean or signify?" "what would you expect?" or even the single word, "Think!" Perhaps the problem-solving types of activities that are often felt to be the best types of "learning experiences" are highly valid under a purposive psychology of learning.

Applications to Instruction

Having dealt with four theoretical positions in the field of learning, must we conclude that they are only of academic interest? It will be recalled that we have said that Thorndike's connectionism has had profound influence on educational methods. Although the other theoretical positions have had much more limited effect on classroom practice, they have not been without influence. It is perhaps fair to say, however, they have not been exploited for their full implications for classroom teaching or curriculum development.[30] How theoretical points of view may be translated into different practices in the teaching of arithmetic and their resulting effects upon achievement has been reported by Swenson.

A similar investigation was conducted and reported by Anderson.[31] He conducted an experiment in which two groups of children learned arithmetic by two methods of teaching, a "drill" method derived from a connectionist theory and a "meaning" method derived from a field theory of learning. The pupils were enrolled in the fourth grades of eighteen Minneapolis schools. Anderson has described the two methods of teaching as follows:[32]

> The drill theory has the following characteristics: (a) Arithmetic is analyzed into a great many units or elements of

30. G.L. Anderson. "Theories of Behaviour and Some Curriculum Issues, "Journal of Educational Psychology, XXXIX (1948), 133-140.
31. G.L. Anderson, "Quantitative Thinking As Developed Under Connectionist and Field Theories of Learning," in *Learning Theory in School Situations* (University of Minnesota Studies in Education, No. 2 [Minneapolis University of Minnesota Press, 1949]).
32. *Ibid.* p. 41.

skill. These units for elements are thought of as being comparatively separate and unconnected. (b) The pupil is to master these elements as relatively discrete acts of skill which need not be understood by the pupil as belonging to a logical system of numbers. (c) The pupil is to master these elements in the forms in which they are most efficiently and effectively used by the adult. (d) The pupil will learn these elements most efficiently and most completely through formal repetition.

The meaning theory, on the other hand, has these characteristics: (a) Arithmetic is a closely knit system of ideas, principles, and processes. (b) This system has an organized, logical structure which can be understood by the pupil. (c) Learning in arithmetic consists in understanding number relations and the mathematical significance of quantitative situations. Understandings of the number system may be called generalizations. (d) Drill or repetition is recognized as valuable for increasing proficiency in arithmetical situations after understanding has been developed or generalizations have been made.

Three hundred seventeen pupils were taught by the drill method and two hundred fifty-eight pupils were taught by the meaning method. Appropriate controls were set up to assure equivalency in learning except for that associated with method. The experiment was conducted over a period of seven months. A detailed testing programme was administered to evaluate the learning during the course of and at the end of the experiment.

This experiment is not being cited at this time to establish that one learning theory is superior to another. It is presented to illustrate that different theories have different practical application to schoolroom learning. However, the results are of significance. Anderson did not find clear-cut differences in the outcomes of instruction under two learning theories. He did find the drill method making greater contribution to pupils who were of initial limited ability but of high relative achievement. The pupils who were of higher ability but low achievement seemed to profit more from the meaning method. McConnell concluded, in his introduction to the monograph in which the study is reported, that the "investigation may... add strength to the hypothesis that certain learning theories are more complementary than mutually exclusive."[33]

33. *Ibid.*, p.5.

Some Common Principles—a Summary

McConnell took the same position as that just quoted above in the Forty-first Yearbook of the National Society for the Study of Education.[34] In this discussion he held that, although there are differences among the theories, there are also points of fundamental agreement and that common principles can be found. In the section that follows we discuss four key ideas about learning: (1) learning is both complex and organized, (2) motivation is an essential feature of learning, (3) response made as we learn can be on a continuum from the random to the insightful, and (4) learning involves processes in which responses are both discriminating and generalized. Following a brief discussion of each of these ideas we quote those relevant principles that McConnell has stated in his Yearbook chapter.

Learning in terms of either stimulation or responding is both complex and organized. This is true whether we think of learning in terms of $S \rightarrow R$ bonds or Sign-Gestalts. Although the psychologist, as a scientific experimentalist, may study or attempt to study a specific stimulus and a specific response, he also finds it essential to account for complex behaviour. The S→R psychologist talks about "chains" of responses; he does not deny that in some fashion an organization is achieved. Hence, we may conclude with McConnell:

1. Both situation and response are complex and patterned phenomena.
2. Descriptions and interpretations of learning, as of all aspects of behaviour, must be made in terms of the mutual relationships among events rather than in terms of independent properties or actions of the parts.

Motivation is an essential feature of learning. On the one hand, it involves need and, on the other, a goal that, if attained, satisfies the need. Although theoreticians may argue about the specific role needs and goals play in the learning process, few would deny the significance of motivation. Hull may say that attaining a goal causes the response that leads to it to

34. McConnell, *op. cit.*, pp. 256-279.

be learned. Thorndike may say that he does not know what causes a reward to be a reward, but that rewards are important. Tolman may say that reaching the goal simply confirms the expectancy that the stimulation carries, but he does say that behaviour and learning are purposive. It seems clear, then, that motivation cannot be ignored as a fundamental part of the learning process. These principles are justified:

3. The organism must be motivated to learn.
4. Responses during the learning process are modified by their consequences.
5. Motivation is the direction and regulation of behaviour toward a goal.

Do we learn by trial-and-error or is learning basically insightful? This might seem to be a point of fundamental conflict between Thorndike and Gestalt psychologists. But differences perhaps are intensified because of the nature of the learning tasks set in the experiments of the respective psychologists. If subjects are learning nonsense syllables, there is little opportunity for insight. Some material that has to be learned, even in school, has little inherent meaning and little relation to other material. Katona[35] has studied the learning of material of various amounts of organization and has shown that learning may be on a continuum from sheer rote memorizing to a high degree of organization. Hilgard has presented the idea of the *provisional try* to describe the learner's reaction to a situation.[36] This concept avoids the dichotomy of either trial-and-error or insight. The learner does the best he can in a situation. If the situation presents no clues for a choice, it is trial and may be an error. If there are clues, the try may be such that it is called insightful. We are thus in a position to accept the following:

---

35. G. Katona, *Organizing and Memorizing* (New York: Columbia University Press, 1940).
36. Hilgard, *op. cit.* (2nd ed.), p. 470.

6. So-called trial-and-error behaviour might be more appropriately described as a process of "approximation and correction" or of "trying this-and-that lead to the goal."
7. Learning is essentially complete (except perhaps for attaining greater precision or reaching a given level of performance) when the individual has clearly perceived the essential relationship in the situation and has mastered the fundamental principle involved in the concrete problem.

   All theorists start with the specificity of learning but provide somewhere for its generality. Learners do discriminate; they do generalize. No psychologist denies that transfer occurs. Thorndike talks of transfer through identical elements. Hull has his concepts of stimulus generalization and stimulus compounds. Discrimination and generalization are key concepts in field theory. We then conclude our list of principles with these two:

8. The transfer of learning from one situation to another is roughly proportional to the degree to which the situations are similar in structure or meaning.
9. Discrimination, as well as generalization, is an essential aspect of effective learning.

This chapter has been intended as an introduction to the psychology of learning. Study of succeeding chapters will enrich the understandings that have begun to develop here.

—G. Lester Anderson

Questions and Exercises (for Discussion and Study)

1 In your opinion, can a "science of behaviour" ever be achieved?

2 If teaching is an art, can a science of the psychology of learning be useful to the teacher?

3 Discuss the pros and cons of the proposition that a teacher should understand theories of learning.

4 Make a list of ten behaviours that you believe are the result of maturation and ten that you believe are learned. Compare your list with that of other students.

5 Secure an elementary geometry textbook and make a study of it as a model of logical development. What are the differences among axioms, postulates, theorems, corollaries, and propositions?

6 What does the word "empirical" mean to you? Consult a dictionary to help you formulate a statement of its meaning.

7 Someone has said that "learning" is a physiological process just as is digestion or breathing. Why should this statement be made?

8 Do you believe that differences in ability to learn will ever be found to lie in the body's chemistry? Why should this question be asked?

9 Criticize the maxim: "Practice makes perfect."

10 What do you believe to be the meaning of "meaning"?

11 Recall incidents from your own learning in which you believe "insight" was and was not manifest.

12 Criticize the maxim: "Spare the rod and spoil the child."

13 Do you believe the principles of learning can apply to learning to play golf and learning college algebra?

14 Speculate as to why the theories of learning described in this chapter seem to say so little about reasoning, thinking, or problem-solving.

References

Brownell, W.A., and H.E. Moser, *Meaningful versus Mechanical Learning: A Study in Grade III Subtraction*. Durham, N.C.: Duke University Press, 1949.

Bugelski, B.R., *The Psychology of Learning*. New York: Henry Holt & Company, Inc., 1956.

Hebb, D.O., *The Organization of Behaviour*. New York: John Wiley & Sons, Inc., 1949.

Henry, N.B. (ed.), *Learning and Instruction*, Forty-ninth Yearbook of the National Society for the Study of Education, Part I. Chicago: University of Chicago, 1950.

——(ed.), *The Psychology of Learning*, Forty-first Yearbook of the National Society for the Study of Education, Part II. Bloomington, III.: Public School Publishing Company, 1942.

Hilgard, E.R. *Theories of Learning*, 2nd ed. New York: Appleton-Century-Crofts, Inc,. 1956.

Kingsley, H.L., and R. Garry, *The Nature and Conditions of Learning*, rev. ed. Englewood Cliffs, N.J.: Prentice Hall, Inc., 1957.

Skinner, C.E., et al., *Readings in Educational Psychology*, New York: Rinehart & Company, Inc., 1937, Part III.

———, *Readings in Psychology*. New York: Rinehart & Company, Inc., 1935, chaps. 12-15.

Swenson, E. J., G. Anderson, and C. Stacey, *Learning Theory in School Situations*. Minneapolis: University of Minnesota Press, 1949.

Thorndike, E.L., Human Learning New York: The Century Company, 1931.

———The, Psychology of Wants, Interests and Attitudes, New York: Teachers College, Columbia University, 1935.

Thorpe, L. P., and A.M. Schmuller, *Contemporary Theories of Learning*. New York: The Ronald Press Company, 1954.

Woodworth, R.S., *Contemporary Schools of Psychology*, rev. ed. New York: The Ronald Press Company, 1948.

9

Nature and Conditions of Learning

The learning process is best understood by noting the changes that are most obviously expressed in intellectual and motor efficiency. Intellectual efficiency is demonstrated when the learner is able to recall information, to apply principles to new situations, or to interpret information. Motor efficiency is evident in the ease with which a task is performed, speed and accuracy being the principal criteria.

Learning is also expressed by attitudes formed, by interests stimulated, and by appreciations developed. It is relatively easy to measure the changes that are expressed by intellectual efficiency and motor skill. It is more difficult to measure reactions that are associated with attitudes, interests, and appreciations. They are, however, important evidences of learning.

Three elements are emphasized in a learning situation: (1) the learning material, which can be selected and organized for presentation; (2) the response to the learning material, which can be measured by testing situations; and (3) the process of learning, or what takes place between the point of presenting the material and the learner's response. This process is important if the teacher's effort in guiding learning is to be helpful. In most classroom situations, however, there is no precise way of knowing how the learner studies or the mental processes involved in meeting requirements. Thus, measurement must necessarily play a large part in a study of the learner's progress. The manner in which tests are planned determines the techniques used.

Techniques of Studying Learning

During recent years, research workers have been concerned

with the need for making their findings applicable to school conditions. For this reason, they have conducted studies in school settings, using typical courses and subject matter. Techniques for measuring gain in these situations may be classified as those that measure *indeterminate gain*, and those that measure *determinate gain*.

Indeterminate gain: In using the technique of indeterminate gain we obtain a measure of present status—the individual's performance at a given time. This technique is illustrated by the wide use of measurement surveys of school achievement. One of the most frequently observed kinds of evidence is to be found in differences in scores on tests administered to different age and grade groups. In one survey an investigator calculated the percentage of pupils in grades four to twelve who were familiar with the meaning of five concepts in social science. The results are presented in Fig. 9.1, which indicates that as pupils advance

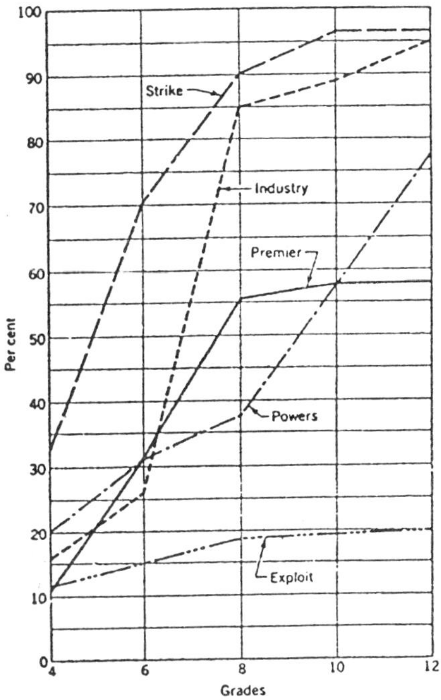

Fig. 9.1 *Percentages of pupils in grades 4 through 12 who recognize the meaning of five concepts in social science.* From S. L. Pressey and F. P. Robinson, Psychology and the New Education (Rev. ed.) (New York: Harper and Brothers, 1944.)

from the fourth to the twelfth grade greater numbers are capable of recognizing concepts such as *strike, industry, premier, power,* and *exploit*.

In using this technique there is no precise way of knowing how far the learner has advanced within a given period, because there are no beginning points to mark off his progress. Neither do we know whether he has made regular or irregular progress up to this time. The technique provides a measure of the status of the different age or grade levels under existing conditions, and affords a means of comparing the performance of individuals or groups.

Determinate gain: A more refined technique than that of one measurement of different individuals or groups is that of repeated measurement of the same individuals over a period of time. Figure 9.2 shows changes in scores of pupils in *reading, arithmetic,* and *spelling* during a five-year period. There is marked improvement in achievement in these subjects as pupils advance form the lower to the higher educational levels, measurements being taken of the same pupils at the end of each year.

One of the striking features of this study is that it was possible to show increments over an extended period of time. Repeated measurements made it possible to gain insight into the rate of progress from one testing period to another. It is a *moving treatment* as contrasted with the static kind of situation illustrated by the technique of *indeterminate gain*.

In more informal classroom situations, use is frequently made of the technique of using two or more testing periods as a means of measuring gain, The first testing, for example, provides a basis for determining what the learner knows at a given time . The second testing affords a basis for measuring his progress. The difference between the scores upon the first and second testing constitutes the gain (or loss) that has occurred.

The technique may be adapted to the subject matter of an assignment, a unit, or an entire course, the only requirement being that there be a pre-test and end-test, so that changes in the learner's performance may be measured. Teachers are interested in knowing the present status of achievement, but they

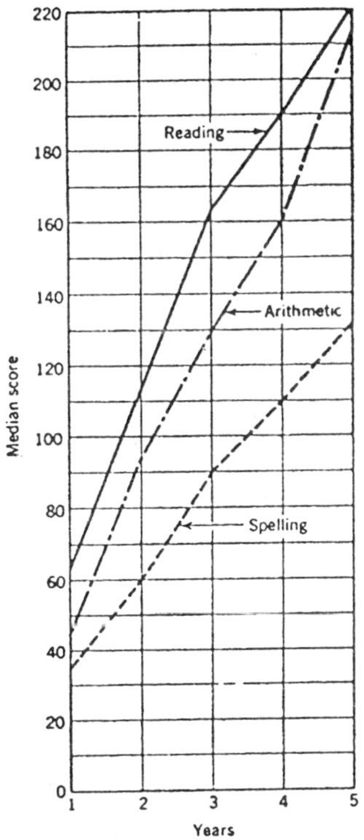

Fig. 9.2 Improvement in three school subjects over a period of five years (Hildreth). From S. L. Pressey, *Psychology and the New Education* (New York: Harper and Brothers, 1933),

are more interested in the change that has occurred during a certain period of time.

Learning in school is a continuous process. It extends through periods of instruction and study followed by testing, after which further instruction and study occur. The results of leaning are confirmed in a regular manner by some kind of evaluation, which may be followed by a consideration of difficulties and the elimination of errors.

Nature of Gains of Learning

Two closely related and interdependent processes make up the gains of learning. Progress depends upon how *acquisition* and *retention* supplement each other. The acquisition process refers to the cumulative effects of instruction when first measured, whereas retention refers to their sustained effects. These two processes are so closely related, that in reality, when we are measuring acquisition we are also measuring retention. Without the ability to retain the effects of previous learning experiences there could be no progress from one practice period of another. It is customary to refer to the mastery of learning material up to the4 first formal testing as *initial acquisition*. The ability to maintain gains after a definite lapse of time following initial acquisition may be referred to as *retention* proper.

Acquiring and forgetting as instruction continues: To keep acquisition and retention in the foreground during a course of instruction requires systematic planning. This includes consideration of the major elements involved in a learning programme: (1) defining the abilities to be developed; (2) selecting and organizing learning materials; (3) selecting activities to be performed by the learner; (4)devising testing situations to measure accomplishment; and (5) plans for giving and using tests. Each of these elements was included in a course of instruction[1] designed for 100 seventh-grade general science puplis.

Two of the abilities to be developed in this course were ability to *recall information* and the ability to *explain data*. The course was organized into nine units based upon the content of a textbook. The activities of the pupils were limited to reading the assignments in the textbook and becoming ready to take part in class discussion. The tests were designed to measure attainment in the two abilities mentioned above. Pupils were informed they would be given the tests at the end of each two-week period of instruction—at the end of each unit. They were not informed, however that, their retention would be checked at two-week intervals.

At the end of the first two-week period of instruction on Unit I, the two types of test were given to measure the amount

1. A.H. Word and R.A. Davis, "Acquisition and Retention of Factual Information in Seventh-grade General Science During a Semester of Eighteen Weeks," *Journal of Educational Psychology*, XXX (1939), 116-125; A.H. Word and R.A. Davis, "Individual Differences in Measuring Teaching Objectives," *Journal of Experimental Education*, VII (1938), 24-30.

of *initial acquisition* that had occurred during this period. At the end of the fourth week (the second two-week period) the pupils were given the two kinds of test on the material of Unit II. They were also given at this time duplicate forms of the tests that had been previously used for the material of Unit I. Consequently, at the time of testing the material of Unit II, the pupils were required to demonstrate their retention of the previous unit. During the remainder of the course the same types of test were given following each unit. The test at each testing period measured initial acquisition of the current unit and retention over the immediately preceding unit.

The progress of these seventh-grade pupils in recalling information is shown graphically in Fig. 9.3, in which average scores of the group are plotted cumulatively. The solid line refers to initial acquisition (scores pupils made on tests of current

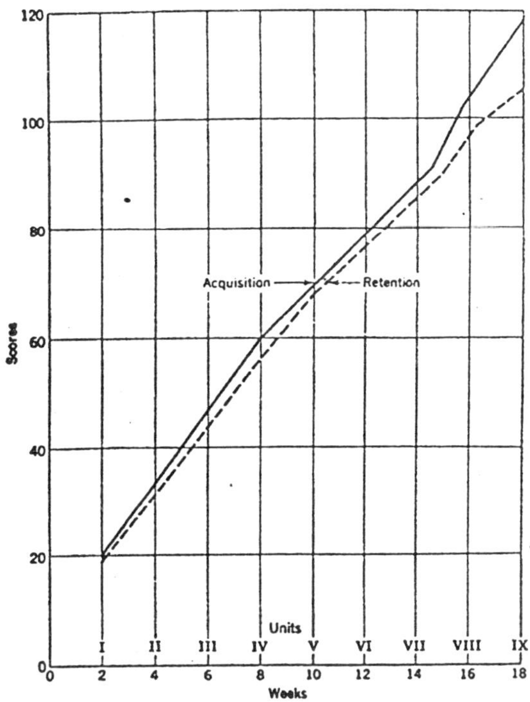

Fig. 9.3 Acquisition and retention scores plotted cumulatively (tests measuring ability to recall facts).

material at the end of each unit). The broken line shows average scores made on retention tests for each two-week period. This figure shows that while the pupils are mastering the material of Unit II, for example, they are forgetting some of the material of Unit, I; while they are mastering Unit VII, they are forgetting part of the material of Unit VI.

By substituting for average scores, the record of an individual pupil in Fig. 9.3 has special meaning. Bill Stewart, for example, would be able to know at any particular stage in this course what his *initial acquisition* and *retention* scores were. He might be told at the end of Unit VII that his initial acquisition score (expressed cumulatively—what he knew once up to that time) was 80, and that his retention score (what he knew two weeks after his first test for initial acquisition) was 75. In general his initial acquisition score would be higher than his retention score because some forgetting would be expected.

The results of the test, ability to *explain data,* are shown in Fig. 9.4. The data are presented in the same manner as those in

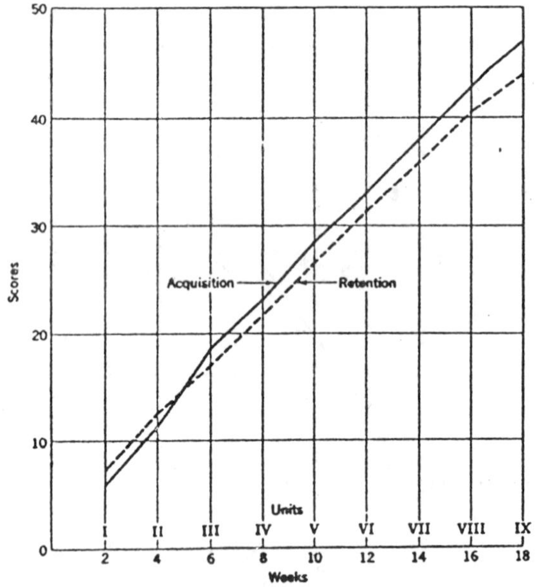

Fig. 9.4 Acquisition and retention scores plotted cumulatively (tests measuring ability to explain scientific data).

Fig. 9.3. The solid line shows average scores plotted cumulatively for initial acquisition, the broken line, the average scores for retention. It will be noted that the level of retention is almost as high throughout as that of initial acquisition. During the early part of the course the retention scores were even higher than those of initial acquisition. The similarity of the curves of Fig. 9.3 and 9.4 suggests that instruction in the ability to *explain data* may have strengthened ability to *recall information*.

The regularity of measuring newly acquired material and retention for two-week intervals doubtless contributed to consistent gains during the course. Since testing itself is an effective means of learning, initial acquisition is strengthened with each successive measurement of retention. Under such conditions retention is relatively high throughout the eighteen-week period.

Acquiring and forgetting after instruction ends: Although functionally similar in every stage of learning, retention that accompanies the acquisition process should be distinguished from that occurring after the instructional period has been completed. We have already dealt with retention as the concomitant of acquisition, pointing out that acquisition involves the combined effects of a certain amount of remembering and forgetting. It is obvious, however, that we cannot leave retention at this point.

In retention studies we are concerned with the same kinds of problem that were involved in acquisition. A principal difference is that a definite period of time has elapsed after the cessation of formal instruction. Two techniques are generally applied in measuring retention in school subjects. One consists of remeasurement of indeterminate gain; the other, remeasurement of determinate gain. The studies of retention in school subjects have either: (1) determined how much was known at the end of a learning period, and how much was known at definite intervals thereafter (retention being measured by objective tests); or (2) measured the gain in a subject or course during the period of instruction (using initial and end tests), and determined how much of the gain was retained after varying periods of time. Of the two procedures, the latter obviously is more accurate. This more refined technique provides for a test at the beginning of a course. The difference between the scores made on the pre-test and the end-test constitutes the gain during a period of instruction. It rules out the knowledge that pupils may possess at the beginning of a learning period.

Study of retention of school subjects in this country appears to have begun in 1906, when W. F. White[2] conducted an experiment on retention of arithmetic during summer vacation, using a group of second and seventh-grade pupils. Since that time, classroom studies have involved many types of subject matter and have included grades from the first through college. We shall refer briefly to typical studies conducted (1) in the elementary grades; and (2) in the high school and college.

Elementary-school subjects: Almost all of the elementary-school subjects have been investigated at one time or another. Standardized achievement tests are generally used to measure achievement. In a majority of studies the technique of indeterminate gain is employed: and end-test at the end of a grade or course, and a re-test after a lapsed interval of time to measure the amount retained. The greater number of studies have dealt with the summer-vacation period of approximately three-months duration.

Bruene[3] administered the Stanford Achievement test in May and an equivalent form the following September to children in the fourth, fifth, and sixth grades. Fundamentals of arithmetic showed a loss of .68 of a school year during the three-month summer vacation. Language usage showed a loss of .31; spelling .29; history and literature .26; and arithmetic reasoning. 07. Two subjects, reading and nature study, showed a gain of .22.

Studies of arithmetic show reasonably consistent results. Kramer[4] reports a median in arithmetic of 39.7 in June; the median for the same group in September is 37. Garfinkle's[5] study of arithmetic during summer vacation shows a decrease in

2. Study reported by M.J. Nelson, Thesis, University of Wisconsin, 1929.
3. M.D. Sterrett and R.A. Davis, "The Permanence of Learning: A Review of Studies," *Educational Administration and Supervision*, XL, No. 8 (1954), 449-460.
4. *Ibid.*
5. *Ibid.*

accuracy and a loss equivalent to almost two years of work for all groups tested. Brooks and Bassett,[6] Bruene,[7] and Kolberg[8] show losses of varying amounts in history during summer vacation. Morrison, [9] on the other hand, shows a gain equivalent to more than one-half school year on items of information, and approximately the same amount on items relating to thinking.

Investigations dealing with retention of elementary school subjects during summer vacation, when there is no prescribed routine and when review and study are voluntary, show a considerable loss in some subjects and gain in others. The subjects showing the greatest loss are usually those least likely to be practised during summer vacation. Subjects such as arithmetic fundamentals and spelling, for example, exhibit the greatest loss; arithmetical reasoning and reading, which may be used during vacation, often show appreciable gain. Improvement has been noted also in the case of world history,, nature study, and certain aspects of science, probably as a result of incidental learning through media such as motion pictures, radio, television, travel experience, and recreational reading.

One of the most ambitious programmes designed to offset the amount of loss during summer vacation is that sponsored by Cook, [10] who conducted a study over a period of twelve years. The subject of reading was selected for special study. The procedure consisted of three steps: (1) giving standardized tests during May; (2) subjecting pupils to varied kinds of reading experience during summer vacation; and (3) giving duplicate forms of the same tests in September, to measure the changes that had taken place. Children who participated in this programme were significantly better than those who did not join. Those who did not participate in one or more reading plans in the programme lost on an average .4 of a school year during the summer. On the other hand, only 5 out of approximately 230

6. *Ibid.*
7. *Ibid.*
8. *Ibid.*
9. *Ibid.*
10. R.C. Cook, "A Dozen Summer Programmes Designed to Promote Retention in Young Children," *Elementary School Journal*, LII (1951-52), 412-417. See also R. C. Cook, "Vacation Retention of Fundamentals by Primary-grade Pupils," *Elementary School Journal*, XLIII (1943), 214-219.

children who read at least two books and worked on assigned materials for six or more weeks showed a loss in reading when re-tested in the fall.

High-school and college subjects: Unlike the data for the elementary grades, which are generally presented as standardized test scores for various subjects, retention studies of high-school and college subjects are often analyzed according to the kinds of ability measured. These abilities frequently include ability to apply principles to new situations and the ability to interpret data as well as ability to recall items of information. The measuring instruments used in many of these studies are locally constructed examinations prepared for the particular purpose. The techniques of both *indeterminate* and *determinate* gains are used.. The time intervals vary widely, but many studies make use of the summer-vacation period.

Frutchey,[11] in studying high-school chemistry, used a pre-test in December followed by a post-test in May. One year later a re-test was given to measure the amount retained with respect to application of principles, knowledge of chemical terms, symbols, formulas, valence, and ability to balance chemical equations. The re-test in this study shows that 84 per cent of the initial gain was retained in the area of general information; 92 per cent in application of principles; and 66 per cent in knowledge of chemical terms. Retention computed on the basis of composite scores amounted to 81 per cent of the initial gain.

Wert,[12] using college students, measured per cent of loss gain over a three-year period in relationship to the gain made while taking a course in zoology. For the three-year period there was a gain of 60 per cent in application of principles to new situations. There was also a gain of 20 per cent in a test requiring the ability to interpret new experiments. On the other hand, there was a loss of 50 per cent on tests measuring terminology, function of structures, and main ideas. A loss of 80 per cent was noted in the test requiring the matching of names with structures.

---

11. F.P. Frutchey, Measuring the Ability to Apply Chemical Principles," *Educational Research Bulletin*, XII (1933), 255-260.
12. J.E. Wert, "Twin Assumptions," *Journal of Higher Education*, VIII (1937), 136-140.

One of the first observations to be made of studies dealing with high-school and college subjects is the rapid forgetting of facts, dates, names, formulas, abstractions, and detailed kinds of information. Figure 9.5 shows typical retention curves for several subjects. In general, these curves indicate that a large amount of subject matter is forgotten within a short time, frequently as much as 50 per cent within a single year. It should be kept in mind, however, that these studies involved use of tests designed to measure the amount of information the learner is able to recall. Of greater significance are results obtained by measuring retention of abilities other than recall of information.

Studies are consistent in showing that abilities of a higher order than memorization and recall are retained over long periods with slight loss. Some of these abilities, as has been indicated,

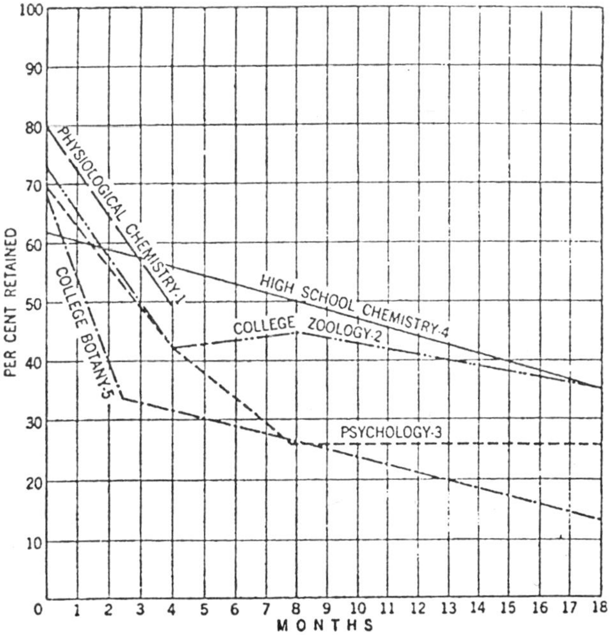

Fig. 9.5 Percentage of subject matter retained at the end of courses as measured by objective tests and at definite intervals after that time. (Curves 1, 2, and 3 after Greene; curve 4 after Powers; curve 5 after Johnson.)

show gain after instruction has ended. Cook[13] has summarized the results of studies that measure such abilities as follows:

> These experiments indicate that learning involving problem-solving relationships and the operation of the higher mental processes are relatively permanent, and that unrelated facts and mere information are relatively temporary. Unless learning involves differentiation and integration of old and new responses into a problem-solving type of mental process or into an organized behaviour pattern it has little permanence or value. How was it learned? is the important question.

Conditions of Learning

Up to this point we have been principally concerned with the processes of acquisition and retention. In the studies reviewed no effort was made to interpret the results in the light of the conditions under which they were obtained. The purpose was to illustrate the processes and to indicate the trend of results.

We now turn to the problem of considering that conditions the affect the learning processes of acquisition and retention. Under certain conditions these processes will be enhanced; under others, inhibited. Interpretation of the results of studies must be made on the basis of the conditions existing at the time. In a similar manner we need to take into account the procedures followed in our teaching if the results are to be appraised. Both research workers and teachers are constantly striving to discover and provide conditions that will be most effective in producing the kind of learning desired.

Providing proper conditions for learning requires careful planning. Much of this planning can be done while preparing a learning programme before instruction begins. In a carefully worked out plan, conditions favourable to learning can be built into the instructional programme. After this has been done, there is need not only for skillfully putting the programme into effect but also for adapting instruction to unforeseen conditions.

Comprehensive treatment of the numerous conditions that affect the learning process would require an entire volume. Our

13. W.W. Cook, "The Functions of Measurement in the Facilitation of Learning," in F.F. Lindquist (ed.), *Educational Measurement* (Washington, D.C. American Council on Education, 1951), pp. 3-46.

purpose here is to consider a few of the significant ones that are largely within the control and direction of the teacher. These conditions relate to (1) organization and presentation of learning material; (2) learning activities; (3) testing; (4) guidance; and (5) emotional and social climate for learning.

Organization and presentation of learning materials: Ranking high among the requirements for success of a course of instruction is the manner in which materials are organized and the meaningfulness of their presentation.

Organization: Organization implies there has been an effort to prepare learning materials so that the learner is able to perceive relationships between one element and another in a learning situation. It also suggests that, while the learner advances from one unit of material to another, he has opportunity to build a background that will help him in learning additional units. When learning materials are properly organized, there is a continuing relationship evident between the units of work. An organized situation is one that makes sense and gives evidence of some pattern.

Proper organization enables the learner to know where he is going and how to get there from the beginning of a course of instruction to its completion. It encourages the learner to view his materials in prospect and retrospect and gives him a feeling of satisfaction when he has completed his work. It establishes the main direction, with appropriate signposts to guide the learner and teacher. It also provides a basis for review and marks off the periods for testing and evaluation.

Modes of presentation: Organization in itself is ineffective without considering the manner in which materials are presented. The meaning that learning materials have for the learner is dependent in part upon the mode of textual presentation, including the length of sentences, the kinds of words used, and the length of paragraphs. It is also dependent in part upon the use of such materials as graphs, charts, pictures, and audio-visual aids. Because of the extraordinary part played by seeing and hearing in the learning process, the discussion will deal with the effectiveness of audio-visual aids.

The need for varied media of presenting learning materials grows out of the inability of words and abstractions to describe or explain. Everyone admits that, if words are inadequate, the next best procedure would be to have the learner come close at hand with the objects or events to be studied. But since this is generally impossible, the next best means is to bring replica of materials directly to the classroom by audio-visual aids.

The function of such aids is to make an appeal to those senses that can respond adequately. If we wish to present the sound of a bird, the most effective mode of presentation would be the bird itself, engaged in producing the sound. If this is not possible we might use some mechanical device for its reproduction. It is extremely difficult to describe colour, smell, physical shape, sound, and motion by means of words. Few persons, for example, can resist the impulse to define a spiral by making motions with their hands. One can recognize the sound of a coyote upon hearing it, and identify certain wild flowers by sight. These evidences of knowledge are non-verbal and suggest that seeing and hearing had more to do with initial impressions than the printed page.

We no longer need to depend upon opinion regarding the effectiveness of varied kinds of presentation. Research in psychology and education is replete with findings dealing with one or another aspect of these different modes. The purpose of some investigations has been to compare the effectiveness of audio-visual aids with conventional methods. In others, the purpose has been to compare one aid with another. In still others, the effectiveness of the slide and silent motion picture has been considered when they are accompanied by the instructor's comments. Effort has also been made to determine the value of the sound motion picture when supplemented before and after presentation by discussion.

Some investigations show that the silent film, with the teacher's commentary, is more effective than either the sound or silent version of the same film. Goodman[14] compared four aids: the *sound* motion film, the *silent* motion film, the sound

14. D. J. Goodman, "Comparative Effectiveness of Pictorial Teaching Aids," *Journal of Experimental Education*, XII (1943), 20-25.

film strip, and the silent film strip. The silent motion film proved superior to the other three; the two film strips were next and about equal in value. The sound film was the least effective.

In Craig's[15] experiment, first-year students in a modern secondary school were shown *silent* and *sound* copies of the same film. The effectiveness of the two kinds of film was measured by tests given immediately after presentation and four weeks later. On the test that measured *initial acquisition*, the differences in favour of the silent presentation with teacher's commentary were marked and statistically significant. On tests of *retention* (four weeks later), similar differences were noted, the differences being in favour of the silent form of presentation. Craig believes the teacher will obtain better results when he uses the silent version of a sound film and supplies his own commentary. In this way he can adapt the film to his purpose, and can alter the commentary as the occasion requires.

The net effect of research on audio-visual aids is that the difference between the effectiveness of one mode of presentation and another is relatively small. There would appear to be a close relationship between the effectiveness of one sense and another. For best results, use of several modes would be preferable to one.

Charts, diagrams, and tabulations in various forms make facts stand out strikingly. Film strips and slides are advantageous in arresting and freezing motion, permitting the learner to concentrate on the specific items. They afford a convenient means of exhibiting charts, maps, pictures, or enlarged cross sections of material. Much of the teacher's own material can be easily converted to slide form.

Considerable progress is being made in capitalizing on the possibilities of the sound motion picture. Many of these newer films are especially valuable for showing steps of a process, of portraying various aspects of life, or the scenery of distant places. Motion pictures are singularly appropriate for depicting movement. Movies in colour make a complete lifelike presentation in many situations, such as a study of animal and

15. G. Q. Craig, "A Comparison Between Sound and Silent Films in Teaching," *British Journal of Educational Psychology*, XXVI (1956), 202-206.

plant life.

Learning activities: Two important facts are so obvious that they may be easily overlooked. It is the learner who learns: learning requires active interest and concentrated effort of the learner. Learning is a result of what the learner does with his learning material and what the material does to him. The teacher often believes that, if the student listens to explanations given in class, learning has taken place. He may be surprised, however, to find what he thought had been taught well is not reflected in his tests and examinations. Unless the learner actively responds to a task, little learning results.

The importance of the learner's activities is demonstrated in Seagoe's[16] review of investigations. The individual who attempts to recall while studying, learns better than when he reads and rereads his material. His efficiency is superior when he takes a test over a piece of material immediately following its study. In science courses the learner who participates in laboratory experiments does better than when his activity is limited to the lecture-demonstration kind of presentation. The lecture-demonstration is generally' superior to lecture-discussion in high schools and colleges. Discussion is superior to the lecture in college classes. The lecture is generally superior to reading independently. Note-taking aids learning because the learner does something with his material at the time that he hears it. If he organizes and edits his notes, he gains more than when simply recording the main points. He learns best when he is most actively identified with a learning situation.

Activities and abilities: The problem of directing the learner's activities must be coordinated with the kind of abilities that we wish to develop. First, we make a decision regarding the kind of abilities that are appropriate for cultivation. Second, we select the activities believed to contribute to development of these abilities. It will be helpful to outline a number of conditions governing the regulation of activities.

1. The learner must have opportunity to practice the abilities selected. If we desire to cultivate, in social

16. M. V. Seagoe, *A Teacher's Guide to the Learning Process* (Dubuque, Iowa: William C. Brown Co., 1956).

science, the ability to comprehend information, there must be ample opportunity to read, discuss, and interpret materials. If one of the abilities is to interpret graphic and tabular data in the social sciences, the learner must have practice in interpretation of such data. If an ability in science is the application of principles, there must be opportunity for identifying and applying principles to new situations. This does not mean that we can be sure the individual's learning is restricted to the abilities suggested by the teacher. It does suggest, however, that we take the most direct route to the cultivation of the abilities selected. We direct practice upon the function to be improved.

2. The activities selected should be within the capability of the learner. This requirement is so obvious that its discussion hardly seems necessary. Experience shows, however, that it is an important problem in teaching. Can the learner perform the activities selected? Are they within his grasp? What activities might be engaged in at the beginning of a course? What activities might serve to develop preparatory skills for different kinds of activity later? These questions relate to the problem of readiness for learning, on which there is abundant research. On a more immediate basis it is our job to discover whether our students are capable of profiting by the kind of activities we select for them. Much of the information needed can be obtained before a course begins by evaluating the kind of learners expected. But even more important information may be collected during the first few class meetings, when we begin to know individuals.

3. Several kinds of activity may contribute to the development of a single outcome.[17] The problem of directing learning would be easy if our job were limited to selecting the task, identifying the response, and directing practice. The learning process is not that simple, however. For example, the learner may be

17. R. Tyler, *Basic Principles of Curriculum and Instruction* (Chicago: University of Chicago Press, 1950).

expected in a given case to develop the ability to solve problems in social science. Obviously, if this ability is to be developed, the learner should have specific practice in solving social science problems. Several activities, however, contribute to the development of his ability. While the learner is acquiring information in social science he may be thinking about the methods others have used to solve such problems. He may also form generalizations from his reading of facts that would assist him in reaching solutions. Almost any activity such as visiting juvenile court rooms, observing city playgrounds or simply reading current events would contribute to his ability to solve problems in this field.

4. A single activity may contribute to the development of several outcomes. The learner who is studying an assignment in social science to acquire information is, at the same time, developing ability to solve problems involved in his reading. He may also be learning to interpret data and to form generalizations. While reading for information he will likely change his attitudes toward certain social issues and discover interests he will later pursue. His specific task may be to become able, as a result of his reading, to recall assimilated information. But in reality, his study results in the development of several abilities or outcomes.

The fact that several kinds of activity contribute to a single kind of ability makes it possible to capitalize on the learner's efforts in attaining a certain outcome. The fact that a single kind of activity contributes to several outcomes holds promise for reaching many goals.

Activities and measured outcomes: Cook[18] has conducted a series of experiments in introductory sociology for the purpose of measuring outcomes in relation to different kinds of activity. He was particularly interested in measuring the influence of

18. L. A. Cook and Cook, E. F., *A Sociological Approach to Education* (New York: McGraw-Hill Book Co., Inc. 1950), L. A. Cook and R. C. Koeninger, "Measuring Learning Outcomes in Introductory Sociology Courses," *Journal of Educational Sociology*, XIII (1939), 208-225.

different activities upon the outcomes of *factual knowledge, attitudes,* and *critical thinking*. In one experiment, he employed the technique of "matched groups," the only variable being differences in the method of teaching. One group was taught principally by the lecture method, labeled the academic-learning procedure. In the other situation, classes were organized into small groups, each group being concerned with a problem chosen by its members. For these students there were few lectures, but many field trips. Certain specialists were also invited to share their ideas in group discussions. The instructor assisted in directing "study-group activities," giving help when needed.

Here we have two contrasting situations. In one, predigested materials are laid out and their mastery is required. In the other, the learner is encouraged to discover his own solutions with as little direction as possible.

The results definitely favour the group working under the flexible work plan. The two groups showed the same average gain of 22.5 points on recall of information. The gain of the group following the flexible plan was 14.8 points on *attitudes*, which was approximately twice that of the academic-learning group. On the test of *critical thinking* the gain for the *flexible* group was 12.1 as compared with 3.5 for the *academic* group. Cook concludes:

> Study after study casts serious doubt on the effectiveness of academic teaching in human relations areas. Students do learn, but what they learn, how much and how permanent, in comparison with group procedures and perceptual learning is not encouraging. The lecture-textbook system is best in imparting information, although retention of facts beyond immediate recall is low. The forgetting is high, for one tends to remember the learnings that are repeatedly used....
>
> Academic learning is probably weak in influencing attitudes and weakest of all in inducing behavioural changes, a point of critical importance in any sort of life-centered school. Ideas do not get translated into values and values into habitual ways of acting. While it is never easy to do, for it depends in part on circumstances beyond a teacher's control, the need to work for this objective is an educator's greatest responsibility.

Some teachers stress one or two kinds of activity, whereas others emphasize several. Many regard reading, listening to explanations, and discussions of primary importance. Still others emphasize projects and problems where information is collected and evaluated. Some teachers require few activities but give tests frequently; others sponsor many activities but give tests infrequently.

Several different kinds of activity are needed to ensure learning and to recognize individual differences. Tyler[19] states that the experiments in teaching zoology show that some students learn principles through certain types of laboratory exercise, others through demonstration and problems, and still others through other kinds of experience. No one type of activity appears to be equally effective with all students. Loomer[20] reached a similar conclusion on the basis of a study of the effects of three types of learning activity in art. He concludes:

> Various attempts must be made to adjust the learning experiences to the way individual students learn.... some learn best through lecture and demonstration... where the emphasis is on verbal learning; others... learn best in a laboratory situation where the actual manipulation allows more motor coordination in the learning process.

Testing: Three overlapping but fairly distinct functions of testing are recognized: (a) the directive function, (b) the selective function, and (c) the motivating function.[21]

The directive function: Testing, more than any other element in an instructional programme, directs the learning process. The teacher may state that certain abilities are to be developed and suggest the activities to be used; but it is the kind of tests given that influences the learner most. Where testing programmes are sponsored by school systems, testing also influences what teachers stress in subjects and their methods of teaching.

The type of test the learner expects to take influences his method of study. He will use certain methods when anticipating

---

19. R. Tyler, "Prevailing Misconceptions," *Journal of Higher Education* (June, 1933), 288.
20. I. C. Loomer, "A Study of Certain Effects of Three Types of Learning Experience in Art as Revealed in the Drawings by the Participants," *Journal of Experimental Education*, XXII (1953). 65-102.
21. W. W. Cook, *op. cit.*

an essay examination and other methods when expecting objective tests. When the student expects an essay examination, he tends to search for relationships and to organize his materials into large divisions or units. He also devotes considerable time to recalling information. The student spends more time in preparing for an essay examination than for the objective type.

Methods of studying also vary with different types of objective examinations. The recall technique requires the learner to supply answers to questions; the recognition requires him to identify answers listed. Knowing that the recall technique will be used, the learner studies his material in detail, making note of such factual data as names, dates, locations, and the results of specific studies. On the other hand, when expecting to be measured by the recognition technique, he is likely to concentrate on principles and points of view. He seems to operate on the belief that if he understands the general theme or point of view he will be able to select from the answers provided. The methods used by the student in preparing for the recognition type of item prepare him for that type mainly; the methods used in preparing for the recall type prepare him for more than recognition.

As a result of different methods of study in anticipation of the two measuring techniques, thoroughness and accuracy of information are affected at the time of measuring initial acquisition. The recall technique makes more rigorous demands upon the learner's accuracy. He also fares better on tests of retention that may be given later.

The selective function: Tests define accomplishment, and enable the learner to determine the rightness or wrongness of his responses. Experimental evidence indicates that the more direct and immediate the knowledge of results, the better. Commenting on the importance of immediate knowledge of results in training programmes, Wolfle says:[22]

> Giving the men in training an immediate knowledge of their results was one of the most useful contributions that psychology made to military training. Instances occurred where men presumably trying to learn a complex weapon never knew what they did well or poorly. In some cases the men got worse rather than better.

22. D. Wolfle, "Military Training and the Useful Parts of Learning Theory," *Journal of Consulting Psychology*, X (1946).

If the learner is right we should let him know; if he is wrong we should tell him wherein he is wrong. In some situations the learner profits most when he is given opportunity to analyze and correct his own errors.

An experiment by Meddleton[23] is an excellent example of an effort to relate testing to the learner's activity. He measured the effect of specific practice upon acquisition and retention of the four fundamental arithmetical processes. Each child in the experimental groups had *daily practice,* using specially prepared sheets of number combinations. Tests for measuring progress were given at approximately three-month intervals: December, 1952, March, 1953, June, 1953, and July, 1953.

The plan of specific practice with the use of systematically compiled work sheets resulted in marked improvement. The superior gains of the experimental over the control groups were maintained after the vacation period. Meddleton interprets his results as follows:

> Whether the children were conscious of it or not, it would appear that the practice material in the basic number combinations has been both diagnostic and remedial. Each child had the opportunity to notice his own errors. Any regular occurrence of a mistake throughout the class could have been observed by the teacher, and led to further consolidatory exercises. Besides this each child was afforded the chance, after corrections, of remedying his own particular number weakness. Repetition of the number combinations at a later date provides a ready estimate of the value of any remedial measures.

The motivating function: Tests also stimulate increased effort. In the high schools many teachers believe tests constitute the principal means of stimulating learning. In the colleges and universities the student's interest in testing is heightened because of the importance attached to a few crucial examinations. The sporadic last-minute efforts of college students toward the end of a quarter or semester attest to the motivating effect of examinations.

---

23. I. G. Meddleton, "An Experimental Investigation into the Systematic Teaching of Number Combinations in Arithmetic," *British Journal oj Educational Psychology,* XXVI (1956), 117-127.

If tests stimulate the learner to increased activity, it would seem that for best results they should be given frequently. Fitch[24] conducted an experiment involving two classes in government at Purdue University. The group used as control consisted of 97 students who took only the monthly quizzes, whereas the *experimental* group consisted of 198 students who took the weekly quizzes in addition to the regular monthly ones. The study was designed to determine the effect on achievement (a) when short quizzes were given in one group over the weekly assignment, and (b) when voluntary discussion groups were provided for both classes. To stimulate learning, discussion groups were arranged so that the students interested in improvement could voluntarily receive additional help.

The group that had frequent quizzes in government consistently made higher scores than the group having only monthly quizzes. Part of this superiority is accounted for by voluntary attendance at discussion groups. The evidence suggests that the frequent quizzing motivated students to attend discussion groups regularly. Frequent testing appeared to motivate students to read more extensively from supplementary sources and to extend their preparation beyond routine requirements.

Some studies show that where tests are given frequently lower ability groups in particular are benefited. They seem to need the extra stimulus of frequent testing and the knowledge of progress revealed. Higher ability groups need less stimulation to learn and are more capable of analyzing their progress.

The motivating effect of testing depends in part upon the learner's possibility of success. For one who is incapable of improving his status, testing may have a negative effect; for one who is capable of doing well, a positive effect. It also depends in part upon the standard the learner sets for himself, whether he aspires to high, average, or passing accomplishment.

Guidance: All of the conditions considered up to this point have dealt with the larger problem of guidance, whether we were

24. M. Fitch, A. J. Drucker, and J. A. Norton, "Frequent Testing as a Motivating Factor in Large Lecture Classes," *Journal of Educational Psychology*, XLII (1951), 1-20.

dealing with the organization of material, the activities of the learner, or the management of tests. We now consider the problem of when to help the learner and when to encourage him to work independently. Guidance is primarily a process of limiting trial-and-error activities by preventing errors and focusing attention upon those activities that assure success. Guidance may either prevent or correct errors, depending upon the time of its administration.

The effect of guidance on learning is well established by experimental investigations. Davies[25] measured the effectiveness of guidance in learning a motor skill. The guidance group was taught by a standard technique of shooting the bow and arrow. The other group practised with no guidance other than minimum instruction in the handling of equipment. The results of the experiment are summarized in Fig. 9.6, which shows average percentage scores for the two archery groups.

In commenting on the striking results of this experiment, Davies points out that the teacher can assist the learner in three

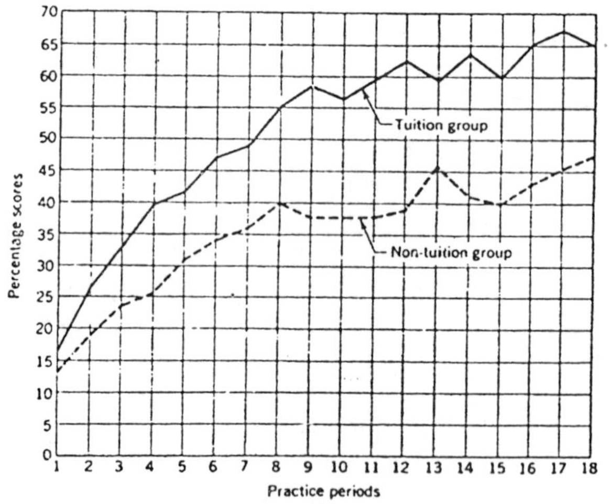

Fig. 9.6 Daily average percentage scores for the two archery groups. (See footnote 25.)

25. D. R. Davies, "The Effect of Tuition upon the Process of Learning a Complex Motor Skill," *Journal of Educational Psychology*, XXXVI (1945), 352-365.

significant ways: (1) He can prevent many errors that characterize the performance of the learner during the early stages of developing a skill. (2) He can direct attention to errors the learner ordinarily does not detect. (3) He can set a good example by demonstration.

Guidance may be introduced at any one of a number of stages during learning. It may be given before the learner has made any attempt to learn, or at any point after he has made several unguided ones. Although the time and place for guidance will vary with the kind of task and the particular needs of the individual, it is most effective during the initial stages of learning. If guidance is given during the initial stages, the errors committed are prevented from becoming habitual. If the learner makes errors and is conscious of their occurrence, they are not likely to be detrimental.

There is also the problem of the amount of guidance. Torrance[26] believes that excessive guidance causes resistance to learning. He states:

> It is not the role of the teacher to force people to learn against their wills. Nor is it his task to trick them into learning. In fact... he is only deluding himself if he thinks he can. The victim of such trickery has ways of dropping material.... The function of the teacher would seem to be to help each student discover and use means of satisfying his needs.... Much failure in school is actually the result of active resistance to over-direction and domination.

Excessive guidance defeats its purpose; there is a point in every learning situation where the efficiency of guidance rapidly diminishes. It is usually desirable to withhold all but the most necessary initial guidance until the learner has had opportunity to survey his task. When it is clear that the learner understands the essential features of his task, guidance should be withdrawn. Between the extreme of giving too much guidance and too little, there is an optimum amount. If the learner is given excessive help, initiative is thwarted; if he is given too little, interest is lost and confidence weakened. One purpose of all guidance is to encourage initiative.

26. P. Torrance, "The Phenomenon of Resistance in Learning." *Journal of Abnormal and Social Psychology*. XLV (1950), 592.597.

Emotional and social climate for learning: Recognition of emotional and social needs of children grows out of our belief that the school should make a contribution to the total well-being of the learner. In a more specific sense, it grows out of the effect that emotional and social behaviour has upon achievement.

Relationship to achievement: For evidence relating to the effect of emotional and social behaviour upon achievement, we shall draw upon two groups of research data: (1) readers versus nonreaders; and (2) retarded versus accelerated pupils.

1. *Readers versus non-readers:* Studies conducted in reading clinics[27] reveal that a high percentage of seriously retarded readers exhibit emotional problems. Two types of non-readers presenting contrasting patterns have been identified by clinicians as the *aggressive* and the *submissive*. The aggressive are quarrelsome, defiant to authority, jealous of their brothers and sisters, hyperactive, and uncooperative in school. Two-thirds of these children are ill-tempered, spoiled, stubborn, and demanding; 50 per cent have had fears for which their aggressive behaviour is probably compensatory; more than half have no friends. Those classified as *aggressive* are bullies or gang leaders. The submissive non-readers resemble the aggressive "non-readers" in their jealousy of brothers and sisters. They do not attempt, however, any of the anti-social acts that are performed by aggressive children. They are quiet, docile, immature, and helpless; many are fearful, anxious, and over-dependent upon adults.

The family histories of these "non-reading" aggressive children reveal an attitude of open and undisguised parental rejection. This rejection is shown by frequent corporal punishment and preference for the child's brothers and sisters. In contrast, the parental pattern of the submissive "non-readers" is predominantly overprotective and restrictive. Often this symptomatic overprotection may be a subtle and disguised form

27. See The Staff of the Reading Clinics of the University of Chicago, *Clinical Studies in Reading*, I (Chicago: University of Chicago Press, 1949), No. 68.

of rejection. The parents may be compensating for feelings of guilt caused by their own previous feelings of rejection. Three-fourths of these "non-readers" show clear evidence of parental rejection or over-protection.

Children having reading disabilities often suffer from severe emotional insecurity and anxiety. The worried, anxious child who is learning to read will have difficulty noticing the fine distinctions between such forms as "b" and "d," and "was" and "saw." He may be wondering whether his mother really loves him, whether she will be there when he arrives home, and whether the children in school will laugh at him when he makes a mistake. No other inadequacy in the learner creates so great a sense of frustration and failure as a reading difficulty. In many difficult situations, an individual may be able to rationalize his deficiency in terms of the unimportance of the problem or in terms of some unavoidable cause to indicate that he is not at fault. It is more difficult to rationalize a reading disability, because every aspect of an academic career is affected by it.

2. ***Retarded versus accelerated pupils:*** Studies indicate that accelerated children excel in interest in school work, effective effort, and possession of desirable traits to a greater extent than retarded children. Investigations of the relationship between nervous-emotional stability and achievement in elementary-school pupils show that the stable group surpasses the unstable group in grade placement. Pupils conspicuously nervous and emotional tend to be retarded in mental and educational age.

Sandlin[28] studied social and emotional adjustment of regularly promoted and non-promoted pupils. He found children who made slow progress did not receive social approval or acceptance from their younger regularly-promoted classmates, especially in the upper elementary grades. They also exhibited feelings of discouragement and failure, anti-social behaviour, and dislike for school activities. They were subject to reproach and

28. A. A. Sandlin, *Social and Emotional Adjustments of Regularly Promoted and Non-promoted Pupils* (New York: Bureau of Publications, Teachers College, Columbia University, 1944).

criticisms from teachers and parents and ridicule from their younger classmates.

3. ***Increasing learning through understanding behaviour:*** Ojemann and Wilkinson[29] were interested in discovering the effect of the teacher's understanding of pupil behaviour upon academic achievement. Two groups of pupils were equated on a number of factors, such as chronological age, intelligence quotient, scholastic record, attitudes, and general adjustment. In the experimental group all possible data were brought together, and the investigator analyzed each pupil's case. As a result of this analysis, he made suggestions for understanding and interpreting each pupil's behaviour for the teacher. No such provisions were made for the control group.

As a result of this procedure, significant differences were found in grade point-averages in favour of the experimental group. There were also significant differences with respect to two other aspects of improvement: Attitudes of the pupils toward the school improved and there was a decline in personality conflicts. The changed attitude of the teachers was even more significant than the quantitative data of the experiment, as illustrated by typical comments of teachers as follows:

> After discovering it was shyness and nervousness rather than sulkiness which prevented L. C. from reciting I made a special effort to see what could be done to help him overcome the difficulty. I seated him so he could be centrally located, praised him at every reasonable opportunity, encouraged him not to do things alone but in company with his classmates, as asking him along with others to pass papers and occasionally to read aloud.

Relationships between pupils and teachers: The extent to which a pupil works in harmony with classroom purposes may hinge upon the attitude the teacher creates in him. It is axiomatic that pupils make better responses for a teacher whom they like than for one whom they dislike. Every word and act of the teacher affects each pupil, often in different ways, creating feelings that include the negative ones of antagonism and unhappiness.

---

29. R. H. Ojemann and F. R. 'Wilkinson, "The Effect on Pupil Growth of an Increase in Teacher's Understanding of Pupil Behaviour," *Journal of Experimental Education*, VIII (1939), 143-147.

Likewise, the teacher is affected by the words and acts of pupils. Certain groups stimulate good teaching more than others. It is no less true of teachers than of pupils that attitudes generated by the classroom setting influence the quality of work accomplished as well as the quality of teaching. The classroom group constitutes a unique situation, representing not only the influence of two levels of maturity, one upon the other, but the impressions that each person creates. Each individual brings with him a pattern of emotional and social behaviour. Each pattern has been formed from experiences outside the school as well as those within the school.

1. ***What pupils like in teachers:***[30] Teachers well-liked by pupils in the intermediate grades are characterized as being: nice, kind, fair, friendly, understanding, willing to help, able to explain clearly. Traits that especially seem to characterize the teacher liked least are: scolds pupils a lot, usually cross, often bossy, difficult to approach with problems, often becomes angry with pupils, and does not see things as children do.

The teacher most liked by junior-high-school pupils is described as kind, friendly, cheerful, with a sense of humour. He is always helpful when assistance is needed and provides opportunities for pupils to help with various tasks. He understands children and their problems, recognizes all children as individuals, is modest and neat in dress, has a clear pleasant voice; doesn't nag, ridicule, or speak sarcastically; doesn't threaten or punish so severely that pupils fear him; is not bossy or domineering; does not arbitrarily impose his will upon his pupils; and finally, allows freedom in the classroom while maintaining respect from all.

High-school pupils regard the following traits in a "good" teacher as most important: knowledge of subject matter, clearness of explanation, fairness. They regard of less importance such traits as humour, good temper, social ability, and neatness.

Opinions of pupils at these educational levels indicate the importance of desirable relationships between pupils and

---

30. P. A. Witty, "Evaluation of Studies of the Characteristics of the Effective Teacher," in *Improving Educational Research* (Official Report of the American Educational Research Association, 1948), 198-204.

teachers in the learning situation. The learner appreciates a school that provides security, shared experiences, recognition of individual success, and opportunities for personal and social adjustment. Witty concludes that children respect teachers who have the following characteristics: (1) the inclination and ability to understand children, (2) the desire to obtain instructional materials from diversified sources to satisfy the varied levels of interest and attainment, and to use different approaches to ensure successful learning for each individual; and (3) the inclination to record and appraise growth so as to encourage the learner to make steady progress.

Symond's[31] study of the characteristics of the effective teacher, as based on pupil opinion, shows that superior teachers liked children; inferior teachers disliked them. The teachers having a superior rating were personally secure and self-assured; inferior teachers were personally insecure and had feelings of inferiority. Superior teachers were well integrated and possessed desirable personality traits; inferior teachers tended to be personally disorganized.

2. ***Democratic versus autocratic methods:*** As has already been indicated, pupils prefer democratic to either laissez-faire or autocratic methods. Adolescents especially resent being treated as less mature than adults; They welcome opportunities to express themselves freely in a group in which they feel secure, and appreciate definite and meaningful assignments, not dictatorial ones. They are most resentful of being given assignments as punishment. To them, the lecture method is suggestive of teacher domination; hence, the lecture is the least liked teaching method. Pupils prefer the discussion method or a combination of discussion and informal lectures.

Lewin, Lippitt[32] and others have conducted studies in which comparisons are made of autocratic and democratic

31. P. M. Symonds "Characteristics of the Effective Teacher; Based on Pupil Evaluations." *Journal of Experimental Education*, XXIII (1954-55), 289-310.
32. K. Lewin, R. Lippitt, and R. K. White, "Patterns of Aggressive Behaviour in Experimentally Created Social Climates," *Journal of Social Psychology*, X (1939), 271-299.

methods of leadership. Their results show that students are more tense when led by autocratic methods. There is also more dominating and bullying behaviour among the students who are led by such procedures. Students being led by democratic methods tend to show increased cooperation toward a common goal. After having become accustomed to democratic methods of leadership, they are eager to share with each other their materials and results.

Several investigators have attempted to apply in teaching some of the techniques and ideas associated with non-directive counselling. This method minimizes the memorization of information and tends to assist the student in learning more about how to think and less about what to think. The instructor withholds evaluation; he provides an atmosphere of free discussion. In using this technique he is particularly interested in the psychological implications of the students' behaviour.

Schwebel and Asch[33] note a tendency for well-adjusted students to approve non-directive teaching and for the poorly adjusted to prefer *directive* teaching. More outside reading was done by those who approve non-directive teaching techniques. The students working under conditions of non-directive techniques tended to place more emphasis upon gains in self-confidence and deeper insight into their own motivation, and had a more tolerant acceptance of others. They also showed more initiative in their work, and a greater tendency to make decisions and to accept the consequences of their actions.

Summary

Learning always involves some change in the learner's behaviour. This change may be expressed by intellectual efficiency or skill in motor performance. It may also be manifested by the less tangible kinds of responses such as appreciation, attitudes, or interests. Two techniques are used in measuring gain in school situations. One of these measures *indeterminate* gain, the other *determinate* gain.

33. M. Schwebel and J. M. Asch, "Research Possibilities in Non-directive Teaching," *Journal of Educational Psychology*, XXXIX (1948), 359-369. See also M. J. Asch, "Non-directive Teaching in Psychology, An Experimental Study," *Psychological Monographs*, XLV (1951).

The learning process includes both acquisition and retention. Without retention of the effects of previous training, no progress could be made during successive periods of practice. Acquisition refers to the cumulative effects of training, whereas retention refers to its sustained effects. Efficiency of learning, therefore, depends not only upon how much is acquired, but also upon how much is retained of what is acquired. Some differentiation, however, should be made between retention while instruction is in progress and retention after instruction has ended.

Forgetting tends to increase rapidly with the passage of time in the case of the ability to recall detailed types of information. On the other hand, higher abilities, such as the ability to apply principles to new situations and to interpret data, are retained over long periods with slight loss.

A principal purpose in all learning situations is to provide conditions that will enhance the learning process. The conditions largely within the control and direction of the teacher include: (1) the organization and presentation of learning materials; (2) learning activities; (3) testing; (4) guidance; and (5) the emotional and social climate for learning.

An organized learning situation is one that makes sense and gives evidence of some pattern. A fairly close relationship exists between the effectiveness of one mode of presentation and another. For best results several modes of presentation are preferable to one. The individual learns best when he is actively identified with learning materials; Several kinds of activity are needed to recognize individual differences and to ensure thorough learning. Three functions of tests are recognized: (1) the directive function; (2) the selective function; and (3) the motivating function. Guidance may either prevent or correct errors depending upon the time of its administration. Recognition of emotional and social behaviour grows out of the concern of the school for the total well-being of the learner.

—Robert A. Davis

Questions and Exercises (for Discussion and Study)

1. How is learning usually defined? How does the educator's concept of learning influence the

instructional and administrative activities of the school?

2. How is learning studied in the school? What aspects of learning are generally involved in learning experiments?

3. How do you account for the fact that true-false and multiple-choice examinations are frequently used to measure the results of learning in informal testing situations? What kinds of mental process are required in these types of examination?

4. Select a subject you are taking and analyze your own methods of studying it. What methods tend to "pay off" best at examination time?

5. Give evidence from your own experience to show that acquisition and retention operate simultaneously. What significance does this fact have for teaching?

6. How may teaching be ordered so that acquisition is at a maximum and forgetting at a minimum?

7. How do you explain the fact that retention studies have tended to stress recall of detailed information?

8. How do you account for the fact that higher abilities, such as the ability to apply principles and to interpret experiments, are retained over long periods with slight loss (or even gain), whereas ability to recall specific items of information is quickly forgotten even though instruction may have stressed such recall? What implications do such findings have for teaching?

9. In the elementary school, activities generally serve the same purpose as tests. In the secondary school and college, however, tests afford the principal means of appraising students. Is there anything wrong with these practices?

10. The exercise you are now doing is one way of learning the materials of this chapter. List three other ways that might be used effectively.

11. What evidence is there for the belief that the best assurance for successful performance on a

comprehensive examination at the end of a course is consistent study from day to day and week to week?

12. When, if ever, is "cramming" justified as a study practice?
13. On the basis of your experience and study of the materials of this chapter, prepare a paper of approximately six pages outlining the conditions that you regard as most effective in facilitating the learning process. In preparing this report, try to recall and evaluate your own experiences in high school and college.
14. Outline a systematic programme for teaching some school subject.
15. Compare the emotional influence of different kinds of teacher—dictatorial, sentimental, indifferent, and intellectually zealous—upon yourself or upon pupils you have known.
16. Outline various disciplinary problems you have observed in school and analyze them as symptoms of (a) chronic emotional distress, (b) conflict with inflexibility of the school programme, (c) developmental difficulty, or (d) lack of intellectual stimulation, particularly at the upper levels of mental ability.

References

Blair, G. M., R. S. Jones, and R. H.Simpson, *Educational Psychology*. New York: The Macmillan Company, 1954.

Brueckner, L. J., *Improving the Arithmetic Programme*. New York: Appleton- Century-Crofts, Inc., 1957.

Burton, W. H., *The Guidance of Learning Activities*, New York: Appleton-Century-Crofts, Inc., 1952.

Coladarci, A. P. (ed.). *Educational Psychology*. New York: The Dryden Press, 1955.

Cronbach, L. J., *Educational Psychology*, New York: Harcourt, Brace & Company, 1954.

Frandsen, A. N., *How Children Learn, An Educational Psychology*. New York: McGraw-Hill, 1957.

Fullagar, W. A.. H. G. Lewis, and C. F. Cumbee, *Readings for Educational Psychology*. New York: Thomas Y. Crowell Company, 1956.

Garrison, K. C., and J. S. Gray, *Educational Psychology*. New York; Appleton-Century-Crofts, Inc., 1955.

———, *Improving Educational Research*. Official Report of the American Educational Research Association, 1948.

Kingsley, H. L., and R. Garry, *The Nature and Conditions of Learning*, 2nd. ed. Englewood Cliffs, N. J: Prentice-Hall, Inc., 1957.

Lindgren, H. C., *Educational Psychology in the Classroom*. New York: John Wiley & Sons, Inc., 1956.

National Society for the Study of Education, *Learning and Instruction*, Forty-ninth Yearbook, Part I. Chicago: University of Chicago Press, 1940.

Seagoe, M. V., A *Teacher's Guide to the Learning Process*. Dubuque, Iowa: William C. Brown Co., 1956.

Smith, H. P., *Psychology in Teaching*. Englewood Cliffs, N.J.: Prentice-Hall, Inc., 1954.

Stephens, J. M., *Educational Psychology*, 2nd ed. New York: Henry Holt and Company, 1956.

Sterrett, M. D., and R. A. Davis, "The Permanence of School Learning: A Review of Studies," *Educational Administration and Supervison*, XL No.8. (1954).

Tilton, J. W., *An Educational Psychology of Learning*. New York: The Macmillan Company, 1951.

10

Motivation in School Learning

There is very little school learning without mental activity on the part of the learner. The most effective learning takes place when there is a maximum of mental activity. Maximum mental activity is best attained through strong motivation.

Motivation is the superhighway to learning[1]

The major problem of the curriculum-maker and the classroom teacher is in knowing and applying the science and art of motivation. How do children learn "in doing what comes naturally"? Can such situations be artfully created? If so, how? What is the best technique for utilizing this knowledge in motivating school learning?

In our present state of knowledge, there is no sure method or procedure to guarantee the desired results in so many easy lessons. However, much data are now available in the literature of motivation and learning that can be of great help in producing more effective teaching.

It is our task to present the best obtainable information based on known facts, experimental and clinical studies,

1. Cf. "The organism must be motivated to learn" (McConnell); "Learning will proceed best if motivated" (Anderson); "Motivation is an essential condition of learning" (Melton); "The problem of motivation is central both to educational psychology and to the classroom procedure" (Harris); "The problem of motivation lies at the very heart of a sound educational programme in a free society.... Motivation is indispensable to learning. It represents the antecedent, dynamic background for both original behaviour and its modifications" (Gates); "Motivation is the central factor in the efficient management of the process of learning. Some type of motivation must be present in all learning" (Kelly); "All motives are learned" (McClelland); "Motivation is the basic problem of psychology in education" (Bernard).

observation, and the experience of successful classroom teachers as concisely as possible within the confines of a single chapter.[2]

A Few Preliminary Considerations

The child is a dynamic, living, growing, developing, maturing personality: Human beings share with all living things the universal, generalized, undifferentiated, more-or-less vague, urge to live. The infant unconsciously and automatically seeks those activities that aid in survival. Gradually this vague urge to survive takes on many manifestations according to the peculiar culture of his group, in short, from his total environment. The teacher is not directly concerned with the hereditary factors in the child. By the time the child starts school he has already a well-developed personality. Many of his attitudes have become more or less stable. Whatever may be said in defence of John Locke's *tabula rasa* theory will certainly not apply to the kindergarten child, for he is already a dynamic, growing, developing, maturing personality.

Nevertheless, as part of the total environment, the teacher has the privilege and responsibility of not only utilizing the native needs and wants in motivating school learning, but also of helping to direct, and, to some extent, shape these dynamic needs and wants according to the ideals of a democratic society. The task of the teacher is doubly important and rewarding.

The child is a total personality: Another factor to be constantly kept in mind is that the child is a total personality; an "integrated organized whole." It is the individual, the self, the totality, that has to be satisfied in the fulfillment of any need and want. This makes possible the acceptance of substitutes (in most cases) and presents the teacher with a multiple-choice situation. When we speak of individual parts such as needs, desires, wishes, likes and dislikes, and so on, it is for the sake of convenience. The totality is too complicated to take hold of in a

2. Due credit will be given to authors for direct quotations and other reference to their contributions. Lack of space precludes a detailed description of the experimental data. For the convenience of those who wish to pursue the subject further, a selected list of references is given at the end of the chapter. Attention is also called to the references in the footnotes. Many of these references contain recent detailed, descriptive, firsthand experimental data.

single grasp. It should not be assumed, however, that these units have any entity or any validity apart from the total organism.

Unconscious and semi-conscious needs and wants: The individual is also motivated by unconscious and semi-conscious needs and wants. Fortunately, many of these can be redirected by proper motivation in formal education. We shall concern ourselves with these as well as the conscious in presenting the practical suggestions for effective motivation of school learning.

Practical Suggestions

Any successful school programme will have to take into account the dynamic nature of the child, his past experience, his total environment plus individual differences, and the manifold needs and wants as they manifest themselves.

The following practical suggestions are presented as tools for the classroom teacher. Care should be exercised to keep them from turning into weapons. "Brain washing," in one form or another, may be used by unscrupulous parties to influence people. Manipulating people, individually and collectively, is becoming a science. Some of the new social scientists talk of the "depth approach" and call themselves motivation analysts, motivation researchers, social engineers, and so forth. The cold war and all propaganda, including the big business of advertising,[3] utilize the art of motivation. The technique of manipulating people is a two-edged sword in and out of the classroom.

---

3. Could it be that sincere, patriotic educators and devoted scientists and investigators are unwittingly playing into the hands of those who would use their findings for selfish and nefarious purposes? This could happen even in the classroom. For a well-documented, factual discussion of the modern technique used in advertising, see V. Packard, *The Hidden Persuaders* (New York: David McKay Company, Inc., 1957). A more favourable account of motivation in depth is presented by J. G. Frederick, *Introduction to the New Science and Art of Motivation Research* (NewYork: Business Bourse, Publishers, 1957). He defines motivational research as "... an attempt to dredge up out of the more or less hidden depths of human nature and human personality if possible some good practical hints as to how to sell people a particular item of goods readily and agreeably." See also L. O. Brown, "What Motivational Research Is and How It Works: Its Advantages and Shortcomings," *Advertising Age,* XXVI (1955), 65-69. The science and art of motivation have come a long way in the last three decades. In addition to the experimental studies by psychologists and educators and the

Maturation. It is useless to attempt motivation in school learning if the assignment is too difficult or the goals too remote for the child's readiness or his maturation.[4] Maturation and motivation must be synchronized. Formal learning can take place only if the learner is physically, mentally, emotionally, and culturally mature enough to understand and carry out the assignment. For example, very young children are influenced more readily by immediate satisfactions, follow the more primitive needs and wants, and are not too strongly motivated by outside incentives. They also have a relatively short attention span.

The connection between motivation and maturation has received a great deal of experimental and clinical study in recent years with remarkable success.[5] Further studies will determine more accurately the degree of maturation required for the learning of specific subjects and also reveal whether retardation or pre-cociousness is due to heredity or environmental factors. Individual differences, however, will always present a problem to the classroom teacher. Children are at present classified in the schools largely according to their chronological age. Although chronological age does set a sort of pattern for maturity, it does

---

discoveries by the motivation researchers in depth, is the newest approach in the form of "subliminal projection," designated by some as a "frightening development." James W. Vicary, head of the firm called The Subliminal Projection Company with headquarters in New York, is the inventor. A message is flashed on a television or movie screen for one three-thousandths of a second. Although this is too fast to see or to register consciously, the subconscious takes it in and acts upon the suggestion. A check on results shows that sales, imposed by this means, were increased from eighteen to fifty-eight per cent.

4. Maturation, as such, is treated fully elsewhere in this text.
5. "Research in child development is providing working generalizations for the classroom teacher. Children differ in their rate of growth.... Growth is an individual matter and must be appraised from the point of view of the nature of the individual. There can be no common expectancy for achievement when it is conditioned by sex differences, the total maturity of the child, and the family from which he comes.... Children as they present themselves in schools have more things in common when viewed broadly than when single attributes are studies in detail. Similarities as well as differences deserve attention in classroom." Quoted from W. C. Olson and B.O. Hughes in A. P. Coladarci (ed.), *Educational Psychology* (New York: The Dryden Press, 1955), pp. 80-81. See also C. Bühler, "Maturation and Motivation," *Personality*, I (1951), 184-211; R. Metroux, "Implicit and Explicit Values in Education and Teaching as Related to Growth and Development," *Merill-Palmer Quarterly*, II (1955), 27-34; E. Stellar, "The Physiology of Motivation," *Psychological Review*, LXI (1954), 5-22.

not eliminate the problems of individual differences and variations in the development of different phases of maturity in the same child.

Bringing assignment within child's experience: Experience is not only the best teacher—it is the only teacher. There can be no learning apart from experience and every experience can be an education. We speak of a self-educated man as though there were some other kind of education. Broadly speaking, all education is self-education. Formal education by the schools merely seeks to improve the quality of the education by improving the quality of experience, for the quality of learning is determined by the quality of experience on the part of the learner.

Learning is also conditioned by past experience.[6] We interpret new experience in the light of the old, Identical environmental circumstances mean different things to different people and are variously interpreted. Their reactions also differ widely. Eyewitnesses at the scene of a crime or accident will give widely different interpretations of what actually transpired. If all witnesses give identical accounts, they are suspected of collusion and their testimony discounted. Learning based on past experience and tied in with the "total pattern" is more effective in comprehension and speed of learning.[7] It is better integrated and longer retained because it is better organized. It is more functional and therefore meets the objective of all school learning in producing approved conduct through the various satisfactorily desirable experiences of the learner.

Respect for personality of the child, appealing to ego-maximization: Ridicule and sarcasm are far from the best means of motivating school learning. Children, as well as adults, have their pride and self-respect. Any attempt to embarrass or

---

6. "... a person is always the product of the sum of his impressions and it is absolutely impossible for him to cut out a period, or segment, as it were, of his life and go ahead. There is no break in the continuity of the psychic life." A. A. Brill, *Basic Principles of Psychoanalysis* (New York: Doubleday & Company, Inc., 1949), p. 60. See also J. A. Blake, "Comprehension Versus Motivation in Child Behaviour," *Understanding the Child*. XXIV (1955), 77-79; A. Mujib, Motivation and Learning," *Indian Journal of Psychology*. XXIX (1954), 115-123.
7. Cf. J. W. Atkinson, "The Achievement Motive and Recall of Interrupted and Completed Tasks," *Journal of Experimental Psychology*, XLVI (1953), 381-390.

humiliate a child, especially in the presence of his classmates, is likely to end in one of two undesirable results—withdrawal or pugnacity. Shame and embarrassment are not healthy emotions. They tend to disorganize the personality of the child. They produce uncertainty, hesitation, frustration, loss of confidence and self-respect. Sometimes they force a child to complete withdrawal from school activities and set up a mental attitude against all learning. In extreme cases, the child refuses to cooperate at all. He will not answer any questions, nor talk or utter a single word in school. In most cases the opposite takes place. The child becomes pugnacious and aggressive, with a hostile attitude toward the school and toward society. He is then ripe for delinquency. It is his way (mostly unconscious) of getting back at his tormentors, be they teachers or parents or authority in general.

Disregard for the personal integrity of the child is unwise,[8] because it threatens just about all of his basic needs and wants—self-respect, freedom from fear and the feeling of failure and guilt, the need for love and affection, for security, for achievement and success, and most important of all, the need of belonging and being accepted. A feeling of frustration is the worst psychological atmosphere for motivating school learning[9].

On the other hand, an appeal to ego-maximization has exactly the opposite effect. We may set it down as a basic principle in motivation that we like those people, objects, and situations that make us feel important. Conversely, we dislike those people, objects, situations that make us feel inferior. Accordingly, we prefer to play those games in which we excel; to associate with people who listen when we talk and who respect our opinions. We diligently avoid situations that are likely to prove embarrassing and which place us in an inferior position. This is why we resent personal questions and being the butt of a joke. Practical jokers who delight in playing pranks on other people rarely can take a joke at their own expense. The teacher

8. See P. M. Symonds, "What Education has to Learn from Psychology," *Teachers College Record* (Columbia University, New York), LVI (1955), 277-285; M. Sherif, *The Psychology of Ego-Involvement* (New York: John Wiley & Sons, Inc.,1947).
9. Cf. K. Wiles and M. Beauchamp, "How Can a School Provide a Good Emotional Climate?" *National Education Association Journal*, XL (1951), 462.463.

can accomplish a great deal more in motivating school learning by appealing to ego maximization than by shaming, ridiculing, and belittling the would-be learner.[10]

Securing attention, creating interest and enthusiasm: The inattentative child is preoccupied and does not hear what is said. He might as well be absent. Securing attention is, therefore, the primary prerequisite for motivating school learning.

It is well to remember that the attention span is very short, especially in young children. The only thing that will bridge the gap is interest and enthusiasm. Interest may exist to some extent on the part of the pupil; more likely it needs to be artfully created by the teacher. Capitalizing on natural interests and cultivating new ones is the mark of a good educational programme. "Intrinsic interest must be achieved."[11] Interest is created by the acquisition of new skills, by encouragement, and above all, by satisfying experience. The wise teacher will take advantage of the slightest show of interest. The best time to explain a subject is when it is presented to an inquiring mind—when the child asks questions. This is the true pedagogical moment; it is better than the "logical" moment according to the lesson plan.

The teacher's own interest and enthusiasm are contagious and will go a long way toward inspiring and maintaining interest on the part of the pupil. As the child grows and develops, he acquires and displays new interests commensurate with his level of maturation. These may be used as points of departure in the development of new interests in an ever-expanding process.[12] The process may be accelerated by offering multiple-choice situations and numerous incentives suitable to the child's abilities and comprehension.

---

10. This topic is treated later on from another angle under praise and reproof.
11. H. G. Wheat, *Foundations of School Learning* (New York: Alfred A. Knopf, Inc., 1955), p. 51: L. Postman, "Perception, Motivation and Behaviour," *Journal of Personality*, XXII (1953), 17-31.
12. J. Pikunas, *Fundamentals of Child Psychology* (Milwaukee: Bruce Publishing Company, 1957), p. 22. "Spontaneous use of unfolding abilities.... The establishment of new patterns in any aspect of life absorbs the child for a long while. This urge to practice unfolding abilities and skills is based upon the principles of intrinsic motivation.... Curiosity for new experiences, exploration, experimentation and knowledge increase steadily and underlie the child's self-expression. Abilities are to a certain degree irrepressible."

Significance of attitude in motivation:[13] Closely related to attention and interest is attitude. Attitude is one's set to react in a given way in a particular situation. It is relatively permanent and wider in scope than interest. Attitude limits and channels motives. In its broader aspects, it is almost synonymous with motive. It is a habitual response to identical or near-identical total situations. A person's perspective—his interpretation of units and segments of experience as well as totalities and general outlook on life—is gravely affected by his interests and attitudes. Attitude is not only a readiness for new experiences: it also creates the contours of the new experience and sets boundaries.

On the other hand, anticipation often overmobilizes attitude to the extent of "reading" something into the situation, exaggerating and distorting the facts. If you are waiting for someone whom you are expecting shortly, any person appearing on the distant horizon will be mistaken for this person, because anticipation and expectation tend to magnify the slightest points of similarity.

Praise and reproof: Many experimental studies have been conducted to determine the relative merits of praise and reproof in motivating school learning.[14] According to Schmidt,[15] there is

---

13. "Attitudes toward alternative acts determine the direction that action will take; and information about the conditions of attitude change will be highly relevant to the problem of controlling motivation": summary by L, M. Soloman of H. Peak. "Attitude and Motivation," *Nebraska Symposium on Motivation*, Sect. 30: 483 (1955), 149-189. See also I. E. Bender, "The Development of a Scale for Attitudinal Motivation," *Journal of Abnormal and Social Psychology*, XLVIII (1953), 486-494; A. R. Mead, "Research About Attitudes," *Journal of Educational Research*. XLVIII (1954), 233-234; I. Sarnoff and D. Katz, "The Motivational Basis of Attitude Change," *Journal of Abnormal and Social Psychology*, XLIX (1954), 115-124; L. W. Doob, "The Behaviour of Attitudes," *Psychological Review*, LIV (1947), 135-156; C. I. Howland, "Changes in Attitude Through Communication," *Journal of Educational Research*. XLV (1952), 498.
14. The analysis of the data collected indicates that: (1) When introverts and extroverts are grouped together, praise and blame are equally effective in motivating the work achievement of fifth-grade pupils. Either praise or blame is more effective in increasing the work output of fifth-grade pupils than no external incentives; (2) If repeated often enough, praise increases the work output of introverts until it is significantly higher than that of introverts who are blamed or extroverts who are praised; (3) If repeated often enough, blame increases the work output of extroverts until it is significantly higher than that of extroverts who are praised or introverts who are blamed.... Praise or blame should not be judged on an either-or basis, but should be used to fit the case." Coladarci, op. *cit*., *p*. 431.
15. "The Effect of Praise and Blame as Incentives to Learning," *Psychological Monographs*. XXIII, No. 240 (1941).

no unequivocal evidence one way or the other. Results prove that both are useful in moderation and may have a bad effect if carried too far or used indiscriminately. "Praise for success and reproof for failure are more effective than indiscriminate praise and reproof."[16] Apparently the personality of the child is a determining factor. Some take to both praise and reproof; others respond best to one or the other. The football coach of a certain college discovered that one of his star linesmen would sulk under reproof and refuse to cooperate, but that praise would build him up to top efficiency.

Other determining factors are age, sex, peculiar circumstances, and most significantly, how the praise and reproof are administered.

Most people accept the opinions of others as to their abilities and disabilities. The tendency is to live up to the standards set for them. Witness the boy in school who said, "I could do better if I were not so lazy." How did he get to think of himself as lazy if he had not been designated so by others? Similarly, the so-called "bad boy" is dubbed such in one class and his reputation precedes him in the next. A clever salesman assumes the sale is made and talks as though he believes the prospect to be well-to-do and has good taste. The customer is more likely to meet the expectations of the salesman rather than admit he cannot afford the purchase. The sociologists refer to this as the "mirrored self." Society is the mirror that reflects our social status, traits of character, and personality. Reputation is important not only as a gauge of what others think of us, but also as a determiner of our own opinion of ourselves.

Rewards and punishments: Rewards and punishments are in the same category as praise and reproof, if we consider praise as one form of reward and reproof as one form of punishment. Much that was presented above will apply here also, except that rewards and punishments cover a wider area. Praise and reproof would constitute one form of reward and punishment.

The objective in both reward and punishment is identical— to affect future conduct favourably. They differ as to methodology. Reward seeks to influence conduct favourably by

16. Wheat, *op. cit*; p. 319.

associating a pleasant feeling with the desired act; punishment seeks to deter or prevent an undesirable act by associating unpleasant feeling with it. If it were not for the anticipated deterrent effect of punishment and the hope of changing motivation, it would have no reason for existing, except as an instrument of revenge and sadism. It would be sheer cruelty. The question is: Just how successful is punishment in school learning and how does it compare in effectiveness with reward as an incentive? [17]

Advantages and disadvantages of rewards versus punishments: In terms of motivating learning, the advantages of rewards over punishments are: (1) they create pleasurable associations that are strong inducements to repeat the desired act; (2) they have the advantage of being ideo-motive through the force of suggestion; (3) being pleasant, they generate interest and enthusiasm; and (4) they appeal to ego-maximization and develop high morale.

Some of the disadvantages of rewards in motivating school learning are: (1) they are mostly extrinsic in motivating the pupil, toward winning a prize instead of cultivating a taste for the thing itself; (2) they afford temptation to cheat; (3) they encourage the wrong attitude ("What do I get out of it?"), expecting something for nothing; and (4) .in most instances only a few children may hope to win, those least needing motivation.

Punishments also have some advantages as well as some disadvantages. The advantages may be listed as: (1) they often act as a deterrent; (2) they serve as a form of discipline; and (3) they are especially useful if (a) they appear as natural consequences of the undesirable act, (b) are used in combination with reward, and (c) if the child can be made to realize that it is the undesirable act and not himself that is being punished.

Some of the disadvantages of punishments in motivating learning are: (1) they are based on fear, not a healthy emotion; (2) they lose effectiveness if the child is no longer afraid or is willing to take the consequences; (3) they are likely to reinforce the undesirable conduct by overemphasis; (4) they create

17. Cf. J. P. Seward, "Experimental Evidence for the Motivating Function of Reward," *Psychological Bulletin*, XLVIII (1951), 97-129.

unpleasant feelings that are negative and associated with failure; (5) the results are not always permanent; (6) they may engender ill-will toward teacher and society; and (7) there is no reliable measure of severity in punishments. Punishments that are considered severe by one pupil may be laughed off by another, and deliberately provoked for the compensation of being in the spotlight by still another.

Success versus failure: Success furnishes its own drive. Like happiness, success is often an end in itself. Many an enterprise is undertaken for the sheer satisfaction of succeeding in that enterprise. Success is, therefore, a type of reward, whereas failure is considered a type of punishment. The success-failure motive runs all through life and is constantly operative in everything we do. It is the chief determiner of morale. Every effort in adjusting to new situations is conditioned by trial and error, or trial and success.

Learning takes place in both instances. We learn by our failures as well as by our successes. We tend to repeat successful attempts. In school learning, both success and failure can be useful within limitations. Failure may be a spur to success. No one wants an easy victory. Every novice hopes to best the champion. On the other hand, if failure is too severe or too often repeated, it is discouraging. It reduces aspiration and learning. As the mercury in the thermometer fluctuates with temperature, so the level of aspiration varies with success and failure as determined in the mind of the learner. What actually happens to us is not nearly so important as what we do about it. Understood failure challenges effort. Understood success stimulates further effort... From what the pupil knows and understands comes the motive for further learning."[18] Success and failure should be so balanced that the child does not lose his perspective. In the classroom the teacher can manipulate the situation so that every child will get a taste of success to temper

18. Wheat, *op. cit.* See also E. L. Lowell, "The Effect of Need for Achievement on Learning and Speed of Performance," *Journal of Psychology*, XXXIII (1952), 31-40; J. W. Taylor, "An Experimental Study of Repression with Special References to Success-failure and Completion incompletion *Journal of Clinical Psychology*, IX (1953), 352.355; E. Douvan, "Social Status and Success Striving," *Journal of Abnormal Psychology*, LII (1956), 219-223; E. G. French, "Some Characteristics of Achievement Motivation," *Journal of Experimental Psychology*, L (1955), 232-236.

the ill-effects of failure. Failure may be considered temporary, with success as the ultimate goal.

Children can be taught to take success and failure in stride through classroom situations as well as on the athletic field. There is also the possibility of setting goals and aspirations out of reach as well as out of grasp. If one's aspirations are out of all proportion to his abilities, he may become discouraged, embittered, demoralized.

Positive versus negative: Most investigators favour reward motivation over punishment, because it is positive, whereas punishment is negative. Experimental studies show that learning with positive guidance is superior to negative guidance. The positive is more definitely associated with success; the negative is associated with failure. The positive is more predictable. It sets up a pattern and tends toward habit-formation. The nervous system is so constituted that once a stimulus is received, its force is on-going, even after the original incentive is dropped.

Similarly, an idea tends to work out in action unless it is hindered by another idea or by a physical barrier. The negative approach of telling children what not to do is unfortunate, because it suggests, emphasizes, and keeps "warm" at the focus of consciousness, the .undesirable act, The idea takes the form of compulsion and the act becomes inevitable. One reason why New Year resolutions are so easily broken is that they are usually negative—'something the person is not going to do in breaking a habit. But stressing the negative serves only to keep the idea so strongly in mind that it gets done despite "will-power."

Another unfortunate feature of the negative approach is that it emphasizes the error and tends to "stamp" it in. In teaching spelling, it is better that the misspelled words not be shown to the pupil. The tendency is to repeat the mistake.

Clear assignments and definite goals: In line with what was said about positive versus negative is the desirability of making assignments and objectives clear and concise. Seeing the goal more clearly is an aid to organization, resulting in better perception of relationships, clearer insight, and superior meaningfulness. Clinical and experimental studies definitely show the effect veness of clear goals and knowledge of results.[19] Knowing how ore is progressing could be an incentive in both success and failure if success is not too easy and failure not overwhelming; otherwise it might have the opposite effect. Athletic coaches usually have a marked advantage in that the pupils possess a clearer insight and understanding of the goals and objectives.

Self-motivation: Knowledge of results, high aspiration, and clear goals are the best preparation and incentive to self-motivation, especially if the pupil is directed and encouraged to set his own goals and seek intrinsic incentives and superior remote goals. There is no better means of developing character and ideal citizenship in a free society.

The teacher can do much by defining and redefining goals and helping the pupils to do this for themselves by presenting the possible choices and letting them choose. Experienced social workers do not tell people what to do. They help the individual to view his problem objectively and in true perspective. They suggest possible alternatives. The final solution is left to the individual.

The will-to-learn: Sell-motivation implies a will-to-learn.[20] A prerequisite to all effective learning is a desire on the part of the learner for knowledge or understanding or for skill. In fact, the speed and efficiency in learning is in direct ratio to the aspiration or will to learn, except perhaps when the urge is intense enough to cause an emotional disturbance and thus interfere with learning. An analogous situation occurs when a person "loses his temper" and renders himself less efficient in a task requiring skill.

In summary of suggestions based on experimental studies on methods of improving the will to learn. Book and Norvell offer the following:

---

19. See H. C. Birch, "The Relation of Previous Experience to Insightful Problem Solving," *Journal of Comparative Psychology*, XXXIX (1945), 15-22; M. L. Fitch, *et al.*, "Frequent Testing as a Motivating Factor in Large Classes," *Journal of Educational Psychology*, XLII (1951), 1-20.
20. See L. D. Cohen, "Levels of Aspiration Behaviour and .Feelings of Adequacy and Self-acceptance," *Journal of Abnormal and Social Psychology*, XLIX (1954), 84-86; J. P. Seward, "How Are Motives Learned?" *Psychological Review*, LX (1953), 99-110.

1. Demonstrate to the learner by figures and facts that desire for improvement is a condition of advancement; (2) Make the learner feel that it is worthwhile to exert an effort, and that if he does, he will be rewarded by success; (3) Have a reliable method of measuring progress; (4) Keep the learner succeeding so that he may be assured that he has not yet reached the limit of performance; and (5) Show that others have improved and developed beyond the learner, or when needed, that others have failed for a time.[21]

Unconscious needs and wants made conscious: One significant means of strengthening the will-to-learn and improving aspiration is to help the pupil make his unconscious and semiconscious needs and wants conscious. According to Brill, many of our actions are guided by our unconscious.[22] An appeal to emotion is often more effective than an appeal to reason.

Moreover, the unconscious is a truer index of the real innermost wishes and desires, and it never lies. One need not be a psychoanalyst nor concur fully with their theories and practices to take advantage of the many valuable findings by Freud and his followers. Helping the pupil to clarify his unfelt goals and objectives, as well as his pressing immediate needs and wants, gives him a better insight into the reasons for learning. It will also serve to accomplish another major goal of school learning, namely, self-appraisal.

Self-appraisal: Under or overevaluation of self can be tragic. Many people live mediocre lives because they do not know "their own strength." They have a sense of false modesty concerning their abilities. On the other hand, the person who overrates his capabilities is constantly running into rebuffs and failure for attempting the impossible. Proper appraisal of one's own potentialities is essential to a happy and useful life. It is also central in the learning process.[23]

---

21. Quoted by P. T. Young, *Motivation of Behaviour* (New York: John Wiley & Sons, Inc., 1936), pp. 209-210. See also W. F. Book and L. Norvell, "The Will to Learn, An Experimental Study in Incentives," *Pedagogical Seminary*, XXIX (1922) 305-362.
22. Brill, *op. cit.*, p. 12.
23. See Cohen, *op. cit.*, p. 84-86.

The school programme and the classroom teacher can do much in aiding the pupil to appraise himself and his talents properly. In fact, much of this appraisal is unavoidable in a system of grades, promotions, special rooms, awards of one sort or another, and graduations. The schools and colleges are selective agents for placement bureaus and employment services that rely heavily on the candidates' record in school and the recommendations of their teachers. Our immediate concern is with directing motivation in school learning so as to achieve proper self-appraisal and accelerate learning all along the line. "To the extent that self-evaluation leads to self-knowledge and realistic goal setting, it can be an important part of the motivational setting of the school."[24]

Means and ends: The so-called average person, as well as the child is motivated more strongly by immediate needs and wants than by remote ones. The lure of the immediate is greater because it is already on its way to accomplishment. The orientation is favourable. It is like drifting with the tide. In terms of inertia, it represents a body in motion; it needs no initial push or pull. On the contrary, it will take energy to inhibit or divert. With the very young child, one cannot and need not go much beyond the immediate. But as the child matures, he should learn to modify an immediate want for a more remote goal by visualizing the end result more vividly. This will abridge some of the distance and make the remote seem imminent. Some of the enthusiasm and satisfaction of anticipating the distant goal may be borrowed and appropriated to the means motive. The child who is told he must keep his room neat and tidy and stop teasing the cat and little sister if he wants a bike for his next birthday is offered a lesson in self-discipline. Even a very young child can discipline himself by eating meat and potatoes and drinking milk first in order to get later the ice cream and cake for dessert.

Values, ideals, life goals: Choice, as between an immediate and remote goal, or any choice, involves values. Values are meaningless without a hierarchy of values. If everything were of equal value, then nothing would be of value. And a hierarchy of values implies some sort of philosophy of life. Goals ultimately

24. Young, *op. cit.*, p. 65.

group themselves into value systems. Value systems are synonymous with life goals. They serve, as standards, as guiding principles, and place boundaries on behaviour. They delineate character and personality.

Ideals, as such, are abstract and cannot motivate anything. It is the personality (the person) that determines behaviour. Personality develops in response to basic needs and wants. The process begins very early in life. Personality, in turn, even while in the early formative period, serves to regulate conduct. Motivation of school learning is very much concerned with the development of character and personality both as to method and ultimate result.[25]

To be effective in character-building, ideals need to be personified. It is much easier to be loyal to a person than to an ideal. "Identification" is made more readily to a person than to an ideal. Children are highly imaginative and decidedly imitative. They identify themselves with imaginary and real people whom they admire and envy. They are hero-worshippers. When they are encouraged to imitate worthwhile personalities, they unconsciously identify themselves also with the traits of their heroes.

Setting a good example: The teacher is a very important person in the school child's life. He personifies the democratic ideal and serves as a model. This is why the personality of the teacher is just about the most decisive factor in the success or failure of the school programme. His influence as a person far exceeds methods and materials in teaching. Some years ago, Hartshorne and May [26] conducted a series of tests for honesty in several types of schools representing diverse ethnic groups and classes of society. They found, among other things, that the personality of the teacher played a decisive role. A certain teacher in one of the schools tested had the highest rating for her classes year after year despite the fact that some of the children coming to her rated lowest the year before coming under her influence.

25. See R. E. Bills, "The Effect of Value on Learning," *Journal of Personality*, XXI (1952), 217-222; G. L. Schwilk, "An Experimental Study of the Effectiveness of Direct and Indirect Methods of Character Instruction," *Dissertation Abstract*. XVI (1956), 1845-1846.
26. H. Hartshorne and M. May, Studies in Deceit (New York: The Macmillan Company, 1928).

Group dynamics: The teacher, although very important, is not the only influence in a child's life. His playmates, parents, siblings, relatives, in short, every person with whom he comes into contact influences his behaviour directly or indirectly. The relatively new science of group dynamics is shedding a great deal of light on individual behaviour in the classroom and in all group contacts.[27]

> Learning in groups seems to be superior to learning in isolation... Group dynamics are more effective when all members of the group are interested in the problem being studied.... Where there are vast differences in motives, group dynamics will be adversely affected.... Children are more cooperative, show more initiative, quarrel less. And display less friction and hostility between the members when they work in a group where democratic leadership prevails.... Group dynamics offers the best means available for development of social skills essential for democratic living, better social understanding and preparing the individual member of the group for democratic citizenship.[28]

Competition versus cooperation[29]***:*** Experimental studies show that among very young children (infants) the cooperative responses are more noticeable than the competitive responses. True cooperation, however, is a learned reaction and takes time to accomplish.

> Rivalry is an effective incentive to use with children of the elementary school grades, as a means of inducing them to better work in connection with their school studies. The interest which this arouses, the outlet for a natural desire to compete with others

---

27. See E. G. French and I. Chadwick, "Some Characteristics in Affiliation Motivation," *Journal of Abnormal and Social Psychology*, LII (1956), 296-300; I. E. Morrison and I. F. Perry, "Acceptance of Average Children by Their Classmates," *Elementary School Journal*. LVI (1956), 217-220; A. Zander and A. R. Cohan, "Attributed Social Power and Group Acceptance; A Classroom Experimental Demonstration," *Journal of Abnormal and Social Psychology*, LI (1951), 490-492; W. H. Crockett, "Emergent Leadership in Small Decision-making Groups," *Journal of Abnormal and Social Psychology*, LI (1951), 373-383; A. Mintz, "Non-adaptive Group Behaviour," *Journal of Abnormal and Social Psychology*, XLVI (1951), 150-159.
28. A. I. Gates, *et. al. Educational Psychology* (3rd ed.; New York: The Macmillan Company, 1948).
29. See M. Deutsche, "An Experimental Study of the Effect of Cooperation and Competition upon Group Processes," *Human Relations*, II (1949), 199-231; B. M. Phillips, *et al.*, "Effects of Cooperation and Competition on the Cohesiveness of Small Face-to-face Groups," *Journal of Educational Psychology*, XLVII (1956), 65-70.

of equal ages, and the training which it gives in the building up of a cooperative spirit as opposed to selfish 'individualism, justifies its use.[30]

Competition and rivalry satisfy basic needs in the individual and the race. We speak of competitive games and often refer to the game of life as such, for, from the cradle to the grave, we are competing for something or other. Competition and rivalry are rooted in the *elan vital,* the evolutionary urge. They constitute the push in the struggle to survive and the desire for supremacy. Competition runs all through life. A man must compete for the means of livelihood, for his social position, for his friends, in fact, for everything that is worth-while. Civilized society has not eliminated rivalry; on the contrary, it has extended the field from the purely physical and biological to the intellectual, social, moral, and spiritual.

Rivalry as a principle of motivation is universally recognized. We make practical use of it in the home, the shop, the school, the playground, the athletic field, and in commerce and industry. It is the greatest urge for increased production and for social control. Our present concern is to determine the role of rivalry and competition in motivating school learning. For information on this point, we rely heavily on experimental studies and statistical research.[31] The object is to utilize the advantages and avoid the pitfalls. The advantages are: (I) it provides zest and meaning to life; (2) it is positive and satisfies a basic urge; (3) it builds up morale and ego-maximization; (4) it stimulates growth, development, and maturation; (5) it could lead to self-improvement, for competition can be .against oneself as well as against others. The chief danger is that if competition is too "keen, the individual is likely to suffer defeat, humiliation, frustration, and possibly demoralization.

Cooperative rivalry: The paradox of cooperative rivalry may be the answer to raw competition. It is achieved through group competition that contains both elements. Members of a group cooperate with each other while the group competes with other

30. Young, *op. cit.*, pp. 406-408.
31. Cf. D. Katz, "Group Morale and Individual Motivation," in J. E. Hulett, *et al.*, *Problems in Social Psychology*, pp. 153-157; W. E. Blatz, "Competition," *Bulletin of Child Study* (Toronto), XVII (1955), 1-2.

groups. Groups may co-operate with other .groups in competition with still other groups, and so on. National groups follow this plan in their alliances. Cooperative and friendly rivalry develop team play, community spirit, self-discipline, high morale. It satisfies the urge to belong, to be accepted. And, most important of all, it encourages participation, so essential in a free society.

Participation through participation[32]*:* This could serve as a motto for all schools. Participation is both an ideal method of motivating school learning as well as the most desirable objective in all formal and informal education. In a democratic society, it is not only desirable but absolutely essential that every citizen take an active interest in the welfare of the nation by informing himself on important issues and by casting his ballot accordingly, in short, by participating as fully as possible in the life of the community. Participation, then, is the goal of all our striving in education. The best training for participation as a citizen is participation as a pupil and student. Participation as the ideal means and end in education is what is meant by participation through participation. What was said under group dynamics, goal setting, making methods and materials meaningful to the pupil, and teacher-pupil planning is applicable here.

Appealing to as many motives as possible and to the total personality[33]*:* If appealing to a single motive is effective, then appealing to 'two or more motives is just that much more effective. This is the basic principle of the transfer of learning. It is also significant in the motivation of learning in the first place. "The effectiveness of a given motive in any situation varies directly with the number of cooperating motives or facilitating factors, and inversely with the number of competing motives or inhibiting factors."[34] To make the widest and possibly the strongest appeal, it is useful to capitalize on natural interests, to take into account immediate as well as remote goals, to make the task .as meaningful as possible, to arouse interest and curiosity by displaying interest and enthusiasm and by

32. Cf. E. E. Jennings, "Developing Participation; Some Fundamental Forces," *Personality Journal*, XXXV (1956), 166-170.
33. Cf. I. E. Farber, "The Role of Motivation in Verbal Learning and Performance," *Psychological Bulletin*, LII (1955), 311-327.;
34. Young, *op. cit*; p. 25.

presenting a wide variety of satisfactions and numerous incentives. Much of what was presented above in practical suggestions for effective motivation of school learning is applicable here. A review of these factors is presented in the summary following.

Summary

Using the classroom as an experimental station, the skillful teacher will guide the pupil through new experiences in his drive to adjust and readjust himself to his environment in a democratic society in such a way as to play his best role as a happy and useful citizen. In acquiring such skill, the teacher may profitably explore the practical suggestions presented in the chapter and summarized as follows:

1. Adjust assignments and requirements to the child's abilities, his readiness or near-readiness, to his physical, mental, and social maturation.
2. Bring the assignment within the child's experience and link it up with the present total environment.
3. Respect the personality of the child by appealing to ego-maximization in recognition of the first law of motivation: that life begins and ends with the individual so far as he is personally concerned.
4. Secure attention and create interest and enthusiasm by taking advantage of the "natural" interests of the child and attempt to develop proper attitudes just when the child is ready to be influenced properly.
5. Use praise and reproof judiciously, as prescribed by the experimental findings on the subject.
6. Apply rewards and punishments within certain limitations and recognize that pleasurable associations are more effective and longer lasting than unpleasant and painful experiences.
7. Develop good sportsmanship through proper adjustments to success and failure, create opportunities for success in sufficient instances to offset the inevitable failures, and keep them in such balance that the

individual will be able to take both success and failure in stride.

8. Emphasize the positive approach, not overlooking the limited usefulness of the negative.
9. Be consistent in recognition of the fact that consistency is far superior to severity and pays large dividends in proper habit-formation and character-building.
10. Make assignments clear and concise so that the pupil will have a readable blueprint of his task.
11. Work out desirable goals and objectives through a democratic approach, enlist cooperation as to method and means, as well as ends and objectives, by defining and redefining methods and goals and offering multiple choices.
12. Attempt to secure self-motivation on the part of the pupil, which is not only proven to be more effective in motivating learning, but which will also go a long way in achieving the ultimate end of all school learning by encouraging the initiative and self-direction so important for a free society.
13. Stimulate and encourage a will-to-learn by developing definite purpose, aspiration, and ambition.
14. Make the pupil's unconscious and semiconscious needs and wants conscious; and more urgently felt.
15. Encourage more accurate self-appraisal.
16. Borrow interest and enthusiasm from the end motive to the means motive, introducing the element of play, which is an end in itself, in contrast with work, which is regarded as a means to an end.
17. Personify ideals to make them more tangible through "identification" and a realistic-idealistic philosophy of life.
18. Set a good example in one's attitude to the pupil and the task at hand, for, in the final analysis, the teacher's personality is the greatest single factor in success or failure of motivating school learning.

19. Take advantage of the recent findings on group dynamics and the urge of rivalry and teamwork.
20. Explore the virtues of cooperation versus competition, having due regard for the experimental studies in the field.
21. Develop the art of cooperative rivalry by participation through participation.
22. Appraise the advantages of drill and the transfer of learning, permitting the pupil to "take" the lesson and integrate it as his own experience rather than having it "poured in."
23. Appeal to the total personality and as many motives as possible.

—*M.K. Thomson*

Questions and Exercises (for Discussion and Study)

1. Make a list of primary (natural) needs and wants that are more or less universal for human beings. Arrange the list in order of importance to education.
2. Why is the science or theory of motivation relatively simple and the art or practical application most difficult? Explain fully.
3. What is the significance of the statement that we are all alike in kind, but differ only in degree. Enumerate ten ways in which human beings differ in degree. How would you appraise (account for) this difference?
4. What is meant by social pressure? Describe its place in motivating conduct in and out of school situations.
5. What is the possible fate of motives? Why must some motives be realized; others inhibited?
6. Distinguish between primary and secondary motives.
7. Enumerate factors that lead to clearer insight on the part of the pupil and factors that hinder or hold back such insight.
8. Study ten advertisements in a popular magazine and note the nature of the appeals. Which do you consider most effective? Why?

9. Define "motivation in depth." Illustrate its use in advertising.
10. What is "subliminal projection"? Give an example of its effectiveness in motivating sales.
11. Enumerate the merits and demerits of rewards and punishments in motivation of school learning. Which is more effective? Why? What limitations or precautions would you suggest in the use of rewards and punishments in the classroom?
12. How would you distinguish motivated from non-motivated assignments in school lessons? Which is better? Explain.
13. Discuss the relative advantages and disadvantages of praise and reproof in motivating school learning.

References

Bernard, H., *The Psychology of Learning and Teaching*. New York: McGraw-Hill Book Company, Inc., 1954, chap. 4.

Blair, G. M., *et al. Educational Psychology*. New York: The Macmillan Company, 1954, chap. 7-8.

Bugelski, B. R., *Learning and Motivation*. New York: Henry Holt & Company, Inc., 1956, chap. 9.

Burton, W. H., *The Guidance of Learning Activities*, 2nd ed. NewYork: Appleton-Century Crofts, Inc., 1952, chap. 6.

Henry, N. B. (ed.), *Learning and Instruction*, Forty-ninth Yearbook of the National Society for the Study of Education, Part I. Chicago: University of Chicago Press, 1950, chap. 2.

Jordan, A. M., *Educational Psychology: Growth and Learning*, 4th ed. New York: Henry Holt & .Company, Inc., 1956.

Kelly, W. A., *Educational Psychology*, 4th ed. Milwaukee: Bruce Publishing Company, 1956, chap. 17.

Millard, C. V., *Child Growth and Development in the Elementary School*. Boston: D. C. Heath & Company, 1951.

Olds, J., *The Growth and Structure of Motives: Psychological Studies in the Theory of Action*. Glencoe, III Free Press, 1956.

Remmers, H. H., *et al.* (eds.). *Growth, Teaching and Learning*. New York: Harper & Brothers, 1957, Part II.

Seagoe, M. V., *A Teacher's Guide to the Learning Process*. Dubuque, Iowa: William C. Brown Co., 1956.

Stacey, C. L., and M. F. DeMartino (eds.). *Understanding Human Motivation*. Cleveland: Howard Alien, Inc., 1958.

Wheat, H. G., *Foundations of School Learning*. NewYork: Alfred A Knopf, Inc., 1955.

11

Transfer and Functional Learning

A Statement of the Problem and its Significance for Teachers

All teachers want their students to be able to use the experiences gained in the classroom in meeting situations in everyday life; in other words, teachers want the learning experiences of their students to function as widely as possible in their everyday learning and living. When a teacher becomes interested in developing more functional learning in his students he must think through the problem of transfer of learning and the part it has played in determining educational thinking and practices.

Every student who reads this chapter, in all probability, has had to take certain courses—say, in mathematics or a foreign language—in either high school or college. The people who established such a practice must have had some reason for thinking that certain courses were sufficiently valuable to be a requirement in the programmes of study of all students. The principles that guided the thinking and practice of these earlier educators have been formulated in the Theory of Formal Discipline. This theory has influenced and is perhaps still influencing educational thinking and educational practice more than any other one thing that could be mentioned. Many students have heard some of their high-school or college teachers try to answer questions as to the value of studying the subject that they were teaching. The answer most often given, perhaps, has been that the study of a certain subject sharpens the mind; it improves the memory or the reasoning ability. The writer, a short time ago, heard a university professor say to a large group of university students that mathematics and the languages are the meat and potatoes of the educational diet;

other courses of the curriculum would have to be labeled a salad or a dessert; some few courses might have the distinction of becoming a vegetable. One might readily surmise that the above-mentioned teacher taught either mathematics or a language, and he would be right. Such a statement is a clear index of the basis of the educational thinking of this man.

The doctrine of formal discipline has also had marked influence on educational practices in the elementary schools. How have courses in arithmetic become so filled with topics that students rarely meet in their life situations, and with problems that are largely confined between the covers of textbooks? Spelling books have contained ten to fifteen thousand words although students need to know how to spell only three to five thousand. The additional words have never been used by students, but, being hard and difficult, have therefore been included to "discipline the mind." Pupils have been required to learn the name of every cape that projected into every ocean on the globe, not for any useful purpose in life, but to "train the memory."

Teachers and prospective teachers certainly need to have a clear understanding of a theory that has so profoundly affected educational thinking and practice. Shall teachers continue to let the principles embodied in the theory of formal discipline affect their thinking and practices in solving classroom problems? Or shall they abandon this theory, and endeavour to put in its place a sounder and more vital set of principles? It must not be forgotten that every sound practice has back of it sound principles. In dealing with this problem, Mursell says:

> Our attitude toward transfer [of training] determines our attitude towards teaching. If we retain the disciplinary prepossession, instruction ceases to be an art, the whole problem of procedure vanishes, and only drive remains—external drive at that. If we give it up, at once there emerges that great and exacting responsibility to meet which our whole vast armament of modern educational techniques has been devised. Hence we are bound to feel that the topic is one of the most immediately practical with which it is possible to deal.[1]

1. J.L. Mursell, *Psychology of Secondary School Teaching* (New York: W.W.Norton & Company, 1932), p. 91.

Two terms have been used: *formal discipline* and *transfer of training*. A better understanding of the problem will be obtained if a clear distinction is made between them.

Advocates of the theory of formal discipline have assumed the mind to be made up of *faculties*. Its adherents have often spoken of the faculty of memory, of reasoning, and the like. This theory has further postulated that if the faculty of memory or reasoning is trained by the study of a foreign language or mathematics, so much improvement in remembering or reasoning will result that the student will be better able to remember or reason in every situation where such activities were called for. It has been further assumed that the improvement comes about automatically as the result of studying such a subject, and that the improved faculty, memory or reasoning, functions in a better manner in the newer situations.

Transfer of training is concerned with the question of whether or not the learning of material A—say, mathematics—aids, hinders, or does not affect the subsequent learning of material B—say, physics or chemistry. This theory assumes nothing about faculties of the mind, but is concerned with how the organism meets situations, B, C, D, and so forth, after having had an experience in situation A. Educationally, it is concerned with finding out how the organism can benefit to the largest degree from its experience in situation A when it finds itself face to face with situation B, C, D, and so forth.

The teacher who faces this problem from the standpoint of transfer of learning and forgets about formal discipline realizes that the responsibility rests on his shoulders for so teaching his subject that his students learn to transfer their experiences to as many situations as is practical. He realizes that such teaching is the main way to increase the functional learning of his students.

For the teacher who desires to understand this problem thoroughly, it is wise to become acquainted with the historical and scientific attacks on the problem.

The Attempt to Solve the Problem Scientifically

Our educational system in the United States developed from the top down. Harvard College was established as a vocational school to train ministers. A curriculum was set up to meet the assumed needs of the ministers of those days. After a time, students other than those preparing for the ministry were admitted to the college. The curriculum was not changed materially, but the college people justified having other students study the same subjects by citing the disciplinary value of those subjects. Preparatory schools arose to train students to study the established curriculum. When elementary schools were established, they soon came to be thought of as preparing students to study in the secondary schools. Thus, the theory of formal discipline came to be the all-pervasive American educational philosophy.

This doctrine was tacitly assumed to be correct by practically all American school people until about 1890. In this year, William James published his *Principles of Psychology*. In his first volume, he briefly told how he had tested his ability to memorize 158 lines from Victor Hugo's *Satyr*. He then trained his memory by practicing 20 minutes a day for 38 days in learning the first book of Milton's *Paradise Lost*. At the end of this period, he again tested his ability to memorize 158 lines on the *Satyr*. It took more time to memorize the second 158 lines than it did the first![2] James induced four other people to try a similar test of training their memory, and they obtained about the same result as did James. Thus occurred the first significant challenge in American education to the doctrine of formal discipline.[3]

Certainly any intelligent, wide-awake teacher wants to know whether he is justified in believing in formal discipline or transfer of training. Of course, one who accepts formal discipline necessarily assumes that transfer of training takes place, but one who believes in transfer of training need not in any sense assume the existence of formal discipline. Such an important question should not be decided on the basis of opinions of any group, but upon whatever scientific information is available. A summary

2. W. James, *Principles of Psychology* (New York: Henry Holt & Company, Inc., 1890), Vol. I, pp. 666-668.
3. What James actually pointed out was although native retentiveness was not improved by practice, memory efficiency might be improved through a mental reorganization or arrangement of experience. While challenging the doctrine of formal discipline, he actually gave support to the efficiency of generalized experience.

of what science has to offer towards the solution of this problem will now be presented.

The initial scientific attack of James on this problem stirred up a deep and widespread interest among psychologists. Evidence of this interest is found in the some 300 or more studies on the problem that have been published since 1890.

A teacher of Latin might ask how one could scientifically determine whether or not students who study Latin have an improved English vocabulary of Latin derivatives. In order to answer this question, he would have to secure a large group of students who have studied Latin. Another group of students would now have to be obtained comparable in number, intelligence, and educational training to the first group, but without the experience of studying Latin. Next, he would measure the size of the Latin-derivative vocabulary of both groups. If the Latin group showed a significantly larger vocabulary, the teacher would be justified in assuming that Latin had transferred to the English vocabulary. A better way to make such a test is to select two fairly large groups of high-school freshmen who have not studied Latin. Presumably the two groups are equal in educational training. In order to equate the two groups in intelligence, administer a reliable intelligence test. Now measure the size of the English vocabulary of each group, noting particularly the number of words of Latin origin known by each group. The two groups then attend high school for one or two years. Keep the programmes of studies of the two groups comparable, except that one group is to study Latin. At the end of one year, and also the end of the second year, measure the size of the vocabulary of both groups, with special attention to the number of Latin derivatives known. If the Latin group possesses a considerably larger Latin-derivative vocabulary, it may be inferred that the study of Latin has aided in the building up of a larger vocabulary. Such a result is called *positive transfer*. If the non-Latin students show a knowledge of a larger number of Latin derivative words, it may be assumed that the study of Latin has hindered the building up of a Latin-derivative vocabulary. This result is called *negative transfer*. If there is no difference in the size of the Latin-derivative vocabulary of the two groups, it may be said that Latin has had no effect in increasing the size of the vocabulary. In this instance, the teacher may say that there has been an absence of transfer.

Summary ot Scientific Experiments

Many different kinds of materials have been employed in efforts to determine if transfer of training is a demonstrable fact. One or two illustrations of these various types of materials will be presented.

Sensorimotor materials: One experimenter tried to determine whether learning to tread a pathway through a maze with a stylus aided, hindered, or had no effect in learning several other mazes.[4] He also tested the effect of learning the several mazes upon the maze; that is, he measured the transfer effect of maze A upon mazes B, C, D, E, and F, and also the transfer effect of mazes B, C, D, E, and F, upon maze A. Both human and animals subjects were used in this experiment. The results showed that maze A aided in the learning of the other mazes, and the other mazes aided in the mastering of maze A. The degree of positive transfer varied from 19 to 77 per cent. The degree of transfer also varied with the direction of learning; that is, the amount of transfer in going from maze A to the other mazes differed from the amount in going from the other mazes to maze A. A very interesting result was found in testing the effect of maze A upon maze F. Each maze had four sections. Maze F was highly similar to maze A, but section 3 was made a blind alley. Learning maze F after learning maze A was similar to learning four verses of poetry and then having to say verses 1, 2, and 4. Three criteria were used to measure the effect of eliminating section 3 in maze F. All three measures showed this section to be interfering in the learning of maze F, yet there was a 19 per cent transfer from maze F. On the basis of this result, the author concluded that the transfer effect is a composite process consisting of both positive and negative elements, and that the final result will be determined by the predominance of one or the other of these elements.

The results of the foregoing experiment prove that there is a positive transfer from one sensorimotor material to another; but it can hardly be said that these results favour the doctrine of formal discipline. Although maze A aided in the learning of the other

4. L.W. Webb, "Transfer of Training and Retroaction," *Psychological Review Monographs*, XXIV, No. 104 (Princeton, N.J.: Psychological Review Company, 1971).

five mazes, one would hardly be justified in claming that the mental functions involved in mastering maze A were so improved through this experience that the subjects could better learn all other maze patterns. Was it not shown that the degree of transfer varied from 77 per cent to only 19 per cent? In the instance of the smallest degree of transfer, an interfering element was proved to be present. It is highly probable that a maze could be constructed with so many negative elements that maze A would interfere in its mastery. This experiment also proved that the degree of transfer is determined in part by the second earned activity. Maze A was not equally valuable as an aid in attacking the other mazes. This fact implies that the study of Latin may be more efficacious for doctors or ministers than for lawyers or businessmen. Formal discipline has maintained that the first learned activity, the subject studied, so improves the faculties that the person will benefit in whatever line of future work he engages.

Perceptual materials: Many experiments have been made with perceptual materials, such as measuring the benefit of estimating one length line upon one's ability to estimate lines of different length, or of estimating areas of one size upon the success of estimating areas of different sizes. Most of these experiments have little significance for teachers. However, some experiments by E.L. Thorndike and R.S. Woodworth have had considerable influence on educational thinking. As a result of his studies in this field, Thorndike developed his Theory of Identical Elements to explain transfer.

Memory materials: Experiments dealing with memory materials are many. An English psychologist by the name of Sleight has made one of the best experiments in the field.[5] He tested the effect of memorizing poetry, tables, and prose substance upon the ability to memorize dates, nonsense syllables, poetry, prose (literal), and prose (substance) letters. The results of this experiment were extremely varied. Little or no transfer was manifested in some instances; in other instances, a small amount of positive transfer occurred; whereas in still others, negative transfer resulted. On the basis of his elaborate work with transfer in memory materials, Sleight made a number of conclusions, two of which are mentioned because they are quite contrary to the assumptions of formal discipline. These two conclusion are:

---

5. W.G. Sleight, Memory and Formal Training," *British Journal of Psychology*, IV, Nos. and 3 and 4 (1911), 386-457.

1. There appeears to be no general memory improvement as the result of practice, nor any evidence for the hypothesis of the general memory function.
2. There would seem instead to be a very large number of related and unrelated memory functions of a more or less complex kind.

Although a number of investigators using memory materials have found a considerably higher degree of positive transfer than did Sleight, the results do not prove that extensive practice produces any general improvement in memory. The memory function is a complex process, and the transfer results depend more upon the specific activity exercised and its relation to the memory activity to which it is transferred.

Reasoning material: It appears to be rather difficult to perform experiments on transfer with this type of material. Nevertheless, several interesting experiments have been made in this field. One experimenter used school children to determine the value of training to solve arithmetical reasoning problems in solving other logical problems.[6] Two groups of children were given certain logical tests. Then one group was trained for ten weeks in arithmetical reasoning. The other group carried on its ordinary school work without emphasis upon arithmetical reasoning. According to the author, the practiced group did 30 per cent better in logical reasoning than did the unpractised group. Thus it can be assumed that training in arithmetical reasoning can be carried over in a helpful manner to solving other logical problems.

A somewhat different kind of experiment to test transfer value of learning to reason was made by Barlow.[7] He claims that skill in reasoning is improved by teaching definite methods of reasoning. He trained one group of seventh- and eighth-graders how to analyze verbal problems and how to state general principles. He found that this training resulted in substantial gains on reasoning problems that were quite different in content from those used during practice.

---

6. W.H. Winch, "Transfer of Improvement on Reasoning in School Children," *British Journal of Psychology*, XIII, No. 4 (1922),370-381.
7. M.C.Barlow, "Transfer of Training in Reasoning," *Journal of Educational Psychology*, XXVIII (1937), 122-128.

Another investigator[8] tested the value of a course in geometry for training in reflective thinking. He discovered that, if definite methods of reflective thinking were stressed in the learning of geometry, there would be a resultant improvement along such lines in other learning situations. If the course in geometry was taught with no such emphasis, no general improvement in reflective thinking resulted.

Ideals: There have been several experiments with ideals. One teacher emphasized neatness and accuracy in arithmetic papers to a third grade group of children.[9] The arithmetic papers were scored for accuracy and neatness, and improvement was noted along both lines. Nothing was said to the children about being neat in their other papers. However, their papers in spelling and language were scored for neatness and accuracy, and neatness and accuracy had decreased rather than improved in these papers. In another investigation, great emphasis was placed upon neatness in all papers handed in, and the children were told the advantage of neatness in other aspects of life inside and outside of school. In the other studies of these children, nothing was said about neatness. The papers were rated for neatness, and improvement was noted in classes other than those in which neatness had been emphasized. The author concluded that ideals can transfer.

School subjects: Several experiments have tested the transfer value of elementary-school subjects. Large claims have been made for the disciplinary value of studying formal grammar. One student analyzed these claims, and then made fifty-four tests to measure these abilities.[10] Two groups of seventh-grade children were equated in intelligence. The tests were then given to both groups. Next group one studied grammar for three months, while the

---

8. G. Ulmer, "Teaching Geometry to Cultivate Reflective Thinking: an Experimental Study with 1239 High School Pupils," *Journal of Experimental Education*, VIII (1939), 18-25. For an interesting discussion of transfer and productive thinking,see H.G.Birsh and H.S.Rabinowitz,"The Negative Effect of Previous Experience on Productive Thinking," *Journal of Experimental Psychology*, XLI (1951), 121-215.
9. W.C. Bagley, *Educational Values* (New York: The Macmillian Company, 1911), p.189. See also W.C. Ruediger "Indirect Improvement of Mental Functions Through Ideals," *Educational Review*, XXXVI, No.4 (1908), 364-371.
10. T.H. Briggs, "Formal English Grammar as a Discipline," *Teachers College Record*, XIV, No. 4 (1913), 1-93.

other children studied language and composition. At this time, the tests were again administered. Then group one studied language and composition for three months and group two studied grammar. At the end of this three-month period, the tests were again given to both groups. The grammar groups improved in only one of the abilities measured, the ability to see likenesses and differences.

Does training in arithmetical computation transfer in such a manner as to show an improvement in arithmetic reasoning? An English experimenter selected two groups of ten-year-old students who were equal in their ability to solve reasoning problems in arithmetic.[11] One group practiced arithmetic computation thirty minutes a day for ten days; the other group practised drawing. At the end of the ten days both groups were tested for arithmetical reasoning ability, and both groups did equally well. On the basis of these results, the author concluded that students may study arithmetical computation without any guarantee of improvement taking place in reasoning in arithmetic.

A much larger number of studies have been made in an effort to determine the transfer value of high-school subjects. One study, using over 8,000 students, attempted to determine the effect of a year of study in high school upon the improvement of intellectual activity,as measured by a very elaborate intelligence test given one spring and a second form of the same test administered a year later.[12] The students showed a gain of 23 points on the second test. Approximately 50 per cent of the gain was due to the previous experience in taking the first test, and about 50per cent to the high-school course pursued for a year. Certain groups of subjects appeared to contribute more to the gain than did certain other groups. The highest 1 per cent of the students in initial ability on the first test gained 20½ points. while the lowest 1 per cent in initial ability gained only 1½ points. On the basis of these latter results, the author claimed that the intelligence of the students was a larger contributing factor to improvement than were the subjects studied in high school for a year.

11. W.H. Winch,"Further Work on Numerical Accuracy in School Children: Does Improvement in Numerical Accuracy Transfer?" *Journal of Education Psychology*, II No. 5 (1911), 262-271.
12. E.L. Thorndike, "Mental Discipline in High School Studies," *Journal of Educational Psychology*, XV, No. 1 (1924), 1-22, 83-98.

A more recent study endeavoured to determine the transfer value of high-school subjects to intelligence by obtaining measures of correlation between intelligence test scores and achievement test scores at the beginning and the end of the school year.[13] The author of this study also used a measure of the significance of differences between the correlation as an indication of the presence of transfer.

Many studies have been made in an endeavour to determine the transfer value of a specific high-school subject Many individuals have assumed high-school mathematics to have large disciplinary values. One student found that a course in descriptive geometry transferred 32 per cent to other geometrical materials, but only 7 per cent to non-geometrical materials.[14] Does taking work in science improve one's ability in careful observation? A teacher of botany measured students' ability to observe, and then trained them for a period of time in observing botanical materials. The amount of transfer from this training was 33.9 per cent to other botanical materials and 5.4 per cent to non-botanical materials.[15]

The classical investigation, which was carried on from 1921 to 1924, endeavoured to determine the value of studying Latin. This investigation stimulated a number of experiments on the transfer problem as it concerns Latin. In addition to these studies, several others have been made with Latin. It has been demonstrated that high-school freshmen who studied Latin for a year gained in a knowledge of English words of Latin origin about 2½ times as much as did freshmen who did not take Latin.[16] Latin appears to transfer somewhat to the improvement of reading; those students who studied Latin for a year gained more in reading ability than did non-Latin students.[17] Experiments have shown

13. A.G. Wesman, "A Study of Transfer of Training from High School Subjects to Intelligence," (Teachers College Contributions to Education, No. 909 [New York: Bureau of Publications, Teachers College, Columbia University, 1945]).
14. H.O. Rugg. "Experimental Determination of Mental Discipline in School Studies," *Educational Psychology Monographs*, No.17 (Baltimore: Warwick & York, Inc., 1916).
15. N.P. Hewins, "Doctrine of Formal Discipline in the Light of Experimental Investigation," *Educational Psychology Monographs*, No. 16 (Baltimore: Warwick & York, Inc., 1916).
16. E.L. Throndike and G.J. Ruger, "Effect of First Year Latin Upon a Knowledge of English Words of Latin Derivation," *School and Society*, XVII, No. 453 (1923), 260-270.
17. E.L. Throndike, "Effect of the First Year Latin Upon Ability to Read English," *School and Society*, XVII, No. 424 (1923), 165-168.

that the study of Latin causes an improvement in students' knowledge of the English language about 10 per cent higher than the improvement of those not taking Latin.[18] Latin increases the ability to spell words of Latin origin, but the transfer is negative in relation to spelling words of non-Latin origin.[19] Students who have studied Latin and then study French or Spanish have an advantage at the beginning of the latter study over students who come to French or Spanish without any knowledge of Latin. However, this advantage lasts for only about one semester. After that time both the Latin and non-Latin students do equally well in the study of modern languages.[20]

Some studies have been made that attempt to test the transfer value of French in studying English.[21] French aids somewhat in increasing the rate of reading English. English sentence structure and vocabulary are improved very little by the study of French. Teachers of French should meet this challenge by improving their methods of teaching so that larger transfer values will result.

Many other studies on the problems of transfer have been made. However, this sampling of the experiments will the student or teacher some idea of the extent and vigour of the attack on the problem. At this point it will aid the student if consideration is given to other aspects of the problem.

General Consideration of the Evidence

Authors of the studies referred to above have been concerned with proving the fact of transfer. The illustrations selected did show transfer. In summarizing the results from all

---

18. E.L.Throndike and H.A.Rugger, "Gains Made in Ability in English by Pupils Who Study Latin and Those Who Do Not," *School and Society*, XVIII, No. 467 (1923), 690.
19. W.W. Coxe, "Influence of Latin on the Spelling of English Words," *Journal of Educational Research*, VII, No. 3 (1923), 244-250, and IX, No. 3 (1924), 223-233.
20. L.E.Cole, "Latin as a Preparation for French and Spanish," *School and Society*, XIX, No. 491 (1924), 618-622; and J.J. Kirby, "Latin as a Preparation for French," *School and Society*, XVIII No. 463 (1923), 563-569.
21. C. Woody, "Influence of the Teaching of First Year French on the Acquisition of English Vocabulary," *Studies in Modern Language Teaching (Modern Foreign Language Study*, XVII; New York: The Macmillan Company, 1930), pp. 146-179; and O.H. Werner, "Influence of the study of Modern Foreign Languages on the Development of Desirable Abilities in English," *Studies in Modern Language Teaching (Modern Foreign Language Study*, XVII; New York: The Macmillan Company, 1930), pp. 97-145.

the experiments from 1890 to 1935, Orata states that 28 per cent show considerable transfer; 48 per cent, appreciable transfer; 9 per cent, very little transfer; 3.6 per cent, no transfer; 7.2 per cent, transfer and interference; and 3 per cent, interference.[22]

On the basis of all this experimental evidence, one can conclude with confidence that positive transfer does take place. This fact has been proved again and again by many experimentations under varying conditions. One should be careful at this point, however, and not jump to the conclusion that formal discipline has been proved experimentally. It must also be remembered that absence of transfer and negative transfer have been proved in several experiments. Furthermore, the degree of positive transfer varies from a very slight amount to 92.9 per cent. It has been estimated that 5.4 per cent of the experiments prove that the degree of transfer varies with the conditions under which the experiments were made. These last-mentioned facts hardly fit in with the theory of formal discipline.

With all of those facts before him, no intelligent teacher should be willing to assume tacitly that the subject he teaches, in and of itself, is having the wonderful effects that formal discipline has assumed that certain subjects do have. On the other hand, the teacher should be concerned with whether or not his subject has large or small value to students in meeting other situations of life, no value, or even negative value to students solving certain problems. Such considerations force one to raise the question of the possibility of improving learning conditions in the classroom so as to increase the degree of positive transfer of the subjects being taught there. A number of experiments make some contribution to the solution of this problem.

Conditions of improving transfer: One experimenter endeavoured to test the transfer value of training in the *methods* of memorizing.[23] He administered certain memory tests to three groups of students. One group received no training in memorizing. A second group of memorized poetry and nonsense syllables. The third group spent 43 per cent of its time listening

22. P.T. Orata,"Transfer of Training and Educational Pseudo-Science," *The Mathematics Teacher*, XXVIII, No. 5 (1935), 267.
23. H.Woodrow, "The Effect of Type of Training upon Transference," *Journal of Educational Psychology*, XVIII No. 3 (1927), 159-172.

to instructions on how best to memorize, and the remainder of the time memorizing poetry and nonsense syllables. At the end of the training period all three groups were again given the memory tests. The second group did very little better than the first group. The third group, having received an emphasis on methods, showed a considerably larger gain in the second test than either of the other two groups. This experiment proved that instruction in the methods of learning will considerably increase the degree of positive transfer when students have to master similar meterials in a comparable situation.

Another experimenter wished to measure the value that training to define scientific words had for defining ordinary words.[24] Three groups of students were used. The ability of each group to define ordinary words was measured. Group A, the control group, received no training. Group B was trained for a time in a routine method of defining scientific terms. Group C devoted thirty minutes of its training period to instruction in the technique of definition and to an understanding of the process of defining. Group B profited very little from its training. Group C, however, showed marked inprovement in defining ordinary words as shown by a significant reduction in the number of errors in their definitions. Again, instruction in methods of meeting a situation proved to be significant in increasing the amount of transfer.

Evidence has been produced to prove that students' knowledge of English words of Latin origin can be considerably increased by giving special attention to such material during the teaching of Latin.[25] One group of students was taught Latin in the ordinary way. In the class work of the second group, ten minutes a day was given to the history and derivation of words of Latin origin. After a period of time, gains in the vocabularies of Latin derivatives of the two groups were measured. The second group gained about twice as much as did the first group. Another study dealt with the same problem, but in addition tried to discover if

24. G.P. Meredith, "Consciousness of Method as a Means of Transfer of Training," *Forum of Education*, V, No. 1 (1927), 37-45.
25. A.A. Hamblen, *An Investigation to Determine the Extent to Which the Effect of the Study of Latin upon a Knowledge of English Derivatives can be Increased by Conscious Adaptation of Content and Method to the Attainment of This Objective*, Ph.D. thesis (Philadelphia: University of Pennsylvania, 1925).

equally good result could be obtained by students studying English without Latin.[26] The group studying Latin with special emphasis on Latin derivatives showed decidedly the largest gain.

Two groups of boys were taught to shoot a target 12 inches under water.[27] One group was given an explanation of the principles of refraction of light under water. The other group was given no such instruction. In shooting at the target 12 inches under water, both groups did equally well. Now the target was shifted to 4 inches under water. At this depth the instructed group did much better than the uninstructed group. One of the authors of this experiment claimed that the instructed group generalized its knowledge of the principles of refraction of light under water to targets at different depths. Hence, when the target was changed from 12 to 4 inches under water, this group adjusted to the new situation much more readily.

At a later date this experiment was repeated, having the boys shoot at targets 6 inches and then 2 inches under water.[28] The results from this experiments confirmed the result found by Scholckow and Judd.

Fifty-two classes of second-grade children were used in an experiment to determine the transfer effect of instruction in three types of two-place addition numbers to tasks involving addition and subtraction of two- and three-place numbers.[29] Four different procedures were employed. Group A practised without specific instructions. The other groups practised, but their methods of instruction varied. Group B was taught to generalize the process consciously and formulate a general method of procedure applicable to other types of problems. Group C was taught by a method called *rationalization*, which means understanding the

26. R.I. Haskell, *A Statistical Study of the Comparative Results Produced by Teaching Derivations in the Ninth Grade Latin Classes and in the Ninth Grade English Classes of Non-Latin Pupils in Four Philadelphia High Schools*, Ph.D. thesis (Philadelphia: University of Pennsylvania, 1923).
27. O. Scholckow and C.H. Judd, "The Relation of Special Training to General Intelligence," *Educational Review*, XXXVI, No.1 (1908), 28-42.
28. G.Hendrickson and W.H.Schroder, "Transfer of Training in Learning to Hit a Submerged Target," *Journal of Educational Psychology*, XXXII (1941), 205-213.
29. J.R.Overman, "An Experimental Study of the Effect of the Method of Instruction in Transfer of Training in Arithmetic." *Elementary School Journal*, XXXI, No. 3 (1930), pp. 183-190.

underlying principles of the process. Group D was taught a combined method of generalization and rationalization. Groups A and C obtained an equal amount of positive transfer, around 60 per cent. The percentage of transfer in the case of Groups B and D was about 72 per cent. Whenever the generalization method was taught, the transfer was increased about 20 per cent. These result pointed to the conclusion that, in teaching arithmetic, it is not adequate simply to teach the facts and processes; students must be taught how to apply these facts and processes to other phases and problems of arithmetic—that is, to generalize the procedure to a variety of problems in which it is usable.

The attitude students have toward the matter of transfer at the time of possible transfer of an experience has been shown to be of considerable significance in increasing the amount of positive transfer.[30] The significance of this factor was tested in three instances. Two groups of students were used each time; both groups were given the same training. The experimental groups at the time the transfer was ready to be made were given certain instructions that the other groups did not receive. In the first case, the students were told to use the method of study they had acquired while learning the materials of certain paragraphs. In the second instance, the students were instructed to use their knowledge of Latin in determining the meanings of the words in the test they were about to take. In the third case, the students were instructed to use their recently acquired knowledge of description geometry in answering the questions in the tests about to be given, In all three cases the students in the experimental or instructed groups showed a significantly highly degree of positive transfer than the uninstructed groups. The authors of this experiment admitted that other factors affecting the degree of transfer were probably present, but they maintained that the attitude of readiness set up by the instructions given was of considerable significance. If the amount of transfer can be increased so readily by such simple devices as were used in this experiment, certainly the classroom teacher can find many ways, if he is vitally interested in doing so, of increasing the transfer value of the materials he is teaching.

30. M.F. Doresy and L.T. Hopkins, "The Influence of Attitudes Upon Transfer," *Journal of Educational Psychology*, XXI, No. 6 (1930), 410-417.

One would suppose that the degree of mastery of the material learned is one condition that affects the amount of transfer. This is equivalent to saying that one has to learn a subject before he can use it in another situation. A few studies have been made in an endeavour to determine what significance the degree of mastery of materials has upon the degree to which those materials can be used in other situations. One author tested the effect of learning syllables on the mastery of similar and different syllables.[31] The transfer effect of the degree of mastery was determined by repeating the first learned syllables 2, 6, and 12 times. In the case of 2 repetitions, the material was slightly learned; in the second instance, the syllables were almost learned; and then they were completely learned. The conclusion drawn from this study was that the degree of positive transfer is proportional to the degree of integration if the first-learned material, and that in learning to make an old response to a new stimulus a marked degree of positive transfer results when the integration of the initial learning is complete.

Much interest is displayed nowadays in the question of the application of knowledge. What is the relation of the amount of information a person possesses to his ability to apply his knowledge? A study was made that attempted to discover the relation between the amount of information possessed in several fields of science and the ability to pass accurate judgements on scientific problems of everyday life.[32] Groups of eighth-grade, ninth-grade and junior-college students, as well as adults and elementary-and high-school teachers, took part in the experiment. The groups had received varying amounts of training along scientific lines. The author drew several conclusions that have some significance for the problem of transfer of training. (1) One's ability to apply knowledge is not directly proportional to one's knowledge of facts, (2) The presence of prejudice or superstition decreases the application of facts. (3) Scientific interest stimulates acquisition of knowledge but does not affect ability to apply knowledge. These statements lead one to surmise that, in addition to facts themselves, the application of those facts has

---

31. R.W. Bruce, "Conditions of Transfer of Training," *Journal of Experimental Psychology*, XVI, No. 3 (1933), 343-361.
32. E.B. More, "A Study of Scientific Attitudes as Related to Factual Knowledge," *School Review*, XXXVIII, No. 5 (1930), 379-386.

to be taught. Applying information is an example of the transfer of information and experiences. This study concluded with the following important statements:

> When the facts are known, the fewest errors are made in the situations in which a person had the most experience. It follows then that the methods in the teaching of science should present facts and principles in relation to as many of the important situations in daily life as possible.

The two last-mentioned studies become very significant when one considers the proven fact that so many of the subjects learned in school are relatively soon forgotten. Perhaps the cause of such results is the slight or partial learning of school materials. It is hardly possible for students to have much success in transferring experiences that are so slightly mastered. The teacher can assure himself of larger transfer values by working out methods that result in a more complete learning of the school subject taught. It is highly probable that the teacher is justifics in assuming that one of the best ways of more nearly completely learning a certain body of subject matter is to teach its application to as many situations as possible.

A sufficient number of students has been sited to convince anyone that the degree of positive transfer is affected by a variety of conditions, and that the teacher can increase the transfer value of his subject by giving due heed to these conditions. It has been proved that the methods used in learning, the methods of instruction employed, the attitude of the learner at the time the transfer is to take place, the generalizing of an experience, and the degree of mastery of material are all extremely effective in increasing the degree of positive transfer. All of these conditions are usable in the classroom. Certainly, a good teacher will want to make use of all possible procedures that increase the value of the subject he is teaching.

The most significant generalization that can be made after a review of the experiments on transfer is that if one simply attempts to prove the fact of transfer without any particular attention to the conditions affecting transfer, a relatively small degree of transfer is likely to occur. On the other hand, if one pays attention to the conditions affecting transfer, and deliberately works to enhance the transfer values, the degree of transfer can be increased to a very marked extent. The foregoing statement is equivalent to saying that if a teacher teaches the facts of arithmetic only, that is about all the children learn. However, if he also teaches children to apply the facts of arithmetic to a variety of situations, they will learn to transfer their arithmetic experiences to various aspects of their lives. This last statement emphasizes the of repeated saying of psychologists, "Learn the materials in the way you expect to use them, for the children learn to do exactly what they do." Applied to the problem of transfer, this principle means that the children must be taught to transfer the experiences of the classroom if the teacher expects them to be able to carry on that type of activity in situations outside the classroom.

How does Transfer Take Place?

A large majority of the experiments cited in this chapter show some kind of transfer. Many of the experimenters have attempted to explain how transfer takes place. They have endeavoured to get at the cause or causes of transfer. Such explanations have much significance for school people. If the teacher knows what causes transfer, he can tell better how to set up conditions in his teaching that give the causes a chance to become operative in the experiences of his students. Have the investigators been able to point out the cause of transfer? The two most widely known explanations will be presented in an attempt to answer this question.

One of the earliest explanations was offered by Thorndike in his Theory of Identical Elements. He maintained that one mental function alters any other only insofar as the two functions have identical elements as factors. He also cited the use of the same neural bonds in the two situations as the cause of transfer. Many other writers have employed the idea of identical elements as the cause of transfer. Some have simply stated the explanation in a general claim for identical elements. Others have given their explanation in terms of identity of content, identity of procedure, and identity of aims or ideals.

The other often-mentioned explanation is known as the Theory of Generalization. Judd, the author of this theory, maintained that transfer takes place in a person to the extent that he generalizes his experiences. He derived the theory from the experiment in which boys shot at a target under water. The boys who had been given explanation of the principles of refraction of light under water did better when the target was changed in depth from 12 to 4 inches because they had generalized their knowledge of the principles of refraction by applying them to targets at varying depths. A large number of writers have used this theory as the basis of their statements as to the cause of transfer.

These two theories hardly answer the query as to the cause of transfer; they merely appear to be descriptions of where and how transfer may take place. One would hardly expect an experience with arithmetic to transfer to a situation where no numerical relations are involved. If Latin transfers, it should be to other language situations and not to purely mechanical experiences. One generalizes an experience by transferring it to a variety of situations to which it is applicable.

At the present time there is no adequate theory of the cause of transfer. However, the two theories mentioned above do have considerable practical significance. The theory of identical elements emphasizes that an experience can be transferred only to similar situations, where some of the elements of the first experience are applicable. The theory of generalization of experiences stresses the significance of transferring an experience to as many similar situations as possible in order to understand its applicability to all situations.

A brief survey has been made of scientific attempts to solve the problem of transfer of training. The scientific attack on the problem has large value, but no one can maintain that the problem is adequately solved, for neither the varying conditions that affects the degree of transfer nor the causes of transfer are known as yet. However, the teacher should not be discouraged, because the problem is not primarily a scientific or theoretical one for him, but mainly an *educational* problem. The teacher is concerned with the question of obtaining the largest possible value from the experiences he is giving students by teaching them to make the largest possible application of these experiences. These statements lead to a consideration of the following topic.

The Meaning of the Scientific Results for the Teacher

Although it is true that the problem of transfer of training has not been completely solved by the application of scientific techniques, the results are sufficiently convincing to have a considerable meaning for teachers. Anyone who is genuinely interested in the problem of teaching will find that these results have significance for his thinking about educational problems. These results are very valuable in enabling him to improve his teaching methods and procedures.

In the early part of this chapter, a statement was quoted from Mursell to the effect that one's attitude toward the problem of transfer determines his attitude toward teaching. A teacher who continues to hold to formal discipline as a basis for thinking about educational problems will be inclined to do some of the following things. He will defend the privileged position of certain subjects in the curriculum. He will justify the fact that these subjects are required of all students on the ground that they discipline the mind. Such an argument has often been heard in defense of requiring all high-school or college students to study a foreign language, mathematics, or some one science. This teacher is likely to make the subject he is teaching unduly difficult for his students, arguing that it is the study of the subject itself that has value, and that the harder the task, the more discipline the mind becomes in attempting to meet that task. Again, this teacher, in arguing for the disciplinary value of the study of the subject itself, will ignore interest and motivation, for interest makes the task easier to learn and hence less discipline will result. On the same basis, the introduction of modern methods of teaching will be ignored or resisted. As long as one thinks the value lies in the subject itself, methods of teaching it are irrelevant, for the desired results will be obtained by coming into contact with the subject matter of the course regardless of the method employed.

Should a teacher refuse to be guided in his thinking by the concept of formal discipline, he will immediately become interested in the direct values of the subject he is teaching. He will also be interested in its indirect values. For example, the Latin teacher will be primarily interested in teaching his students to read Latin; he will also look for the largest number of values that Latin may have in the other language experiences of his pupils, and he will teach his students how to apply Latin to these language situations. Such a teacher will no longer think of the mind of the child as made up of faculties of memory, reasoning, and the like, but will consider the child's mind a unit that organizes its varying experiences into patterns of behaviour that will enable the child better to meet the situations of his life; the good teacher will want to aid the pupils to organize the best patterns of behaviour. This teacher will become vitally interested in children. What is best for the varying needs of his students now has first place in his thought; the subjects being taught has secondary consideration. All subjects become means toward obtaining valuable ends; all subjects are tools that aid the students to secure certain recognizable values.

Such a position compels a teacher to be concerned with all that modern psychology has to offer on the learning processes that go on within pupils while they are acquiring the experiences of the classroom. Interest and motivation are all-important in helping the teacher to facilitate the learning of his students. Modern methods and procedures are extremely significant to this type of teacher, for he wants to know every procedure that will enable him to help the children obtain the greatest values from their experience and contacts with him.

This point of view does not mean that a teacher will not be interested in teaching his students to work hard. He will believe in hard work, but not just for its own sake. He will teach pupils to work hard in order to obtain the largest possible direct and indirect values of the experiences that are being given to them.

It has already been emphasized that the modern point of view in regard to transfer of training places a great deal of importance upon methods and procedures.

The first thing school people need to do is to decide what values they want to see realized in the lives of the students both in and out of school. What habits and methods of organizing experiences are most worth-while? What ideals, attitudes, appreciations, interests, and motives are of greatest significance? After these objectives have been derived, what knowledges and skills will be most effective in realizing them? The determination of the methods and techniques that will aid the most in realizing these ends becomes the all-important issue.

Classroom methods should be worked out in the light of the so-called Laws of Learning. In the elaborate experiments by Thorndike testing these laws, the most significant result was that repetition in and of itself is not significant. The Law of Effect, however, was proved to be highly important. It is the kind of repetition that counts. Practically, these results mean that the mere repetition of certain subject matter will not produce the momentous outcomes that have been claimed by the advocates of formal discipline. In order to attain the direct and the transfer values of the subject being taught, the teacher will have to set up in the classroom a situation that will motivate the learners. The teacher should seek to get the pupils to want the values that the procedure was set up to effect.

Too often teachers have worked on the principle that the fixing of habits is a desirable educational outcome. That is exactly what will happen under such a method of teaching. The students learn to repeat the materials in the particular situation of the classroom and are unable to apply them when opportunity is offered elsewhere. The situations of life are constantly changing, highly variable. This means that pliability, not rigidity of habits, and skills should be the end sought, and that classroom procedures should be organized accordingly.

For example, a high-school youngster asked his parent to let him repeat certain rules in algebra that had been assigned to be memorized. The child asked whether he had repeated the rule correctly. The parent replied that he had.

"Every word?" said the pupil.

"Not every word, but you stated all of the essential ideas."

"I have to say it with every word just as the book has it or the teacher will give me no credit."

This teacher did not seem to realize that an overemphasis on the exact wording of the book worked toward establishing within the child a rigidity of habit that interfered with his fully understanding the principle and able to apply it to variable situations where it would be needed.

Such a teacher needs to become aware that understanding the meaning of rules rather than remembering their exact language is the more important outcome of his teaching. This teacher should become acquainted with the work of Katona, in which some experimental evidence supports the idea that much more transfer value is possible when material is learned in an understanding manner.[33] Katona stresses very strongly, in the discussion of his experimental results, the value of learning with understanding for transfer effect.

This teacher would do well to read "Learning and Instruction," Forty-ninth Yearbook, Part I, especially the chapter on the general nature of learning, in which an excellent description of learning, emphasizing such matters as learning and maturation, learning and experience, and the direction and guidance of learning is presented.[34]

He would also do well to read the chapter on how children learn information, concepts, and generalizations, and also the chapter on how children learn the principles and techniques of problem-solving. In these pages one will find strongly emphasized the need and importance of the teachers' coming to have a clear understanding of what psychology has revealed about the learning process of children, and how necessary it is for him to direct the learning of his pupils so that the meaning of information will be acquired, broad concepts and generalizations will be developed, and the use of these experiences in solving problems in and out of classroom will be learned. If this teacher really understands these three chapters he cannot continue to believe that fixing exact details of knowledge in the student's memory will give such wonderful learning outcomes as have claimed by adherents of the theory of formal discipline.

McGeoch emphasizes the above-mentioned points in their relation to transfer of training:

> The learning of complex, abstract, meaningful materials and the solution of problems by means of ideas (reasoning) are to a great extent functions of transfer. Where the subject sees into the

33. G. Katona, *Organizing and Memorizing* (New York: Columbia University Press, 1940), Chap. 5 pp. 108-136.
34. G.L. Andreson and A.I. Gates, "The General Nature of Learning," Fortyninth Yearbook of the National Society for the Study of Education,Part I (Chicago: University of Chicago Press. 1950), pp. 12-35; also in the same volume, W.A.Brownell and G.Hendrickson, "How Children Learn Information, Concepts and Generalizations," pp. 92-128, and R.L.Throndike, "How Children Learn the Principals and Techniques of Problem Solving," pp. 192-216.

fundamental relations of a problem or has insight, transfer seems to be a major contributing condition.[35]

Undue emphasis upon rigid grammar in the study of language may hinder the student in meeting adequately the highly variable situations involved in reading a language. Better results would probably be obtained by using a method that taught the students to deal fluently with the changing meanings in reading, employing grammar in this situation or that to clarify the meanings in readings or the material being read. Several studies have shown that a knowledge of English grammar is more valuable in the study of a foreign language than it is in an understanding of English.[36] Something is radically wrong in a situation of this kind. Teachers have taught grammar by a method that produces a large transfer to foreign languages but only a relatively small degree of transfer to English. Such results suggest a much needed change in the procedures of teaching grammar.

The teacher of science should be mainly concerned with the use the students make of the materials covered in his course. If this is to be accomplished, something more than merely teaching the facts of science in a routine manner must be done. Strong claims have been made for the value of science in training students to think scientifically and in developing in them a scientific attitude towards the problems of life. There is no guarantee that such results will be obtained unless teachers of science devise methods that stimulate students to carry over the materials of the science course to a solution of a great variety of problems that arise in everyday life. The following incident illustrates the lack of transfer value of an intensive study of science. A friend visited a very eminent scientist one evening. Many problems of science were discussed. The friend's interests were so aroused, he was so intrigued by the profound insight and keenness of thought of the great scientist, that the

---

35. J.A. McGeoch, *The Psychology of Human Learning* (New York: Longmans, Green & Co., 1942), p. 446.
36. J.W. Shafer," Modern Language Student vs. English Grammar," *Modern Language Journal*, XIV. No. 2 (1929), 95-102; D. Starch, "Measurement of Efficiency in English Grammar," *Journal of Educational Psychology*, VI, No. 10 (1915), 615-626; and E.R. Coverley," English Grammar and Foreign Language Failure," *Education*, XLVI, No. 10 (1925), 612-616

conversation lasted until the wee hours of the morning. A few evenings later, the two were together again at a meeting in which a very difficult social problem of the community was being discussed. The great scientist left his science in his laboratory and his keen methods of thinking in his study. He attacked the social problem in an emotionally biased and prejudiced manner; he used a method of thinking that any ordinary, ignorant man of the street might employ, a procedure in which any educated man should be ashamed to indulge. The friend came away from the meeting disillusioned and saddened by the fact that the study of science had failed to exert a broadening educational influence upon his friend. Science is not to blame for such results, but rather the methods employed in teaching science.

Numbers and number relations have played a large part in the development of civilization, and they continue to be important in the life of today. Hordes of students who have studied arithmetic, algebra, and geometry have no understanding and appreciation of the role of numbers. They have been drilled on tables, combinations, and formulas, but have never been taught the significance and meaning of the materials upon which they were drilled. Teachers need to learn that application is part of drill. Drill can be motivated by using materials in a variety of situations while fundamental facts and principles are being learned. It is one thing to teach a student that $3 - 0 = 3$, or that $0 + 3 = 3$. It is another thing to get the student to understand that whenever zero is added to any number the result is not increased. It is still more difficult to get students to understand that in *any* aspect of life, when nothing is added nothing results; in other words, something cannot be got for nothing. Such a principle can be learned; therefore, it can be taught if the proper methods are employed.

The teacher should not be hesitant about teaching his subject so as to increase the transfer values, or fear that by so doing he will lessen the direct values of the materials. The two sets of values are intimately related. This relationship is forcefully stated by Mursell:

> When the ability is most intelligently taught and organized for its own sake, it is thereby taught and organized in such a way as will facilitate transfer; and its converse: When we deliberately

work for the transfer of some ability, we facilitate its acquisition in its own right.[37]

In the final analysis, transfer of training is an educational problem. The solution of the problem on an educational level rests in the hands of the classroom teacher. This task of the teacher is beautifully described in the following significant statement.

> Do we want transfer, and if so, what, in terms of ideals, attitudes, beliefs and habits, do we want transferred; and what provision should we make in method of learning and teaching, administration and the like, in order to bring about transfer in the form and amount we desire?... First, the teacher should know what it is that she wants the children to transfer to other fields, second, she must learn by experience or experiment how to teach for transfer, and third, to go ahead and do it.[38]

Summary

The theory of formal discipline has been described and its influence upon educational practices has been pointed out. Transfer of training has also been described, setting it in contrast to formal discipline. The validity of formal discipline as an adequate educational theory was first questioned by William James about 1890. Since then more than 300 experimental studies on the problem have been made. These studies experimented with the transfer of learning of a great variety of materials, including those of sensorimotor materials (e.g., mazes); perceptional materials (e.g., estimating areas); memory materials (e.g., poetry and prose); reasoning materials (e.g., arithmetical reasoning problems); ideals (e.g., neatness and accuracy); and school subjects (e.g., grammar, Latin, and geometry). The results of these studies have proven that positive transfer, absence of transfer, and negative transfer do take place. The positive transfer results may seem to support the theory of formal discipline, but the fact that the degree of transfer varied from a very slight amount to 92.4 offers little proof. Add to this fact the absence of transfer and negative transfer, and it can be said that the experimental results have given little or no support to the theory

---

37. J.L. Mursell, *Psychology of Secondary School Teaching* (rev. ed.; New York: W.W. Norton & Company, Inc., 1939), p. 104.
38. Orata, *op. cit.*, pp. 278, 281.

of formal discipline. Other experiments have dealt with improving conditions for effecting transfer. It has been shown that giving instructions in the learning of materials and explaining principles and their use affect the amount of transfer. The student's attitude toward transfer and the degree of his mastery of material also affect the amount of transfer.

Several answers have been offered to the question: How does transfer take place? Thorndike gave his Theory of Identical Elements, maintaining that one mental function alters any other only insofar as the two functions have identical elements as factors. Judd expounded the Theory of Generalization. He maintained that transfer takes place to the extent that a student generalizes his experiences. Neither of these theories offers an adequate description or the cause of transfer.

The teacher should realize that the problem facing him is one of practical or educational significance, rather than one that is scientific or theoretical in nature. For him the problem is one of teaching students how to make as large an application of learning experiences gained in one situation to other situations as may be practicable. The teacher must decide what values, ideals, attitudes, knowledge, and skills students are to get in their educational experiences. He must understand how students learn these things most significantly and how they transfer their learnings, and, furthermore, he must consciously teach students how to transfer their learning to a large variety of situations.

—L.W. Webb

Questions and Exercises (for Discussion and Study)

1. Of what value to teachers is a knowledge of the scientific attack on the problem of transfer of learning?
2. Why do schools continue to teach so much formal grammar when its supposed beneficial effects are not substantiated by experimental results?
3. In this chapter a distinction is made between formal discipline and transfer of learning. Do you think such a distinction is justified? Give reasons for your answer to this question.

4. Enumerate the direct and the transfer values of the subject you teach.
5. List the things you could do to increase the transfer values of the subject you teach.
6. What subjects in the high-school curriculam have sufficient direct functional value to all students to be required for graduation?
7. Assuming that you will give up formal discipline as a basis of your philosophy of education, make a statement of the principles that you will put in its place.
8. A high-school teacher of geometry asked his pupils to read the preamble to the constitution of the United States to discover the basic assumptions therein. Was this a good assignment in the teaching of geometry? Justify your answer.
9. Give a critical evaluation of the following statements:
   (a) If all the students in a certain secondary school who had studied geometry were found to be superior in reasoning to those who had not, this would be sufficient evidence to prove that training in geometry was responsible for greater ability in general.

   (b) The amount of improvement in the capacity in which the student is trained is probably never accompanied by an equal amount of improvement in his other capacities.

   (c) We may conclude on the basis of experiments in transfer of training that all training is entirely specialized.

   (d) The study of formal grammar can be justified by the improvement that it produces in reasoning.

   (e) The transfer effect from any mental function to any other mental function, or from one school subject to any other subject, may be substantially modified by conscious effort in that direction.

(f) Students who plan to study French should always have a year or more of Latin as a foundation.

References

Andrews, T.G.,L.J. Cronbach, and P. Sandiford, "Transfer of Training," in W.S. Monroe (ed.), *Encyclopaedia of Educational Research*. New York: The Macmillan Company,1950, pp. 1483-1489.

Barlow, M.C., "Transfer of Training in Reasoning," *Journal of Educational Psychology*, XXVIII (1937), 122-128.

Brownell, W.A.,"Theoretical Aspects of Learning and Transfer of Training," *Review of Educational Research*, VI (1936), 281-290, 337-339.

———, and E.E. Mosher, "Meaningful versus Mechanical Learning: A Study in Grade III Subtraction" Duke University Research Studies in Education, No. 8, 1949.

Bruce R.W., "Conditions of Transfer of Training", *Journal of Experimental Psychology*, XVI (1933), 343-361.

Dorsey, M., and L.T. Hopkins, "The Influence of Attitude Upon Transfer, *Journal of Educational Psychology*, XXI (1930), 410-417.

Gagne, R.M., H. Foster and M. Crowley, "The Measurement of Transfer of Training," *Psychological Bulletin*, XLV (1948), 97-130.

Judd, C.H., *et al.*, *Education as the Cultivation of the Higher Mental Processes*. New York: The Macmillan Company, 1936.

Kingsley, H.L., and R. Garry, *The Nature and Conditions of Learning*, 2nd ed. Englewood Cliffs, N.J.: Prentice-Hall, Inc., 1957, Chap. 17.

McGeoch, J.A., and A.L. Irion, *The Psychology of Human Learning*, 2nd ed. New York: Longmans, Green & Co., Inc., 1952, Chap. 9.

Orata, P.T., *Theory of Identical Elements*. Columbus: Ohio State University Press, 1928.

Swenson., E.,G.L. Anderson, and C.L. Stacey, "Learning Theory in School Situations," University of Minnesota Studies in Education. Minneapolis University of Minnesota Press, 1949, p. 103.

Thorndike, E.L., "Mental Discipline in High School Studies," *Journal of Education Psychology*, XV (1924), 1-22, 83-98.

Ulmer, G., Some Suggestions for Teaching Geometry to Develop Clear Thinking," Kansas University Studies in Education. Lawrence, Kan.: University of Kansas, 1942, Vol. 2, No 7, p. 22.

12

Learning Motor Skills and Knowledge

Perceptual-motor Development

Motor development begins in utero at a time when the surface stimuli elicit movements of distant muscles. Previous to this time, stimuli have to be applied directly to the muscle tissue to obtain movement. With the beginning of nerve tissue development, there is "transferred" stimulus – hence, movement in other portions of the organism. From this period on, there are movement responses to stimuli, and growing integration of stimuli situations with satisfactory functioning.

Bodily control begins at the head end of the human infant: The baby learns to hold the head erect, to fixate with the eyes, to reach toward a regarded object, and to grasp it with greater and greater precision. By the time he has gained the ability to reach and grasp, he has probably also developed a crawling method. Posture develops posteriorly until he can sit erect. Posture continues as a part of the developing pattern in crawling, and then in walking. These early elementary motor developments (crawling, prehension, and walking) of infants seem to progress in a similar way regardless of special practice, or of parental encouragement and coaching.

Motor development during the first fifteen months: The sequence of elementary motor development, for the first fifteen months of the normal infant's life, seems to be very much the same from infant to infant. Normal development includes sitting alone, crawling, prehension, and walking. The rate of achievement of these respective developments varies from infant to infant. These variations, unless in an extreme degree, have little significance for prognosis of future traits or abilities.

Eating and drinking skills: The skills involved in the use of untensils for eating and drinking are not easily acquired by the child. It takes the average child about fifteen months to acquire the ability to pick up a cup of liquid and place it to his mouth. The completed skill of drinking from the cup without spilling takes much longer. Eating habits are gradually acquired. They are acquired more rapidly if the child is permitted much practice without forcing, and without much censure for spilling things or "making a mess."

A stimulating environment; guidance: As rapidly as possible, the infant should be exposed to challenging environment that stimulates him to use his developing powers in a variety of ways. What the child needs is equipment, space, opportunities, and help.[1] Blocks and marbles, scooters, roller skates, toy wagons, and the like are often used. Situations that encourage climbing, jumping, running, and swimming foster his development. Skills are frequently facilitated by guidance in new techniques. Interested children prefer to be helped toward successful techniques. Success leads to interest and more opportunities for later practice. Interest, itself, is partly dependent on adequate skill for satisfactory accomplishment. Lack of skill means backwardness, reluctance to participate, and being "left out" (fewer group invitations to participate), hence less chance to "catch up." Moreover, early advantage in learning may mean permanent superiority.

Skill instruction for the preschool child: Experiment with preschool music training (vocal) has indicated that the preschool child is ready to profit from such training. Very early training seems to expand the child's range, develop favourable attitudes and interest that increase later practice, and prevent the acquisition of habits that interfere with later development. The

1. T.D. Jones, "The Development of Certain Motor Skills and Play Activities in Young Children" (Child Development Monographs, No. 26 [New York: Teachers College, Bureau of Publications, Columbia University, 1939]).

superiority of the trained preschool children over the untrained persists in later school years.[2]

The possibilities of development under conditions of suitable environment and parental encouragement are revealed in the early moter-skill development of many primitives peoples. Mead comments that all children among the Manus of New Guiena are expected to swim at three years of age and climb about like young monkeys even before that age.[3] Children of three punt the large canoes. Mead says:

> There is not a child of five who can't swim well. A Manus child who couldn't swim would be as aberrant, as definitely subnormal as an American child of five who couldn't walk.[4]

We seem to have erred in the direction of offering too few opportunities and experiences to the developing child. Children in their second and thirty year of nursery and kindergarten experience have been reported to be unchallenged and bored by the apparatus and equipment.[5] They tend to lose their enthusiasm for attending; or they attempt to add their own "special features" to the activities in attempts to increase the challenge. The apparatus and skill of the average kindergarten are reported to be geared to the developmental level of the three-year-old.[6]

Skills advance in hierarchies: Just as the child in the crawling stage of development builds his climbing of an incline on the crawling pattern, and as the child of the walking stage builds his climbing on the walking pattern, so the more mature child of adolescent builds his new movement patterns on the basic acquirements and skills that have been previously developed. The learner puts together bits of former movement patterns into new adjustments, much as he puts together bits of

---

2R. Updegraff, L. Heiliger, and J. Learned, "Part III: The Effect of Training on Singing Ablity and Musical Interest of Three-, Four- and Five-Year-Old Children," *Studies in Preschool Education* (University of Iowa Studies in Child Welfare, New Series), I, No. 346 (1938), 14: 83-131.

3. M. Mead, *Growing Up in New Guinea* (New York: Mentor Book, The New American Library of World Literature, Inc.) p. 26.
4. *Ibid.*, p. 27.
5. M.V. Gutteridge, "A Study of Motor Achievements of Young Children," *Archives of Psychology*, No. 244 (1939).
6. *Ibid* .

former experience in imaginative thinking. As in imagination, his new pattern must be taken from what he has previously experienced, and is limited in the new situation by the fitness of the previously experienced part.

Skill learning is chiefly the integrating of simpler movements into a new pattern for some purpose: Coordinating the hand and foot movements with visual perception in driving an automobile is an example of reorganizing known movements and percepts into a new pattern. Learning to do a folk dance, to execute military drills, to go through a stylus maze without error, and to trace a star outline while looking in a mirror are other examples of putting together into new patterns bits of perceptual-motor behaviour already learned. The problem is chiefly one of selecting and integrating simpler, previously learned movements rather than one of learning new movements. Strengths, speeds, precisions, and endurances continue to develop throughout childhood and early adolescence. But these are largely incidental acquirements accompanying the coordination of movements in skill patterns to fit the child's ideas and purposes. The greater the variety of specific movements and skill patterns the child goes through in his early maturing and developing period, the more likely he is to possess the motor movement equipment to meet the numerous demands of adult life.

Both school and life require much motor-skill learning: Modern civilization demands speed and precision of movement. Awkwardness is dangerous in many of our industries, in driving through traffic, and even in our rugged sport. Grace and poise are prized socially, and the lack of them is an embarrassment. Grace implies a body so sensitized to movement impulses as to bring about unconscious, perfectly coordinated nicety of control. Social prestige and popularity seem to be somewhat related to one's relative rank in strength and skill acquirements, particulary during the developing years. The child's social maturity seems to be realated, to a degree, to his motor development.

A major portion of school time and adult life is occupied by motor activity. School includes writing and drawing; typewriting and shorthand; laboratory work and industrial work; domestic science and manual training; plus sports, games, and physical education. The boy pounds nails, saws boards, digs earthworms, and goes fishing; or plays marbles, ping-pong, and quoits. He carves boats, builds airplanes, collects bugs, and plays ball. The man hunts, fishes, and tries to lower his score in golf or beat his neighbour at tennis and billiards. He raises roses or vegetables, mows his lawn, or does his own car and house repairing. He begins each day with all the motor activities of rising, dressing, eating, and driving his car to work. Even the office worker has typewriting, accounting, or chart and blueprint drawing as possible activities. The physician has surgery; the chemist, weighing and measuring. Machinists, carpenters, tradesmen of all kinds, and labourers in all the industries rely on motor skills.

The little girl plays house, dresses dolls, sews on doll dresses, plays jacks, glides about on roller skates, begins to dance, plays tennis and golf, practices on the piano, or goes horseback riding. The woman cooks, sews, bakes, sketches a landscape, hikes unbelievable distances while shopping, plays her favourite sport, or raises her favourite flowers.

Skill improvement depends on intent: Improvement in skill means performing the skill faster or more precisely, or both. But it also may mean performing more gracefully and in an appealing tempo, as in the dance, in figure skating, or in the free exercises of gymnastics. Improvement in a skill depends *on practice with intent to improve.* Without the intent to improve, practice establishes a lower level or, what is more frequent, permits gradual retrogression in level of performance. In general, motivation and purpose, and method and equipment, establish the level of the skill finally attained. The levels are rarely established by any physiological limit of the individual.

Cursive handwriting of the average adult serves his purpose without rating high in legibility or beauty of flowing lines. Skill practice for entertainment and recreation does not imply improvement. Many vocational skills, communication skills, and recreation skills remain at a low level because they serve the individual's purpose at that level. Many of us type at a habitually slow pace or speak with careless syntax and slurred syllabus.

Adequate spacing of practice periods: has valuable results. Spacing tends to keep the learner free of pressure and worry.

Moreover, motor skills seem to grow together to some degree during periods of no practice. The periods between practice seem to etch more clearly the major phases of the skill and dim the non-essentials. Mental rehearsal may bring to the attention points to stress in the next practice. However, the teacher, with his ability to analyze, is more likely to detect the parts needing greater emphasis. The frequency and length of practices for most rapid learning vary with the stage of learning, the complexity of the skill, and the strenuousness of the activity. In general, short daily practices are the most practical for the beginner. Twice-a-day practices of less strenuous skills may be adavantageous. The maintainance of a great refinement in complex skills seems to require long and frequent practice.

High levels of a skill: Skill levels become much higher if the motivation is intense and the rewards are high. Practices at the advanced stages of skill are usually longer. The analysis of performance may be quite detailed. Much time will be spent on polish of parts. The learner acquires the ability to concentrate well, to be quite resistant to distraction. The span between cue perception and motor performance becomes longer; for example, the reader's eyes are considerably ahead of his voice in oral reading. Likewise the typist or the pianist reads far ahead of the responses of his fingers. More and more, the attention is focused on cues and results with less and less attention on the performance habits.

Retention of skill: High levels of skill performance such as piano playing, conversing in a foreign language, or even putting in golf seem to drop down rapidly during longer intervals without practice. Regular practice, and a pre-performance review of the skill, seem to be necessary to maintain the high level of performance.

Skill lessons for the beginner: The beginner needs the mental image (or idea) of the act but not a detailed analysis of movements. Much of the selection and combination of movements into a pattern to serve the learner's purpose is done without consciousness of the precise selection made. As quickly as the beginner can get the general idea of the act, he should begin his practice trials and revisions. These first individual movements he makes are only partially identified, if at all. They are continually adjusted and changed, anyway, as learning progresses. Only the gross errors need correction at this stage; minor errors are unimportant. Many minor adaptations will be made below the awareness level of consciousness.

Various procedures are used to give the beginner the idea of the skill: for example, demonstrations, directed observation of the skill performers, rapid or slow-motion movies of performances of the skill, diagrams, drawings, still pictures, or sketches. As soon as he seems to have the idea, he should be subjected to lots of active practice. There will be some additional learning by the highly motivated student because of his mental rehearsal between active practices. However, there is no substitute for the physical trials.

The teacher should avoid detailed verbal explanations in the early stages. Word explanations have very little meaning for the beginning learner of a motor skill. Some teachers try to move the child through the pattern—by guiding his hand in writing, for example. Such guidance seems to be helpful only when the learner actively tries to help himself to follow the movement desired. Usually the learner profits more by trying the form-pattern himself, seeing his gross errors, and correcting them as best as he can, thereby clarifying his idea of the pattern to a greater extent.

Form: The attainment of a high level of skill necessitates the adoption of a form that employs sound mechanics and which is adapted to the structural and functional characteristics of the individual. Form is the "way to do it," the design of performance, the work method. For the individual, it answers his major question after he has a purpose, namely, how to achieve the purpose most effectively. The individual often adopts a form by imitation. However, there is a diversity of forms among the experts to whom one might look for a model, particulary in the details of the work method.

The teacher may very well guide the student into some form that has proved highly successful for others in the past. For example, the handwriting teacher prescribes the student's posture at his desk, his method of holding a pencil, the angle of the paper; and helps maintain, by the direction, a balance between the student's arm and finger movements. The teacher of typewriting tries to fix the student's body posture, arm, wrist, and the finger positions, and keyboard fingers habits.

If the learner, through much undirected practice, has already adopted a manner of performing but is handicapped by inefficient habits of form and technique, it may be necessary to start him over again at almost a beginner's level. Although there will be some interference from his inefficient habits, he almost always acquires the more efficient form more quickly than a complete beginner.

Certain characteristics of skill: deserve special mention. First, skill is specific to the activity, not a general motor ability. Second, a skill is somewhat general in form of expression, that is, it is never repeated precisely the same way in all details of the movement pattern. Moreover, the well-developed skill is adjustable to changing environment conditions. Third, the complex skill, even when developed to a high level, fluctuates in efficiency from performance to performance. Variability of performance in the complex skill never disappears. Fourth, the form used in a skill is, to a considerable degree, an individual matter. Differences in body levers, muscle tonus, strengths, speeds, and learning environment vary the form adopted by different individuals performing the same skill. Even experts with similar form will vary in the minutiae of the movements involved.

Although bright students may profit more by verbal directions and may seem to learn motor skills faster, the difference is probably due to the method rather than the *slight* relationship between academic intelligence and motor skill. Strength and physical or social maturity may affect the rate of learning. Before puberty, sex seems to make little difference in ability to learn motor skills. Different physical development, differences in rates of growth, and a somewhat different social milieu may cause differences after puberty both between the sexes and within the same sex.

Perceptual Learning

First cues to percepts: At birth, the infant is unable to focus his eyes or perceive objects in his environment. His hearing is dulled by mucus. Tactual stimuli affect him, but his response is "random" activity, a few reflexes, and some withdrawal movements. He gradually begins to focus his eyes, to hear sounds, and to become conditioned to certain adapted responses. The sight of the mother and the sound of her voice become to the child a part of the situation in which certain organic stresses, such as hunger and physical discomfort, are relieved. Feelings of satisfaction ensue. Gradually, pleasurable reactions are conditioned to be direct responses to the sight of the mother or the sound of her voice. This learning to respond to the mother as a result of previous experience is perception. His mother, a part of his total environment, has been organized into a stimulus pattern for a set of responses. She has become a cue to preparatory reactions to feeding, or to other activity productive of feelings of satisfaction. "Cue" is used in the sense of a stimulus pattern that guides activity to the recall or reproduction of part or all of a former experience. The organic urges become the infant's earlier learned cues.

Organizing the sensory field, abbreviated cues: Perception involves fusion of various stimuli. The infant's environment at any one time presents to him a mosaic or complexity of stimuli. Usually, the child is simultaneously receiving stimuli from the auditory, visual, cutaneous, and proprioceptive nerve endings; and like as not, the gustatory and olfactory senses are adding their receptions. The child learns to respond to patterns of stimuli; and later to a bit of that total pattern as if the whole were present. The re-experienced parts call forth responses that were originally elicited by the larger stimulus pattern. The principle is not one of substituting one situation for another as a stimulus, but one of substituting some bit or element of the original total stimulus for the whole.[7]

Growth of the perception of the male parent and the verbal symbol for him illustrates this early learning. A large moving object with a rough voice stimulates the infant's sense organs. The large moving object tickles his ribs, gives him peculiar sensations by lifting him high in the air or tossing him about,

7. In terms of Gestalt psychology, a perception is a recognition of relationships between figure and ground. Such a recognition from reduced cues is termed *closure*, a subjective completion of the whole.

turns him over a shoulder, and adds sensations of motion to pats on the back when he becomes vociferous with colic. An occasional jab from whiskers mixes into the stimulus pattern.The mother is absent and the same large stimulus pattern furnishes him with a bottle and a change of clothing. Pleasurable reactions become attached to the growing stimulus pattern—this adult. The baby kicks and squirms and makes various sounds with his vocal organs. He utters, "da." The exercise is enjoyable, it gives him an auditory stimulus, and he says, "da," again. The object with the deep voice comes into his field of vision and repeats the "da-da." The infant's efferent speech pattern is not yet quiescent; the stimuli tend to discharge in the direction of the lowered potential of the body-part that has just been active. The auditory stimulus of his own sound of "da" is followed by repeated "da-da" sounds from the deep voice. The infant says, "da-da" again as an outlet for energy aroused by the complex of stimuli. He is rewarded by being picked up, patted, and, in general,"fussed over." The "da-da" has a good start as a conditioned stimulus cue to be attached to this large moving object, deep voice, and the feeling-of-satisfaction responses. After other rewardings of a similar nature, "da-da" or a modification, becomes a conditioned symbol for experience with this adult.

Growth in definiteness of percepts: Others males with deep voices enter the senseory field of the infant. He utters, "da-da," but the results differ. Many repetitions of presentations of satisfying treatment by this one male, and negative results with others, cause an individuation in the particular stimulus pattern. The particular pitch of the voice, the bald head, the mustache, or other sensory cues limit the stimulus pattern that produces the symbol "da-da" to the stimulus object that gives the child the pleasurable reactions and relieves his stress. By some such process, "dad" may become significant to the youngster.

Conditioning to a nurse, brother, or sister would follow the same principles. The example of conditioning to the male parent illustrates the principles of perceptual learning, but is by no means a typical example. Fear frequently enters the situation of conditioning to the male. Many infants have little opportunity to develop perception of the male until a later stage. Perception, however, develops from just such simple beginnings as these.

The infant learns to recognize his bottle, and to say, "bottle" or, "hot" in connection with it. He watches lights and moving objects. He chews his rubber ring and shakes his rattle. He learns to respond in specific ways, either overtly or implicitly, to things in his environment. Annoyances cause him to turn away or withdraw until stimuli are outside his sensory field. Statisfactions keep him in the presence of the stimuli, and result, therefore, in frequent persistence of stimuli.

The infant seems to begin perception by organizing his sensory field into a somewhat vague and indefinite figures. First, he seems to distinguish people from objects; and then familiar people from strangers. His early perceptions of the world around him grow chiefly from his handling and manipulating, exploring, crawling over or climbing over, and the like. He bites, pounds, or throws the object. The object with which he is fed is bright and shiny. He pounds with it, throws it on the floor, and is fascinated by its shine; so the perception of "spoon" grows. He finds a wooly moving object that emits yelps and barks. It runs away and comes back. It paws him and chews his shoe. Thus, the perception of "dog" develops. Objects of his environment give off light, make sounds or movements, are useful to him in his activities, and become attached to his response patterns. His environment is becoming differentiated into perceived objects.

Verbal cues associated with perceptions: The perceived objects are becoming associated with a verbal sound that he can recognize when heard, and which he gradually learns to make himself. By such early conditioning, the perceptions become identified by words. It is important that, as the child develops, he be taught to pronounce word-names associated with perceptions with distinctness and correctness of articulation. This perception of precise pronunciation prevents later confusion of words as he attaches the verbal symbol to the printed symbol. Moreover, clear enunciation prevents many later difficulties in spelling.

Attention precedes perception: The child perceives only what he "pays attention to." He is most likely to observe large things, noisy things, lights, moving objects, bright colours, or things that cause him discomfort. He observes those things in which he is interested. His needs, his motives, and the social situation will all affect his observations.

Abbreviated cues and mental constructs: As was mentioned earlier, the cues essential for recognition decrease with experience. Prompt recognition requires more experience, or more cues. The older child recognizes daddy's shape in the distance, but the younger child needs the closer approach, and the filling in of a few more details of the image, to complete the recognition.

That a stimulus may be a cue or a set of cues instead of the whole stimulus pattern is a basic principle of habit perception. The perception has stabilized with experience and occurs as the slighter cue arouses the mental construct. The rest of the figure, not revealed by sense stimuli at the particular moment, is "seen" but the "filling in" results from the interaction of the stimulus cue with the individual's memory traces.

Teaching precise observation: When the child starts kindergarten at the age of three, he may be able to enumerate things but his observation of detail is still too meager to permit him to describe things. The key to more rapid development of perception during the preschool age is richness and variety of material for active exploration. The kindergarten experience is very valuable because it does enrich perceptual practice.

The school can help perceptual knowledge by directing the child's attention, by arousing interest in observation, by telling him what to look for, by asking questions that require better observation in order to answer, and the like. Camping and outdoor education are experiences rich in observational training. The regular grade-school work can be helped by fields trips, simple science lessons, and construction projects. Discussion of his observations will help clarify his perceptions.

The child can learn to be on his guard against subjective bias in perception by having such instances pointed out to him; for example, the thin person is likely to look taller than he actually is. The short person can be made to look taller by high heels, a high hat, or dress lines. Speeds of large objects, in comparison with smaller, are underestimated. The teacher should look for likely misinterpretations in the material that the pupil is to observe, and give him examples of them. The demonstration of illusions in the particular field of observation tends to make the student more cautious and critical in his observations. The advantages of the demonstration method of teaching beginning science, as contrasted with the laboratory method, are partly due to the directed observation.

Errors in perception: There are, of course, many inaccuracies in observation. The child's desires and fears, his past experiences and expectations, have a great influence on his misinterpretation of stimuli. Noises in the dark are attributed to bears, Indians, or burgals; a friendly dog's pursuit is interpreted as a ferocious attack; the cottage cheese is seen as ice cream until taste corrects the illusion. Early confusions occur in words of similar form. The letters "b," "d," and "p" are confused by the beginner.

Although misinterpretation is much less frequent in adults, mental sets, interests, or expectancies will alter their perceptions as well. Perceptual maturity makes the normal adult less likely to perceive objects at great variance with reality unless the cues are insufficient or the mental stress is great. Slight auditory cues heard at night, situations of excitement such as a traffic accident or a robbery, or even the behaviour of young couples as viewed by elderly critics are examples of stimulus patterns frequently misinterpreted.

Perception difficulties may be due to sense defects: The large number of pupils suffering from eye and ear defects makes an examination of every school child's eyes and ears imperative. Lack of progress is never safely diagnosed unless such examinations are made. If money is not available for examination by specialists, the school nurse or teacher may secure the eye chart and conduct the examination herself. An ordinary watch may be used to check hearing.

But there is much lack of progress without sensory defect as a cause. Errors are not uncommon due to the fact that the teacher is trying to cover too much content in the time allotted. Errors often result from too rapid observation, or from attempting to observe situation too complex for the individual's present stage of development.

Complex perceptual habits: Man has invented an immense number of memory aids and symbolic methods of communication in the form of words, music scores, formulas, telegraphy codes, semaphore signals, architectural designs, and the like. The child is confronted with the task of rendering many of these symbols so familiar as to guarantee prompt recognition. One of the child's first problems on entering school is the recognition of printed words, and the attaching of them to the appropriate oral symbols and to the objects they represent. He must reduce this perception of the printed symbols to the promptness of habit, or else the delay in recognition will interfere with his association of these individual perceptions into sentence meanings. Phrase perception instead of word perception is a somewhat larger unit in the hierarchy of perceptual habit. The larger unit of perception makes it possible to carry the span of attention over a greater area and, by checking each word interpretation with more cues from the remaining context, to improve comprehension.

The teacher should remember that rapid perception, to function efficiently, must be developed into a habit reaction. Moreover, experience with the pattern to be established must be repeated many times, in diverse total situations, so that the cues will be recognized in still other novel environments. The repetition establishes the habit reaction of perceptual interpretation in the light of associated cues, for example, other words in the sentence.

Hierarchies of organization in perceptual learning are attained only by continued purposeful practice. Passive exercise of already acquired percepts, and satisfaction with the present level of slower recognition and response, are not conducive to higher levels of perceptual organization.

The child may begin his music reading with individual note recognition; or he may begin with a five-note melody. He learns to recognize the note position and the time. When he starts on the piano, he learns at the beginning to find the keys and follow two notes with each hand while he is recognizing the notes. To become even a mediocre pianist, he must increase this perceptual span to five or six notes at a glance, in the meantime adjusting his total pattern of tempo to allegro, andante, or whatever. If one adds to this the need for tactual-auditory discrimination, ranging from fortissimo to pianissimo, one begins to realize the complexity of perceptual learning involved in the field of music.

Maintenance of high levels of perceptual skill: Even after high levels of perceptual skill are acquired, periodic practice is necessary for their maintenance. Moreover, each perceptual skill seems to be specific. Practice to maintain a high level of perceptual skill in one area does not seem to improve one in another skill nor even help maintain the achieved level of perception in that other skill.

Difficult percepts requiring long experience and maturity include the relative rate of movement of passing or approaching objects, approximations of time span, estimation of distance, size of distant objects, and form. Distance perception has been a slowly developing process that began at a low, vague level with early infant mobility. Its approximation depends upon the apparent size of objects as contrasted with their known size, the distinctness of the image, and so forth.

In so much as the size of the image on the retina varies with distance, size must first be observed by exploration and movement near, around, or over. Then the individual is ready to practice perception from changed positions and distances. At first the youngster sees distant objects as being small. He soon learns to see them as normal but farther away. Less vivid and etched sensing of figures and convergence of the parallel lines come to mean greater distance to him. The cue to direction of sound is the difference of loudness to the two ears; and also, at times, previous experience as to where the sound is likely to be.

Motion is perceived as change of position of the object with regard to the background against which we see it. Better judgement of speed seems to be possible when one permits the moving object to cross the visual field (with the eyes still) instead of trying to follow the object with the eyes.

Directional orientation as regards the compass points is one of the early and very important perceptions to be acquired from geography, outdoor education, or wherever it seems meaningful. Early lessons in drawing seem to help in space orientation and perception.

Perception of form is developed from visual, tactual, and kinesthetic sensations. In a person's attempt to stabilize the perception, he runs his hand over the object or sketches it in outline. He moves his eye focus around its boundaries. He sees the form bounded by different backgrounds. The shape gradually takes on a subjective definiteness, which is superimposed on later cues and thereby produces the completed habit perception. If this form perception problem is combined with distance, size, and motion perception in an unusual atmospheric condition, the individual's subjective interpretation is likely to vary to a considerable degree from the actual objective situation. Dimness of outline has become a part of the cue for distance. Vary clear air or very hazy atmospheric conditions upset this perception in reverse directions. If the reader wishes to experience this perceptual difficulty, let him stand on the wharf some foggy morning, watch the incoming and outgoing ships, and try to identify their size, lines, and specific nature; or let him try to estimate distances on his first arrival in some our western states with their remarkably clear air.

Complex percepts in flying: Early experiences in learning to fly present examples of adult percept formation. Shape perception seems little affected by aerial distance. If the object is recognizable, it is perceived as normal in shape. Past experience keeps the "seen" shape the same as it has been known to be. Size perception of ground objects has to be re-learned before objects can be perceived as normal but distant. Some things present quite different visual patterns when viewed from a plane. A cornfield that looks green from the ground appears from the air as a gray area dotted with green spots. New cues become necessary for recognition. One learns to utilize new cues for example, in distinguishing between flat and rolling terrain. Curves in plow furrows or in hay windrows may be causes to uneven terrain. Roads and fences seen at an angle will show curves that indicate hilly country.

The speed of object below on the earth is very difficult to estimate. A football game seen from the vertical position in the air appears as a slow motion picture of a midget game. A shorter "seen" distance and the same actual time give illusion of slow motion.

The adult understands the reason for this illusion because of his concept of size as affected by distance vision, and time as not being so affected. He has meanings that go beyond his percepts, to concepts and reason. Let us look at the difference between percepts and concepts.

Percepts as related to concepts: There is no fine line of demarcation between higher forms of perception and conceptualization. Perception is usually considered to be recognition of a stimulus or pattern of stimuli. Conceptualization is usually thought of an aura of meaning unified by and emanating from some symbol. Its development has involved abstraction and generalization as to the significant aspects of much previous experience. However, the perception begins to take on the nature of a concept as soon as repeated experiences establish the perception as a mental construct elicited by very abbreviated cues. The "filling in" of the perception is a result of common and significant features experienced many times before. The very nature of the verbal symbol representing an object implies not only repeated experience but experience from which common traits have been abstracted.

Let us go back again and follow the infant's development of meanings to see how the individual matures, from the early organization of sensory stimuli into percepts to the later stages of symbolic thinking.

Growth of Meaning Concepts

Beginnings of ideational learning: The human infant, even before he begins to talk, may look for a toy with which he played at some previous time. Mother knows that infants cry for things that they cannot name. The mother brings one thing and another, only to have them refused or shoved away, until the right object is hit upon. The child feels an implicit want but has no words to express it. Higher animals and children apparently acquire memory traced without the help of language. This is the beginning of ideation. It is not meant to imply that these memory traces are, necessarily, consciously anticipated activities. That they are total pattern responses to some cue lying within the organism itself, or to a combination of cues internal and external to the organism, does not necessarily imply that they constitute awareness activity. The infant did, however, modify the mother's behaviour in the foregoing illustration over a period of time. Some definite and persisting inner want functioned in changing external environment.

The behaviour situation of the human organism at any time is made up of both the external and the internal environmental stimuli and responses. Just as parts of the external situation, such as the sight of the mother's face or the sound of the father's voice, become substitute stimulus cues for behaviour originally initiated by the larger pattern, so internal elements of the original total stituation become substitute stimuli. These substitute stimuli may include mental images. The prevalency of mental imagery in children and primitive people indicates that imagery originates early in the development stage.

Children's symbolism: In addition to learning to communicate with others by movements and gestures, the child soon learns the use of sounds. One child, for example, called his mother and asked for things, refused things, and expressed satisfaction or anger entirely through the pitch and intonation of one "baby word" and his postural attitude. The word he used to express all these meanings sounded like "Goo."

Oral sounds associated with situations—"da-da," "bottle," and "hot"—serve as abbreviated stimuli for responses to the total situation of which they were originally a part. These oral sounds, alone, after association with a situation is established, have meaning through the associated mental images, or through the tendencies toward action that they provoke.

However, when the child learns to repeat words by pure imitation, he may use actual words without their having any meaning to him except as they serve for verbal play. The words that the child does learn have, at first, very vague meanings. The early meanings of a word is, after all, an individual matter both in nature and degree: it connotes what it represented in the *past experiences* of the person using it.

A six year-old boy explained "bad" as meaning not holding the pencil and paper "right" or sitting "right." He said that it was "bad to spill things" and "bad to fight," but not "bad" when he fought "just a little." When presented with an old shoe and asked if it was bad, he replied, "Pretty bad." When asked if his foot could be bad, he chukled and replied, "Could smell bad." He was "sure" that he knew what a dog was, but could not define it. A twelve-year-old described a dog as an animal that had four legs and barked, and hunted animals, but not other dogs "expect for fun." He said that it differed from other animals; also, that it differed from other dogs but in "different ways." When asked if it hunted animals "for fun," he replied that it might play with them before it killed them. When asked if it would eat other dogs, he said, "Not unless it is necessary." He offered "evil" and "criminal" for synonyms for the word "bad."

The egocentric nature of the child's thinking can be noted in the word interpretations of the above-mentioned six-year-old boy. Personal experiencing of social disapproval has conditioned most of his responses to the symbolic cue "bad." This six-year-old boy has progressed beyond mere use of nouns. He is able to use verbs as symbols to express action but, even more, he is beginning to analyze qualities or characteristics of things. He is now using adjectives and, to some extent, adverbs. The characterization of the old shoe as being "pretty bad" and the foot as "smelling bad" illustrate an extension of the meaning into new dimensions beyond the basic meaning.

The twelve-year-old boy shows the advantage to word interpretation of experiencing the symbol "dog" in a great variety of situations. His interpretation of bad as meaning "evil" or "criminal" reveals the more mature development of the concept in its basic meaning.

Differentiation into percepts and concepts: First impressions of an object seem to be of its general form, outline, or framework. The earlier perceptions are of gross similarities, which seem to transfer response patterns. Examples are numerous. Automobiles are just "cars" to many people, indistinguishable as to make, model, or type. To most people, a sheep is just a type of animal. More experience begins to reveal individuality in the specific individuals of the type; and begins to synthesize recurring general traits and aspects. A pet lamb or the old ram who dominates the flock begins to be known as an individual. The sheep as a type begins to be known for its wool production and for its edible flesh. The dog, another animal, is a different type of animal. With successive experiencing, responses suitable for the common elements gain in development. Responses suitable only for individual examples become tied into the recognition construct of a specific perception but dissociated from the class or type symbol. "Rover"is a recognized acquaintance but the various stray canines that roam the neighborhood are "dogs." These latter have certain common characteristics and aspects. Attaching word-symbols to successively appearing characteristics and aspects, or to any objects that have these common traits, epitomizes the experiences and integrates them into a unit of meaning. They become dogs or sheep or cows or horses, depending on certain general traits.

We have moved from gross outline recognition through familiarty with specific perceptions; and then to a synthesis of experiences around a verbal symbol according to aspects or traits. The common aspect may be such a quality as number, colour, or roundness. A word-symbol for the aspect is furnished to the learner by other persons, and is encountered in the varying situations. The symbol becomes attached to the responses to the quality of an object rather than to the object itself. "Red" appears as a part of the situation in houses, flowers, dresses, vehicles, lights, and rouge. Gradually the light stimulus of a certain narrow range in wave length becomes associated with the verbal symbol "red."

Basic meaning: Children's symbols are usually at a lower level of meaningful development than the symbols of adults. The adult, by using a symbol a great number of times, abstracts the common qualities and synthesizes them into the basic meaning. This basic meaning is likely to be the one aroused, unless the individual is attempting to pun or form bizarre associations. Children tend to be more vague and hazy in regard to word meanings. They are likely to use symbols in a way which seems native and foolish to the sophisticated adult. However, give time, the varied experience, error-checking with purposeful observation, and adult guidance, the children will develop basic meanings.

Verbalism without basic meaning: Experience may condition the child to substitite verbal symbols as responses to other verbal-symbol stimuli because of the greater social approval. Such association is no guarantee that the symbol has attached to it the variety of responses necessary to make it functional in specific contextual or environmental patterns. Meaning is specifically related to the child's own experiences. Vicarious experiencing, as an educative practice, implies sufficient awareness of identity between the individual's own personal experience and the "secondhand" experience to make the transferred experience meaningful.

As we try to force a great many concepts on our students in a relatively short time in our schools, we produce rote learning of non-meaningful responses. A concept takes time to develop. The substitution of rote verbalism for understanding is an educational malpractice by no means limited to the elementary school. Too often in the higher academic levels, vagueness of thinking and superficial knowledge are successfully disguised by euphonious polysyllables.

Arbitrary, associative learning: Whenever practicable, learning should be based on meaning and full understanding; however, the student can be saved much time and trouble by the repetitive practice and rote learning of some materials. Spelling is not a procedure based on meaning; neither are many of our grammatical rules. Dates, day of the month and month of the year, number combinations for the skills of arithmetic, and the like are largely matters for rote memorization.

Drill, external motivation, rhythms, and any chance similarities or possibilities of organization may be used to establish associative learnings. Associations that must be correct and immediately available when needed are often best established by such methods. Arithmetical drill is an economical way to learn number combinations. One might very well determine the correct answer to problems involving number combinations by a series of additions and figure countings, but the procedure is too slow and not as apt to be as accurate as the habit responses established through drills. "eight times seven" and "nine times six" do not seem to be types of learning that can be economically established by meaningful incidental use. Memory devices, such as the old rhyme "Thirty days hath September..." or the use of the word "lice" to provide the key for the respective vowels after "I" and "c" in "believe" and "receive," are well-known devices. Who could confuse "stalagmites" and "stalacities" again after hearing the statement, "The mites go up and the tights come down"?

Motivated drill necessary: When arbitray associations are to be established, extrinsic motivation, repetitive practice, and prompt correction of error are the keys to method. Results are measured in terms of speed and accuracy of response. The individual when learning material of this kind will organize it in some manner of his own as he tries to learn it. The method may be rhythm, superimposed meanings, or what not. He is usually the best judge as to his own method. Practice must be continued far into the overlearning stage.

It is difficult to conceive of a rapid method of learning a foreign language for speaking and writing purposes that does not involve much memory work and drill. A person can learn the language by living among those who already speak it. Even so, he learns more rapidly if he drills and practices. Most students are not fortunate enough to be able to learn their foreign languages in countries where those languages are spoken. Yet the good school programme in foreign language, much of which has necessarily been composed of rote or associative learning, has done a great deal to establish basic groundwork in those languages.

No successful methods have yet been discovered by which the teacher can make everything that must be taught meaningful to the child at each particular grade level. To date it has seemed better to drill the child in certain portions of the social heritage that will be required later on. School subject matter, even when not completely understood by the student, should leave him a residue of learning that saves him much time in reacquiring the bulk of the material later, when it is needed.[8] Meanings are, by their very nature, vague at first, depend on accumulating experiences for their development, and take time, as well as experience and use, for their growth.

Rote vs. logical memory: When practicable, the memorization of necessary facts should follow the learning of the

8. Cf. H.E.Burtt's studies of the retention of meaningless Greek in "An Experimental Study of Early Childhood Memory," *Journal of Genetic Psychology*, XL (1932), 287-295.

significance of these facts. This statement is applicable to arithmetic, social studies, or almost any other school subject. For practical purposes, it will be necessary to memorize some material that can be used before one's understanding of the entire material is complete. In science, mechanics, and mathematics, for example, it is frequently economical (in terms of learning time) to accept expert opinion for the correctness of a formula or a method, memorize the formula or method, and proceed to use it.

The foregoing statements should not be interpreted too broadly. It has been found that arithmetic, for example, is learned more easily and rapidly if counting and number work are postponed until certain basic quantitative concepts are developed.[9] A certain level of educational maturity of the student (a mental age of six years and six months is often used instead) has been found to be necessary before the student can be taught reading economically. A mental age of about ten years seems to be requisite to learning geographical names and places with an understanding of space and orientation. The abstract concepts of elementary social science are apparently better learned after the mental age of twelve.[10] In other words, a basis amount of educational maturity is essential in many subjects before even fact memorization is accompanied by meaning in use. When applicable to the material, logical memory requires less expenditure of time than rote memory; also, it is less subjects to loss through forgetting.

The importance of language in concept development: The child's early language is made up largely of nouns. As soon as a noun begins to refer to more than one item of a kind, it is taking on the general framework of the concept. Abstract nouns and descriptive adjectives tend to develop a little later. Meaningful

---

9. W.A.Brownell and G.Hendrickson, "How Children Learn Information, Concepts, and Generalizations," *Learning and Instruction*, Forty-ninth Yearbook of the National Society for the Study of Education, Part I (Chicago: University of Chicago Press,1950), Chap, 5, pp.92-128.
   N.M.Russel, "Arithmetical Concepts of Children," *Journal of Educational Research*, XXIX (1936), 647-663.
   C.L. Thiele, *The Contribution of Generalization to the Learning of Addition Facts* (New York: Teachers College, Bureau of Publications, Columbia University, 1938).
10. T.J. Eskridge, Growth in Understanding of Geographical Terms in Grades IV to VII" (Duke University Studies in Education [Durham, N.C.: Duke University Press, 1939]).

use of either implies a concept of *aspects*. The aspect of quantity (more or less) begins to develop in the pre-school period.

The importance of language in human understanding is almost impossible to exaggerate. The symbol, the core, the matrix that unifies and preserves abstracted, integrated and synthesized experience is usually a *word*. It functions without recall of the pertinent experiences. It is the "shorthand" that allows experiences to be fed into the infinitely complex "electronic computer" of the human mind.

Concepts organize and refine experience: Successful advancement in the field of human learning would be impossible without concepts as tools of thought. Only by their means can experience be labeled, identified classified, and organized. Understanding depends on this association. Unorganized masses of factual material can neither be comprehended nor retained. They must be classified under their appropriate concepts, and mentally field for use.

Science is continually trying to refine its concepts. The analytical process of science—the attention to aspect, relations, characteristics, traits or parts instead of the whole—is a relatively mature mental process. The ancient shepherd had no counting system; so he learned to recognize and remember each individual sheep (by name). Such a laborious procedure of distinction between, and memorization of, percepts has value areas. Political popularity seems to depend partially on remembering individual people. But this process, valuable as it may be at times, is the perfecting of a lower level of mental activity. Much of our knowledge must be retained for use without the presence of memory of the hundreds of original percepts from which we abstracted the knowledge. The concept of science are usually based on the cause or origin of phenomena. When phenomena are inexplicable without a concept, one is formulated. Examples of such formulations are the concepts of gravity, electricity, energy and relativity. The organization of experience into meaningful material depends upon concept formation; completeness of understanding depends on experience adequate to permit precision and exactness.

Suggestions for teaching concepts: In order to foster growth of word-symbol meanings, the teacher should keep in mind that concepts (1) develop through numerous specific experiences form everyday life; (2) grow slowly from the concrete, perceptual level to the abstract, relationship-of-common-elements level; (3) must await educational readiness for learning on a higher, abstract level.

The child should be given adequate opportunity to use his concepts, to express them to the class, to adjust them in the light of errors, and to elaborate on them. Group discussion guided by the teacher, together with study based on key questions, may serve to clarify the child's meanings. In a physics class, for example, one teacher asked his class what effect a reduction of the earth's gravity to that of the moon would have on high jumpers. A social studies teacher asked his class what the effect would be on the school if the students were permitted to govern it by democratic procedures.

Use of a suitable vocabulary is a difficult problem for the teacher. New concepts should be introduced in language that the child, himself, can use functionally. Even so, simple language will not clarify a difficult idea—"The whole is more than the sum of its parts," for example, or "All things are made up of energy."

The teacher can accelerate the formation of concepts by: (1) introducing the concept with examples in which the basic relationship stand out; (2) keeping the early examples as close as possible to the concrete objects and perceptual level of the everyday life of the child; (3) reducing the number of concepts to be covered, and allowing more time and a greater wealth of experience for each; (4) giving regular practice in use, with guidance, motivation, and opportunities for success; (5) directing the child's attention to the general traits or aspects by copious illustrations, examples, pictures, and the like; (6) helping the child to formulate in verbal symbols an expression of these general traits, or aspects, for the purpose of analysis; and (7) helping him to discover what symbolic cues in his *own repertoire* will fuse into the concept if brought together under the focus of his attention.

The teacher should be careful not to abbreviate experience to verbal symbolism too rapidly. Even a parrot can recite learned answers to questions. A person who really understands has had sufficient meaningful experience to fit his own symbols precisely to the situation. A background of much information fosters precision of response. The teacher-formulated answer, memorized but inadequately understood, is not independently applied to new, pertinent situations.

Summary

Sensorimotor behaviour begins with the gross muscular reactions of the fetal response to a stimulus. The development of the nervous system makes possible movement responses to distant stimuli. Motor control of the body develops from the head end of the child, downward and outward. Infant development includes sitting alone, crawling, prehension, and walking. Life demands much motor-skill development. A challenging environment stimulates the child to develop his powers more fully. He needs equipment, space, opportunities, and help. Playgrounds and playrooms, nursery schools and kindergartens, are sources for such experiences.

Skills are built on preceding learning and tend to develop in hierarchies. Improvement in skill depends on intent, adequate, purposeful practice and suitable form. Skills are specific to the activity but, when well learned, adjustable to changes in environmental conditions. Skills are not exact repetitions of the same movement patterns. Fluctuations in performance occur at all levels. Form is, to a considerable degree, an individual matter, although much time may be saved by imitating a form that has proved successful for many others in the past. The teacher can short-cut the learning procedure by guiding the learner into such procedures, especially in regard to sound mechanics of preparatory position and of basic motions.

The development of perceptual behaviour refers to the growth in ability to recognize previously experienced stimulus situations in an increasingly adequate or socially more acceptable form. The infant's early recognitions are of hunger stimuli, parents, feeding equipment, toys, and the like. Words become attached to experiences and recognized first by sound and, after schooling, word recognition progresses to phrase recognition. A memory "types" correct variations in sensory presentations. Cues from various sensory modalities fuse into complex perception; for example, notes, time cues fuse into each single perception by the pianist. These complex perceptions are prompt, habitual recognitions, and must be so to have the speed and accuracy essential for functional use.

Conceptual behaviour implies that the individual is guided in his responses by symbolic cues representative of the significant features in much previous experience. Whereas the mental construct fill in the sensory perception of the sepcific case, the concept fuses object similarities or aspects into a core of meaning. A symbol, usually verbal, is the expression of, and the integrating factor in, this aura of meaning. The symbols may refer to classes or to aspects. Verbal symbols need a background of direct experience to gain clearness of meaning. Concepts develop by the application of experience to seemingly similar situations and by the readjustment of responses in the new situations. Social guidance accelerates the process by calling attention to common characteristics and furnishing symbols for these characteristics. The concept multiplies the mass of experience reducible to units of meaning. The labeling, classifying and organizing of experience into concept units increases tremendously the possibility of one's grasp of meanings.

In teaching concepts, the appropriate symbols should be associated with the student's firsthand experiencing. The student's observation and analysis can be so directed as to focus on general characteristics. Concepts introduced to the immature student, through the medium of verbal symbolism only, lack precise meaning. The student learns a vagueness of thinking, a substitution of rote statements for meaningful responses. He covers the blemishes in his thinking with verbal cosmetics unwittingly furnished by the teacher.

—John D. Lawther

Questions and Exercises (for Discussion and Study)

1. In ten practice periods at spaced intervals, attempt to learn any one of the following skills which is new to you: ice skating or roller skating, spinning and balancing a basketball on one finger, writing with the pencil gripped between your large toe and its adjacent toe, juggling two or three balls.

2. Check among your family and friends as to their means of remembering: to mail a letter, keep an appointment, an address or telephone number, articles to be bought on a shopping tour, points to be made in a speech or formal argument, location or personal items when they need them. Then compare these findings with your own processes in attempting to recall.
3. Suggest techniques for learning the following:
   (*a*) Major points of this chapter,
   (*b*) Birthdays of family and friends,
   (*c*) Important dates in history,
   (*d*) Quotations to be learned in your literature courses,
   (*e*) A vocabulary list in a foreign language,
   (*f*) A scientific formulas,
   (*g*) How to extract square root.
4. To study the fusion of sensations from various sense organs and past experiences into new perceptions, select anyone of the following foods with which you are either vaguely or not at all familiar, and repeat the experience of eating it until the perception is well developed: permission, pomegranate, guava mulberry, serviceberry, shrimp, snails, sweetbread, clams, eels, lobster, Limburger cheese. Analyze the development of the perception.
5. Determine by experiment how early a child of average intelligence learns to select the larger of two pieces of a desirable edible. Observe the growth of the habit of courting social approval by selecting the smaller piece, in youngsters of kindergarten and primary-school age.
6. Think over your elementary-school experiences in learning the skills of handwriting, reading, arithmetic, spelling. Did the practice procedures differ in: length interest, amount of physical rehearsal, mental practice between drill assignments, imitation of others, learning procedures thought through and planned beforehand?

7. How is the development of skills affected by: A dynamic want to master the skill? Correct practice? Knowledge that progress is being made? A feeling that the skill is not learning? Failure to master the skill? Vigorous health?

8. At what stages of learning can one profit most by longer drill periods, beginning or advanced? At what stage of learning is detailed self-analysis most profitable?

9. How would you teach a youngster to ride a bicycle? To throw a ball for distance? To produce the appearance of three dimensions on a flat-surface drawing? To orient himself and be able to point out North, South, East, and West?

10. A six-year-old with a mental age of nine asks you why the artificial satellite does not fall. Work out your vocabulary, sentences, and illustrations to answer his question so that he will understand.

11. What are the differences in types of learning necessary to answer the following types of questions over the same lesson content:

    (a) A true-false question,

    (b) A multiple-choice question,

    (c) A completion question,

    (d) An essay question as to cause and effect?

12. A group of city children were making an excursion to the country. One asked the teacher, as the bus pulled out of the city into farm areas, "Is there much country around here?" What would you reply to the child to clarify his thinking with regard to the respective extents of urban and rural areas?

13. Should you expect the same results from reading a true-false test aloud to students as from presenting it to them in mimeographed form? Why (or, why not)? What is the value of giving students a test covering a unit of subject matter before beginning the teaching of the unit?

14. Which promotes greater achievement by a student: (a) having the teacher supply the information to students, or (b) letting them discover the facts for themselves? Does the student learn faster by rereading, or by trying to recite after his first reading? Should the teacher supply the wording for the student's conclusions, so as to increase the precision and exactness of the student's concept or generalization?
15. How has your study of science affected your concepts of: distance, time, the nature of matter, energy?
16. What are the implications as to meaning in the following statements:

    (a) "Only those who have lost it for a time, can really understand democracy."

    (b) "The greatest danger to the world is mass ignorance."

    (c) "Knowledge is virtue."

    (d) "Cognition is not volition."

    What change is implied in (a) the concept of democracy? The last three all deal with aspects of knowledge. Explain the concept implied in each.
17. How can students develop a mastery of educational psychology more economically? Would you advise considerable library reading on the subject, discussing it with others, outlining lessons, writing papers for publication, explaining it to others, making experiments, or studying psychology and doing student teaching at the same time? Why (or, why not)?

References

Carmichael, L., *Manual of Child Psychology*, Second Edition, New York: John Wiley & Sons, Inc., 1954, Chap. 9.

Cole, L.E., and W.F. Bruce, *Educational Psychology*. Yonkers, N.Y.: World Book Company, 1950, Chap. 14.

Eskridge, T.J., Jr., *Growth in Understanding of Geographical Terms in Grades IV to VII*. Durham, N.C.: Duke University Press, 1939.

Goodenough, F., *Developmental Psychology,* Second Edition. New York: Applenton-Century-Crofts, Inc., 1954, Chap, 14.

Jones, H. E., *Motor Performance and Growth.* Berkeley and Los Angles: University of Califorina Press, 1949.

Kingsley, H.L., *The Nature and Conditions of Learnings,* rev. by Ralph Garry. Englewood Cliffs, N.J.: Prentice-Hall, Inc., 1957, Chaps. 10, 13.

Leeper, R., "Cognitive Processes," in S.S. Stevens (ed.), *Handbook of Experimental Psychology.* New York: John Wiley & Sons, Inc., 1951, pp. 730-757.

Monroe, W.S. "Child Development-VIII. Language," *Encylopaedia of Educational Research.* New York: The Macmillian Company, 1950, pp. 165-172.

Skinner, C.E., *et. al.* (ends.), *Readings in Educational Psychology.* New York: Farrar & Rinehart, Inc., 1937, Chaps. 7, 8.

———, *et al.* (eds.), *Readings in Psychology.* New York: Farrar & Rhinehart, Inc, 1935, Chaps. 12-13.

———, and P.L. Harriman (eds.), *Child Psychology.* New York: The Macmillan Company, 1941, Chaps, 4, 6.

Trow, W.C., *Educational Psychology,* 2nd ed. Boston: Houghton Miffin Company, 1950, Chaps. 10, 15.

Welford, A.T., *Aging and Human Skill* (New York: Oxford University Press, 1953), Chap. 2.

13

Intelligence

Intelligence is a descriptive concept. It represents a theoretical dimension which can vary from very low to very high value. In common usage the word intelligence is associated with the general behaviour of an individual so that it becomes synonymous with brightness or brainy. A psychologist, on the other hand, uses the word as a theoretical construct. It is an intervening variable which can be inferred and measured by indirect operations and it has certain descriptive and predictive properties. In this connotation, intelligence has no absolute meaning because it can be changed in definition and design so as to suit the needs of the psychologists.

Intelligent behaviour implies the making of value judgements. These value judgements differ in different cultures so that the definition of intelligence derives its meaning from the social context. An individual who is capable of taking quick decisions is considered intelligent in one culture while he is considered impulsive and not so intelligent in another. So, in constructing an intelligence test the psychologist usually attempts to reflect the value judgements of some specific culture. That is the reason why it is widely believed that the intelligence tests cannot be borrowed from one cultural background and be used in another.

Though psychologists have been using operational definitions for the construction of intelligence tests yet they have never given up the attempts at framing one or the other definition of the concept for theoretical use. This, perhaps, will be the right place to consider some of these definitions.

Binet was the first psychologist to devise an acceptable scale of intelligence in 1905 and his 'Measuring Scale of Intelligence, in 1908. The results of his tests agreed quite well with the judgements of experienced teachers who came in close contact with the children tested. During the process of constructing this test Binet defined intelligence as the ability of an individual to direct his behaviour towards a goal, to make adaptations in his goal-oriented behaviour when necessary and to know when he has reached the goal.

According to him comprehension, invention, direction and censorship were the processes that went into the making of intelligence. Thus much emphasis has been placed by him on the problem-solving behaviour. Goddard evolved another definition based on forty years of research and experimentation. He defined intelligence as 'the degree of availability of one's experiences for the solution of immediate problems and the anticipation of future ones'. In this definition again we find the emphasis on past experiences as they can be utilized towards the solution of present and future problems so that like Binet's definition here also the problem-solving becomes the goal.

Terman translated and revised Binet's tests for the English speaking population. For his first revision of 1916—Stanford Revision of the Binet-Simon Tests for use in English speaking cultures—he defined intelligence as an individual's ability to carry on abstract thinking and to use abstract symbols in the solution of all kinds of problems. Considering the emphasis placed on the use of symbols it becomes clear why Terman consistently considered the size of vocabulary to be the best single indicator of an individual's general intelligence.

Most of the tests used for measurement of intelligence today either are a form of Terman's Test or highly correlate with the two versions of his tests. As such the functional definition, in vogue today is the one given by Terman as stated above in this discussion. This definition has much in common with Spearman's[8] description of general intelligence. McNemar has proved that the versions of Binet Scale do measure, to a large extent, one general factor of intelligence.

Terman has often been criticized for making his definition too much related with the social and cultural environment. Use of symbols has been found to be the most difficult process among different mental processes and it has been further found that the kind of social and cultural environment provided to the individual make a lot of difference in the skill at using these symbols.

Inspite of this criticism Terman has collected a large mass of data which goes to demonstrate the predictive usefulness of an intelligence scale based on his definition. There are other psychologists who have based their scales on different definitions, Wechsler and Thurstone are among those psychologists. However, they have yet to demonstrate that their tests have the same descriptive and predictive usefulness.

In the development of his intelligence tests Thorndike[10] implied Terman's emphasis on abstract thinking. Thorndike defined the level of an individual's intelligence on the basis of three independent variables:

1. ***Altitude:*** Other things being equal the difficulty of the tasks that an individual can perform determines the level of his intelligence. An individual who can tackle more difficult tasks naturally shows higher intellectual level than the individual who does not possess the skill to master difficult tasks.
2. ***Breadth:*** The number of tasks that an individual can tackle is another indication of the level of intelligence that he has attained. A large number of difficult tasks indicates higher intelligence while a smaller number is indicative of lower level of intelligence. In this Thorndike has combined the diversity of tasks with the difficulty of tasks. The larger number should also maintain a certain level of difficulty. Comparatively easier tasks even though performed in larger numbers would not be considered an indication of high level intelligence.
3. ***Speed:*** The quicker an individual is in performing tasks of equal difficulty the higher he is considered in his intelligence. Moreover the performance of the task should be correct. The speed is an indication of intelligence provided the responses made during that time interval are correct.

So putting all these factors together Thorndike based his measurement of intelligence on the difficulty of tasks mastered, variety and diversity of these tasks and the speed of these tasks.

Thurstone, as already mentioned, has constructed a series of intelligence tests that combine both verbal and non-verbal components of intelligence. He emphasized seven factors which are involved in the verbal and non-verbal items of an intelligence test. These factors are:

S or the Space factor: According to his theory space orientation, ability to visualise flat or solid objects is highly related with intelligence and is greatly needed in the mechanical aptitude.

N or Number factor: Under this Thurstone expects an intelligent individual to be able to make certain numerical calculations similar to the ones performed by a cashier.

V or Verbal Comprehension factor: This factor involves the ability to deal with verbal concepts the examples of such ability are verbal reasoning and vocabulary or the number of words that are available to the individual at a given time.

W or Word Fluency factor: This is the test of fluency rather than the number of words or the range of vocabulary. An individual can be fluent in spite of the fact that he has a few words at his command and vice-versa.

M or Memory factor: This factor according to Thurstone is supposed to estimate the individual's ability to preserve and reproduce perceptional as well as conceptional material.

Induction factor: Denoting the facility in discovering a single principle or rule that applies to a series of problems.

Deduction factor: For this factor Thrustone could not produce enough evidence but in this factor he visualized the ability to apply a given principle to series of specific problems.

Flexibility and speed of closure: Another factor given by Thurstone which indicated the ability to interpret instructions quickly and facility to size up a situation. Flexibility meant an ability to abandon one pattern in favour of another one when the latter seemed to be more promising.

The factors given by Thurstone have been treated in detail here because at present his theory seems to be the most scientifically established and a reliable one. His theory is considered to be of the most promising nature, and the study of these factors is considered to be an essential for any student of measurement of intelligence.

Developmental psychologists are often occupied with the question of child intelligence versus the adult intelligence. They are interested in knowing if there is a difference between the nature of the two or if the nature of intelligence is the same and the difference is made by the process of development. Thurstone, during his researches, was able to isolate and identify almost the same primary mental abilities in kindergarten children as have been found in adults. Thus he has established the continuity of intellectual growth throughout childhood.

While comparing his factors with Spearman's 'g', Thurstone made the claim that general intelligence is a second order factor, its ability to define the concept clearly is much less than that of the primary factors and also that it is less useful than the primary factors. He further claims that the level of intelligence of an individual can be best judged from the profile of primary mental abilities. Such a representative profile allows one to predict behaviour trends that cannot be deducted from a single score of intelligence as is given if we contribute to the 'g' factor.

Though we have stated that Thurstone's approach seems to be the most promising one for the measurement of intelligence yet we have no way of predicting whether it will collect the same amount of valuable material as was collected by Binet and Terman. This can be shown by the time only.

The definitions given so far, have often been, criticized by the subsequent psychologists on account of one or the other omission. Guilford[5] has criticized these definitions on the basis that they are too narrow and neglect the important concept of creativity, on the other hand these definitions have been criticized for the neglect of the social values. Creativity or the original responses are emphasized because they are considered to be of prime importance for the socially important concept or genius. There is no doubt that the current definitions have omitted the social values as a factor of intelligence.

On the other hand there are psychologists who believe that the theoretical construct of intelligence should be broad enough to include the conative and personality aspects of man's behaviour. Wechsler has expressed the opinion that general intelligence is influenced by certain conative factors like drive, will, perseveration and persistence; it is also influenced by certain emotional factors like anxiety and impulsiveness and by other more general personality characteristics.

Summarizing the discussion we come back to the original statement made that intelligence is a descriptive concept and that there is no specific definition of the concept. The definitions are made for a specific purpose, usually for the construction of an intelligence test and as such vary from time to time and from author to author. A theoretical construct may be changed at any time to suit the needs of the scientist and the intelligence is such a theoretical construct.

Measurement of Intelligence

History

Before testing came into existence intelligence was assessed by mere observation of the individual concerned. This question raised is that of the standard used for these estimates. Presumably the standards would differ with each individual observer. This led to the need for a uniform standard of estimates and so the measurement of intelligence.

Towards the last days of the 19th century Alfred Binet a French psychologist was busy experimenting with the teachers' estimates of children's intellectual level, their acceleration rate etc. He observed that all teachers resorted to asking some sort of questions. The questions asked were different with each teacher. He also observed a remarkable discrepancy in the teachers' estimates of two children even when the questions asked and the responses given were identical. This difference, Binet suspected, was dependent on the bias which the teachers held about individual children. However, this experiment hinted at a few essentials of intelligence testing. In the first place, it pointed out that questions can be asked and the responses given to these questions can be used as an estimate of an individual's intelligence. It was also clear from this demonstration that the question asked should be one single criterion used of assessing these responses.

Before this Galton in England and Cattell in America were trying to develop a method of estimating intelligence through certain physiological indices. In their laboratories one would come in for a series of physical measurements including tests of sensory acuity and reaction time. Their contention was that a complex process like intelligence can be measured in terms of psycho-physical tasks. Binet, however, was working on the theory that the differences in the ability to think and reason, to solve difficult problems, to make use of past experiences in new situations can best be measured by setting situations in which the subject has to make use of these.

In 1896 Binet and Henry published a paper in which they described a test that they planned to use with school children and by which they claimed to measure each of the following 'facilities'.

1. Memory
2. Mental imagery
3. Imagination
4. Attention
5. Comprehension
6. Suggestibility
7. Aesthetic appreciation
8. Force of will as indicated by sustained effort in muscular tasks.
9. Moral sentiments
10. Motor skills
11. Judgement of visual space

This and other articles of Binet appeared hereafter in which he reported that these tests were systematically tried with school children of different ages. The two factors that they were interested in investigating were:

1. Whether the scores on these tests improved with age or not.
2. Whether consistent differences were obtained in the scores of children rated bright and those rated dull by their teachers.

After repeated experiments with different tests Binet found that younger children could not perform certain tasks and if they could then their method of tackling the problem was not as neat as the one used by older children. He was bothered by the fact that some children scored a zero. The question that faced him was: Does it mean that the intelligence of this individual is at zero level? He argued that the use of zero cannot be made in the absolute sense, so that the scoring in mental measurement must consist of psychological units and that if zero is used it should be used in the relative sense. Thus we find that Binet was busy solving most of the statistical problems that we consider today in the process of standardizing a test.

At this time Ebbinghaus was studying memory. He was interested in the study of factors that helped in the process of memorization and also what the process itself was. His method of studying memory through nonsense syllabaus led to the test for memory. These included the tests for measuring the span of visual appreciation, memory for digits, for list of words and sentences etc. Most of these later formed a part of an intelligence test.

There were many other attempts at intelligence tests besides the ones discussed here. The need seemed to be for a comprehensive test which would measure all these abilities and still be so short as to be manageable within a reasonable length of time. Many tests that were tried did not come out with the increase in scores with the age nor did they show much relationship with the school success or the teacher's estimates of these pupils.

By the beginning of the 20th century Binet had accumulated a large amount of data about the way children respond to different tasks. He had compared this performance of younger children and children from lower grades as well as higher grades. He had evidence for some tasks that were useful for his purpose and also for those that were of no use at all. In brief he had a good knowledge of what kind of tasks the children are usually able to do. So far nobody had devised a plan to put these tasks together and frame the test. So Binet had to be the first one to attempt this task.

In 1904 the French Government appointed a Commission to evolve special measures for the care and the education of the retarded children. Binet was entrusted with the task of screening such children. He had the help of Simon, his colleague, in this work. With the time factor involved, they could not insist on perfect scientific techniques. So they laid down four general rules for the construction of their first scale. (i) It should not make any pretence of measuring each of the faculties stated above, it should achieve an overall measure of the general intelligence of the individual. (ii) It should not take too much time in administration. (iii) Items should be selected on the basis of a very general and wide definition of intelligence. (iv) Items should be arranged according to their difficulty without considering their nature.

Their second test, published in 1908, was only partly based on the 1905 scale. At the time of the first scale, Binet was primarily interested in the diagnosis of the subnormal children, intelligence testing of average normal children was of secondary importance. By 1908 his interest had undergone a change. He was now interested in the intelligence testing of normal school children. As a result some of the items included in 1905 scale and meant for use with the idiots were eliminated from the subsequent scale.

In 1911 another revision of Binet scale appeared. This scale had five tests each for ages three to ten with additional groups of five each provided for ages twelve to fifteen. In this test an additional allowance for tests passed above the basal year was provided. Such an allowance consisted of 0.2 years for each test passed, thus permitting the use of fractional parts of a year in computing the mental age of an individual.

Summarizing the above account we find that Binet through his experiments had devised a complete method of standardizing an intelligence test which the psychologists now follow with complete assurance and scientific justification.

The value of Binet's scale was recognized by his contemporaries in the form of attempted translations for use with different populations in other countries. In 1906 the first of such attempts was made in New Jersey by Goddard.[3] He required a diagnostic instrument for use with the inmates of the training school at Vineland. The final form of his translation of Binet appeared in 1910. It proved to be very useful for the guidance of the pupils who had spent a lot of time and faced repeated failure due to the lack of guidance.

Goddard, however, was not the only American psychologist awake to the importance of Binet's work. Others had also taken note of it and were busy attempting a suitable translation for the English speaking children. Standford University Revision of 1916 was an evidence of this. Besides the translation, Terman[9] supplied psychology with a new concept of I.Q. For some time the intelligence testers had realized the limitations of mental age as a measure of intelligence. So when Terman provided this ratio as the measure it was accepted with great satisfaction and is in use even today. The psychologist had by now understood the need of changing tasks with different populations and from time to time with the result that Terman and his colleagues felt the need of another revision by 1937. This brings us to the age when individual testing has established itself well and is widely used for the purpose of diagnosis and screening of individuals with different levels of intelligence.

World War I brought another problem before the psychologists. The need of testing the soldiers was felt but individual testing was impracticable. So the psychologists got busy with working out group tests. Army Alpha and Beta tests were the outcome. Beta test was constructed for use with the illiterates while Alpha was for use with educated soldiers. These tests strike one with their apparent simplicity of tasks and the high degree of effectiveness with which they served the purpose in army.

Gradually the psychologists felt the need of tests that could be used with people who could not make use of language but still needed to be tested. Non-verbal tests were the result which are used with deaf people with a certain amount of effectiveness.

This marked a sudden-spurt in the testing movement. Tests are now being devised for educational skills, mechanical skills, aptitudes for different fields and also for the understanding of personality and its components.

In India the earliest attempt at intelligence testing can be traced back to Rice, an American professor working at Lahore. He translated Binet Scale into Hindustani—the generally used language in North-West of India at that time. The test was available in cyclostyled form—with the norms—in late thirties.

The movement caught notice of some Indian psychologists and as a result we get individual as well as institutional attempts at construction and standardization of tests. Sohan Lal gave a battery of tests as an individual worker and later as the head of Psychological Bureau at Allahabad. His work includes intelligence test for Hindi-speaking population and achievement tests in Arithmetic and other school subjects.

Bhatia[1] was responsible for a well standardized test which is popular with many a psychologist today. Kamat have us another test of intelligence which is reliable for use with children.

Besides Allahabad Bureau, Central Institute of Education, Delhi took translation and calculation of Indian norms for a number of tests. Individual Test of Intelligence, Group Test of Intelligence, Jenkin's Culture Free Test were some of the instruments.

The language variation in India led to construction of tests in regional languages. Faculty of Education and Psychology, of M.S. University of Baroda was active in this line and added group tests of intelligence, Achievement Tests in various subjects and the translation and adaption of W.A.I.S. for the Gujarati speaking population. At present there are a number of tests available in Hindi as well as in regional languages. Some of these tests are well standardized and reliable for use while the reliability and validity of others is doubtful. To assess the value of all available tests the Government of India organized a workshop in 1962 the purpose of which was to analyse and evaluate the existing tests. As an outcome of this attempt the psychologist in India has a directory of tests which gives complete analysis together with the final rating of the test.

Standardization of Tests

Before setting out on the task of test construction a psychologist has to be clear about his defintion of intelligence. The theory by itself may not be of much significance but it is of great significance inasmuch as it determines the nature of items and the determine the level of intelligence. It is these items and the tasks that determine the level of intelligence. The statement that intelligence is what the intelligence tests measure, is made bearing the above fact in mind. Each test, however, cannot afford to measure anything and call it intelligence. Certain criteria have to be evolved before the test items can be made. Terman developed the following criteria for selection of items for his 1937 revision of Binet's test:

1. The percentage of children passing the tests should increase with increase in chronological age;
2. They should be easy to administer and score;
3. They should reflect experiences common to all children and should be free from the influence of advantages enjoyed by only a few of them;
4. The test items should sample according to the performance of this sample for the inclusion in the final form of the test.

The items are selected according to their difficulty value as well as their discriminative value. We consider the difficulty value because we do not want a lot of too easy items to be included in a test, neither do we like to have items on the test that are too difficult for this particular age group. Discriminative value of an item is judged from whether it can discriminate the bright from the dull in a consistent manner. According to these two criteria the final form of the test is determined.

Next stage is that of the final administration for the standardization purposes. Now a substantial representative sample of a particular age level is required for administration. Their performance of this form acts as the norms for this group. The performance of any one child of this age can be compared with the standardization sample and his level of intelligence determined accordingly. The precise intellectual level of a particular child has often been expressed, by the psychologists, in terms of mental age.

The mental age is operationally defined as the average performance of a group of children of a particular age who are representative of the total population. So the mental age of ten year would mean the average performance of chronologically ten year old children who are representatives of some defined population. Mental age is a very useful concept for the precise statement of the level of intelligence. This enables us to place each individual child more or less accurately in his age group as well as within a group of his own mental level.

From the mental age, intelligence quotient was the next step—a ratio which is easier to handle and a better index for comparative purposes. It is calculated by the simple formula $\frac{M.A}{C.A.} \times 100$. The ratio of mental age and chronological age multiplied by hundred gives a number estimate of the individual's intelligence. It does not need the interpretation of mental age for individuals with different chronological ages, I.Qs. of 140, 60 or 106 are self explanatory.

During psychological researches it has been found that many of the biological traits and characteristics of human beings are disturbed along a normal probability curve. Height and weight have been found to be disturbed in this fashion throughout the world. Likewise the administration of Revised Stanford Binet Scale demonstrates that the I.Qs of a larger number of children on this test approximate a normal probability distribution fairly closely. By accepting the fact that the I.Q.s are normally distribution fairly closely. By accepting the fact that the I.Qs are normally distributed we can make very definite statements about the I.Q. obtained by one particular individual if we know the mean and the standard deviation of the test. Terman, after considering the normal distribution yielded by his data, has given the following classification of the intellectual level according to the I.Qs. obtained:

I.Q.	*Classification*
Above 140	'Near' genius or genius
120 – 140	Very superior intelligence

110 - 120	Superior intelligence
90 - 110	Normal or average intelligence
80 - 90	Dullness, rarely classified as feeble-mindedness
70 - 80	Border line deficiency, sometimes classified as dullness and often as feeble-mindedness
Below 70	Definite feeble-mindedness

Of the feeble-minded, those between 50 and 70 I.Q. include most of the morons (high, middle and low), those between 20-25 and 50 are ordinarliy to be classified as imbeciles and those below 20 or 25 as idiots. This classification gives us a broad outline within which specific value judgements can be passed.

The concept of evaluation is also useful for the prediction of one's intellectual level at a future date. A child has an I.Q. of say 90 at the age of 6 years; by applying the I.Q. formula we can calculate what his mental age would be when he reaches the age of 12. This information is very useful for planning the education of this child and determining the exceptions of the parents.

In recent years however, some of the psychologists have started moving away from the concept of mental age. Mental age works fine while we are dealing with younger age levels but when we come to testing the adults then it brings us into little difficulty. Usually, the tests are made for the school children and include the items which are suitable for them. So when we apply the same test and the same norms to adult population, often we get a case where the subject with a chronological age of 40 will score a mental age of say 15. Straight application of the I.Q. formula will yield an I.Q. of 15/40 X 100 = 75/2 app. 38. Does it mean that we label the individual a feeble-minded? Such situations have been saved by the theory of intellectual growth. As mentioned in the section on 'Development' the child develops in various fields as he advances in age. If we draw the developmental curves we find them going up rapidly upto a certain age and then level up leading to a definite decline after a particular age. The chronological age till when the intellectual ability shows rapid growth can be determined from these curves. For calculation of I.Q. of individuals beyond this age the denominator is set constant at this optimum age of growth.

Wechsler argued against all this and based his test and its scoring on entirely a different basis. He feels that mental age holds no meaning in the intelligence testing. Instead, the score of an individual as compared with the scores of his age group is of much more importance. He further argues that most of these tests are prepared for children so that the tasks included in them have no meaning for the adult population. With this rationale Wechsler constructed two different tests for use with children and adults. His standardization procedure was also different from other tests in the sense that he developed separate norms for different age levels. In each age group he included men and women in equal numbers. He also tried to include subjects from different vocations and different backgrounds, and developed scaled scores for each one of these representative age samples.

Instead of comparing a particular subject with the general norms of the test, which would imply the comparison of a subject with those at the peak of their development, Wechsler advocated comparisons within the age peers. Thus the I.Q., according to Wechsler scale, of an adult of 22 years will be based on a group of like youths and that of a subject fifty years old will likewise be based on an older group rather than on a population that he resembles very little.

The reasons for this kind of treatment, given by Wechsler are the variation in individual experiences, knowledge and daily activities at different age levels. With the rise in number of people getting higher education we find that I.Q. of those who have not had formal education would not compare well with the younger group. Similarly older people simply because they have lived longer and have accumulated experience will do better in certain aspects of the test than the younger group. This justifies the comparisons within age peers. Thus an I.Q. of 160 within sixty year old may hold the same meaning as 120 in a group of 18 year olds.

I.Q. as the ratio between the mental age and chronological age, according to Wechsler, may hold good while working with children but it does not work to complete satisfaction when applied to adults. He, therefore, devised the concept of deviation I.Q. which was applicable both to child and adult scale.

The calculation of deviation I.Q. is based on the average score being considered equal to 100 and the standard deviation set at 15 I.Q. points for each group. Thus for any age group the distribution of I.Q's has a mean of 100 and a standard deviation of 15.

An important advantage of this method is that it makes I.Q. validity constant from one group to another. The I.Q. of a given magnitude always has the same meaning with regard to a subject's standing relative to his age peers. Any I.Q. can be counted in terms of the deviations from the mean.

Description of Some Well-known Intelligence Tests

Tests for Infants

There is a great deal of controversy about the use of intelligence test for infants. The criticisms for the use of such instruments are based on the fact that children at this stage cannot give expression to the highly abstract concepts so that the only functions that you can test at this age are the sensory motor ones. So the items consist of showing the infant a coloured toy and making note of whether he pays attention to it or not and if a sound is made whether he looks in the correct direction or not.

Gesell[2] has developed a large number of infant scales which he prefers to call developmental scales. However, when the nature of items on these scales is studied one finds very little difference between these items and the ones on other intelligence tests for infants. These developmental scales are most widely used in the psychological field because of the wide influence of Gesell's work and the number of books that he has written. At the infant stage the predictio.. of intelligence is considered to be very low, yet the wide publicity of such scales has provoked curiosity in the minds of parents. They are usually keen to get their infants tested and their intellectual level predicted.

Intelligence Tests for Pre-school Children

Though Binet's test covers the pre-school age range yet many of the psychologists have tried to make tests specially for use with younger children. The younger child is usually not very happy with the formal testing situation so that the tests for him have to avoid the formality and have to include tasks that are more like play than work. One of the most widely used tests, for pre-school children, in the U.S. is the Merrill-Palmer Scale which involves tasks like buttoning, cutting with scissors, handling cubes, etc. In this scale the examiner can get an estimate of the child's failure which is due to the me e social resistance. Minnesota pre-school test is another one very popularily used with children of younger age levels. It is a carefully standardized test and has been used in various experimental situations in order to establish its reliability and validity.

Another test very commonly used and to which reference has already been made is that standardized by Wechsler. His scale for the adult had been known for a long time to the American Psychologists by the name of Wechsler-Bellevue Scales of Adult Intelligence. More recently he used the same type of items in order to prepare a scale meant for children of younger ages. The philosophy and the proceudre of standardization of this scale is exactly the same as Wechsler followed for his scale.

These are some of the tests that used the traditional type of items to test the intelligence of young children. There are efforts on the part of psychologists to test the intelligence of children through play-like activities as well. Goodenough[4] developed an intelligence scale based entirely on the child's ability "To Draw a Man". The scoring of this test is very simple and consists in assigning points for different characteristics of the human figure that the child has drawn. Another test very different from the usual kind is developed by Kohs,[6] which is based on the child's ability to make designs, like the ones presented to him, out of a given number of blocks provided for the task.

It is obvious from the above discussion that all these tests quoted are American in origin. In the section on 'Intellectual Development' we have seen that the intelligence is greatly influenced by the cultural conditions provided to the subjects and the kind of training given to them. Also we know that the skills developed and the tasks usually indulged in are different from one environment to another. As a result each culture and so different countries attempt to standardize or translate intelligence tests for children of their own culture. So the logical question for us would be to ask ourselves what kind of tests are available in our country.

Testing movement in this country is still very young. Some intelligence tests are available in different regions but very often the extensive use of these instruments proves that the test norms are not very good or that the items included are rather poor in quality. Some of these tests, however, are well accepted by now and give good results. Bhatia's[1] Performance Scale gives quite good results with Hindi speaking children and is widely used in some parts of the country. Another attempt that is worth mentioning here is that made at the individual and group scales by the Central Institute of Education. The C.I.E. Individual Scale and group test will be reliable instruments for use as soon as the manual is made available. In the absence of reliable tests in India, the use of the tests meant for children in other countries is common. Usually a concession is allowed in the scores obtained.

Criteria for Tests

Having described a number of intelligence tests, we are now faced with the question of the evaluation of tests. Out of the available tests which one should be chosen for use? How should this choice be made? What are the criteria for this choice?

Validity

The most important characteristic of a test is its validity. A test is valid to the degree that it measures what it is supposed to measure. In evaluating an intelligence test we are interested to know how well it measures intelligence operationally defined. The construct has not been definitely defined and as such no precise measure is possible yet the validity depends upon the accuracy with which a test measures this phenomenon.

Validity has two approaches to it i.e., logical analysis or empirical analysis. Logical analysis aims to judge precisely the factors which a test measures. It attempts to understand the processes which affect scores. Empirical analysis, on the other hand, has a practical bias. It tries to show that the test correlates with another measure which presuambly measures the same variable. Thus an aptitude test in engineering may be proved empirically valid if it correlates highly with the subsequent success of the students tested.

Reliability

No test can be valid without being able to measure accurately. In accuracy of measurement lies its reliability. An automatic conclusion of reliable measuring is that every time it measures in the same fashion and in every population it measures the same phenomenon. Every test has probability of error involved in its administration but the lesser this probability the more reliable that test is supposed to be. Reliability coefficient measures the reliability of the test. Three general principles must be kept in mind about the reliability coefficients. These are:

1. The reliability coefficient depends upon the length of the test;
2. The reliability coefficient depends on the range of scores in the group under study;
3. The test may give reliable measure at one level of ability and unreliable measures at another level.

The degree of reliability required for a good test varies with the purpose of the test. The aim is always to get the highest degree of reliability that is possible. The case is exactly the same as for validity. Though we know that it is impossible to get a perfect measure of a variable yet we desire as perfect a measure as may be possible.

Objectivity

Objective tests are more desirable than the ones which involve subjective bias. Subjectively scored tests are more flexible and are influenced by individual differences among the testers and scorers. Objectivity in administration and scoring allows testing of different groups at different times in precisely the same manner. This permits inter-group comparisons. Subjectively scored tests, on the other hand, may be useful individual work in a clinical set up but it does not permit comparisons with other groups.

For normal population where comparisons with the average are desirable and basic to all educational programming, objectivity of the test used becomes an important criterion for the goodness of a test. Even when a subject has to produce a response, it is desirable that alternative scoring is predetermined for different responses.

Norms

No test can be recommended unless it has worked out norms for use with groups. Authors of tests give tables which are helpful in interpreting the scores on a particular test. These tables are worked out in terms of normal average performance of the group used for standardization of the test.

The data are presented in terms of means, percentiles or standard scores. A tester after he knows the score of a particular individual, can place him well along the standard group. This gives the precise position of a particular individual in the reference group.

Two types of norms are usually calculated. Age norms and grade norms. Age norms give the average performance of persons of each age while the grade norms give average performance of children of different grades. With Indian populations age norms run into difficulty because of the unreliable nature of our age records. Therefore, most of the time authors of tests prefer to give grade norms rather than age norms.

Mode of Administration

Usually individual tests are more reliable than the group tests. The group test does not allow a direct contact between the tester and the tested. So the ambiguities or doubts about directions and the understanding of items remain unclarified. Individual tests eliminate this factor and give a chance of individual assessment. Though the method is time consuming yet it is more dependable than mass testing.

Certain other criteria, though secondary in nature, are important for choosing a test. The clarity of items is one. Unambiguous questions give better results than vague and hazy items. Facility with administration is another consideration. How much time it takes and what specialization it requires on the part of a tester are important factors in the selection of a test. The cost and availability of the instrument are added factors under Indian conditions. A valid, reliable and objective test if not possible to procure is of little use to the teacher in India.

Limitations of Tests

From the detailed description of tests and the discussion on validity and reliability one comes to the conclusion that most of the tests are far from perfect in measurement of abilities. No matter how accurately a test may claim to measure, the measures are never perfect. The validity of the tests determined form the correlation of test scores with future achievement are usually low. Studies conducted in the area have reported correlations between 40 and 50. The relationship, therefore, does not allow categorical predictions. For all practical purposes the interpretations have to be general in nature.

Use of test and interpretation of scores need careful handling because of the possible errors involved in prediction. A number of precautions are necessary before any interpretation can be made. The tester has to be sure that the particular subject is not markedly different from the standardization sample. It is essential that he should be coming from the same home background, socio-economic status and cultural level.

All test results are reported on averages of the groups. Individual differences are all smoothed out so that interpretation of scores of a markedly different individual may not fit into the norms. Standard error of estimate gives only the gross probable limits of the errors committed in a particular case. Thus we find that for all practical purposes the measures given by tests are rough and general. Tests used as the only measure have their limitations. For any useful application, they need to be combined with individual study, clinical records and estimates of teachers' ratings etc.

Summary

Intelligence is an intervening variable which can be measured by indirect operations. Intelligent behaviour implies making of value judgements. Binet can be rightly called a pioneer in intelligence testing. Thorndike felt that the level of intelligence can be determined on the basis of three independent variables viz. altitude, breadth and speed. Thurstone worked out a number of factors which constitute intelligence. Standarization of an intelligence test involves a good definition of the phenomenon, item construction, item analysis and the development of norms from the administration of the final form.

Extensive researches have pointed out that the intelligence of large sample—and so of the entire population—is distributed along a normal probability curve, so the subjects can be placed in different categories according to their intellectual status. Intelligence tests for American population are available for all ages beginning from infancy and going right upto adulthood. Though few in number tests are being made available for Indian population as well. Before a test can be declared 'good' for use the criteria of validity, reliability, objectivity and norms have to be considered besides the factors like mode of administration, cost and availability of the test. In spite of all the values which a test may hold tests have their limitations.

Questions for the Students

1. What is the best definition of intelligence? Distinguish between an absolute and operational definition.
2. What are the dimensions of intelligence according to Throndike? Elaborate each one of them.
3. How will you fit Thurstone's factors into Spearman's 'G' and 'S' factors?
4. Discuss the process of standardization in test construction.
5. What is the predictive values of infant tests? What age would you set as reliable for prediction purposes?
6. What makes a test 'good' for use? What factors will you keep in mind before choosing a test?

References

1. Bhatia, C.M. Performance Tests of Intelligence under Indian Conditions. Oxford University Press, Bombay; 1955.
2. Gasell A. *et. al.*, The First Five Years of Life. Harper, New York; 1940.
3. Goddard, H.H. A Measuring Scale for Intelligence. The Training School, 1910, 6; 146-155.
4. Goodenough, F.L. Measurement of Intelligence by Drawing. Yonkers, World Book, 1926

5. Guilford, J.P. Creativity. Amer. Psychologist, 1950, 5; 444-454.
6. Kohs, S.C. Intelligence Measurement: A Psycholgical and Statistical Study Based upon the Block Design Tests. Macmillan, New York; 1923.
7. McNemar, Q. The Revision of the Standford-Binet Scale: An Analysis of the Standardization Data. Hougton Mifflin, Boston; 1942.
8. Spearman, C. The Abilites of Man. Macmillan, New York; 1927.
9. Terman L.H. The Measurement of Intelligence. Houghton Mifflin Company, Boston; 1916.
10. Thorndike, E. L. *et al.*, The Measurement of Intelligence. Teachers' College, Columbia University.

14

Personality

Personality is the total being of a man. It Includes his physical as well as mental make up. Sensations, reflexes, instincts, emotions, perceptions, imagination, memory, intelligence, reasoning, will and character are included in the term personality. It includes besides one's relations to others. A great part of our personality is social in nature. The various factors that constitute personality are joined in a unity. A man's personality is made up of all the experiences that he had from childhood up to manhood. Everyday we are changing, yet all this change does not break our continuity with the past. In so far as there is a unity in all our pursuits and past experiences there is a personality that can be said to exist in us. "We are not the same today as we were a year ago. Many things happened in the year. If we should compare ourselves, now with what we were a year ago, in some ways we would hardly recognize ourselves. Yet we are the same personality."[1] The essence of personality lies in the unity of our experiences.

Elements of Personality

There are several factors that contribute to our personality. It is impossible to name all the factors. The factors have received greater or less importance or less importance at the hands of different psychologists. Some have classified personalities according to the prominence of some of these factors, whereas others have classified differently giving prominence to other factors. We shall here take note of a few elements that constitute personality. The elements generally are:

1. Morgan and Gilliland: *An Introduction to Psychology*, p. 305.

(i) Personal appearance.

(ii) Intelligence.

(iii) Emotionality.

(iv) Temperament.

(v) Character and moral traits.

The above elements taken together constitutions the personality of a man. It is obvious from the nature of the elements that some of them are congenital and others acquired. Intelligence, emotionality and temperament are congenital factors, whereas much of personal appearance and character and moral traits are acquired. The acquired factors are determined by environment and education, the congenital factors, on the other hand are not so determined. Yet great modifications may be made in the intelligence, emotionality or the temperament of a person through proper education. The congenital factors may be so trained as to do social good or they may take shape so as to do social harm. We have dealt with most of the acquired traits of personality in the previous chapters of this book. We have also dealt with intelligence. We shall be here primarily occupied in the remaining traits of personality, namely the emotionality and the temperament of persons. From the point of view of emotionality, personalities may be divided as "stable-minded" or "unstable-minded"; from the point of view of temperament they may be classified as "classic" or "romantic" and "extrovert" or "introvert".

Classification of Personality

Personalities are classified into *stable-minded* and *unstable-minded* by Trottor (in his book *Instinct of the Herd*). "The stable-minded has fixed opinions generally consistent with those of the 'herd' to which he belongs. He does not readily change them, or conceive them as open to question. The unstable-minded is more changeable, being sensitive to experience."

Ostwald conceived of personalities as belonging to either the *romantic* type or the *classical* type. "The man of romantic type is especially differentiated by the extraordinary rapid character of his thought. He and his occupation are varied. The classical type, on the other hand, is distinguished by a slower form of thought." His development is relatively slow and he sticks to one pursuit. The romantic type has greater personal influence, a greater power of inspiring audience or students. He is anxious to gain early popularity. The classical type neither seeks nor gains early popularity. He usually publishes his work late. Rousseau and Voltaire belong to the former type; Newton and Kant to the latter.

The great German thinker Jung has classified personalities into two main types—the *extrovert* and the *introvert*. The two types are as nearly opposed to each other as can be. The gaze of the extrovert is directed outward, that of the introvert inward. The former is objective, the latter subjective. The extrovert has facility in self-expression; the introvert lacks it. The extrovert tends to have more self-confidence than is justified by the facts; the introvert tends to have less. The extrovert is self-seeking in the sense that he likes other people to think and act as he does—he may be a propagandist; the introvert is detached and remains content to go his way and let others go theirs. The extrovert is stimulated by publicity, and tends therefore to perform least when he is under observation; the introvert, on the other hand, is more often paralysed by the presence of an audience his best work being done when he is unobserved. The extrovert contemplates opportunity in light of the scope for self-expression, while the introvert regards it as primarily from the point of view of responsibility. The first thought of the one type generally is the second thought of the other."[2] The extrovert is pushing, seeking opportunities, the introvert is cautious and would often let go opportunities even if they come. The one is gregarious, the other solitary. In the extrovert the fundamental function is feeling and the possibilities of thought tend to be unconscious. The extrovert is primarly a man of action, whereas the introvert is pre-eminently a thinker. Alexander, Napoleon belong to the former type, Kant,[3] Newton[4] and Wordsworth to the latter. Pandit Madan Mohan Malaviya and Pandit Jawahar Lal Nehru are the best representatives of the former class; Rabindra Nath Tagore and Sir Radha Krishnan of the latter. Psychologists have

2. Crichton Miler: *Psycho-analysis and its Derivatives*, pp. 152, 153.
3. Kant was so cautious about taking up responsibilities that when during his youth a young lady offered her hand for marriage to him, he went on thinking for over a year but could not make up his mind till the lady's patience was exhausted and she married another person. His first important work was published at the age of sixty-six.
4. Newton did not publish his main work *'Principia'* for a long time when ultimately the work was published he did not rejoice over it. He wrote to his publishers that the publishing of the work would fetch him popularity but the studies which he loved to pursue would decline.

admitted that it is hard to distinguish the two types of personalities. In everyone of us there are tendencies of each type. A good way of discovering what tendencies predominate in oneself is just to follow the injunction of a psychologist given to an audience bearing on the subject of personality. "A good way for you to distinguish whether your main tendency is towards introversion or extroversion is this: If, as I talk, you wonder which type you yourself are—you are an introvert; if you wonder which your neighbour is—you are an extrovert."[5]

Jung has further divided the above two main types into four sub-divisions according to the predominant psychic function. The functions, according to Jung, are thinking, feeling, intuition and sensation. Every individual has all the four functions, but one of them may be predominant. It is the 'superior function', the others are then 'inferior' ones.

The thinking type is rational, logical, detached; the feeling type is mainly guided by feelings. The intuition type depends on unconscious inference; he is quick and alert. The sensational type is mainly influenced by sense impressions. Each function has its opposite pole (see fig.), is the inferior function, and vice versa.

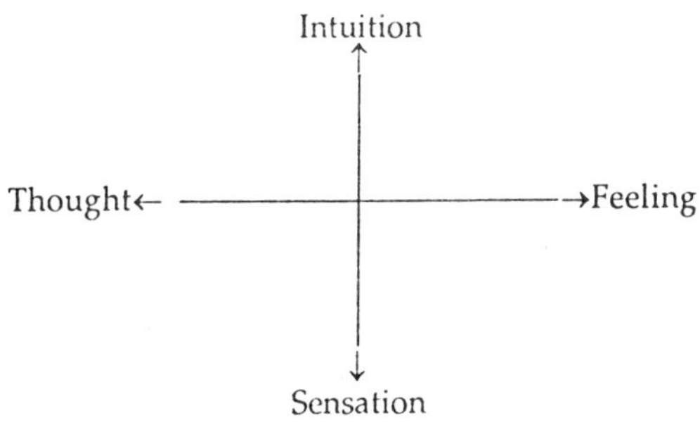

Similarly intuition and sensation are poles apart. Thus, both cannot be dominant in the same man. There is, however a combination of psychic functions that are intermediary to the polar opposites. Thus if the superior function is sensation, thinking and feeling will be better developed than intuition.

There may be a combination of thinking and sensation; this gives *empirical thinking type,* or combination of sensation with

5. Morgan and Gilliland: *An Introduction to Psychology*, p. 310.

feeling, giving *emotional feeling type*. Other combinations give the *intuitive feeling type* and the *speculative thinking type*.

When the above four psychic functions are combined with the two general attitude types—the extrovert and the introvert we get quite a complex division of personalities in eight different types—the introvert thinker and the extrovert feeling type; the introvert feeling type and the extrovert feeling type; the introvert sensational type and the extrovert sensational type; the introvert intuitive type and the extrovert intuitive type. It is difficult to explain here the natures and aptitudes of all the various types as conceived by Jung.[6] There are good points and weaknesses in each type.

Educational Significance

The different types of personalities are congenital. By education one cannot change the type but by education each type may attain perfection after its own kind. We have to recognize the congenital temperamental differences among individuals and give education to each taking note of the differences. We have to provide the proper environment for the growth of the special aptitudes of the child which ultimately depend on the type of personality that he is. We should see that the extrovert does not suppress altogether capacity for reflective thinking or allow it to die of disuse; similarly the cultivation of feeling should not be ignored in the introvert. Life situations demand different kinds of adaptations, some requiring more thoughts, others more feelings, and the individual who lacks in the capacity for proper adaptations suffers.

What education has to aim at, as pointed out by G. H. Thomson, is to create none of the undesirable types. It has to see that somehow the congenital disadvantages are compensated for by proper training. The individual has to be enabled to adjust himself effectively to changing environments of life. When this does not occur, unity of personality is often broken and a crisis

6. "The introvert thinker" is essentially subjective, theoretical and may display intellectual power. "He is tactless because he lacks intuition; callous because he lacks feeling, inhuman because he is devoid of sensation. He seeks seclusion and is afraid of criticlam. He first evolves a theory in his mind then goes out to find facts to support it."

occurs. Educational efforts should be directed to avoid this and create a happy well-balanced personality.

'The extrovert thinker' is a realist and deals in facts. He is in quest of a formula and when he finds one he makes most of it. He tends to become fanatical and intolerant. This is the commonest type among politicians. As a scientist, he gathers facts rather than formulates theories.

'The introvert feeling type' and 'the extrovert feeling type' are more common among women than among men. The former are intensely moved by feelings, they have strong likes and dislikes. They cannot express their feelings properly and hence are often misunderstood, seem to be selfish when they are not. 'The extrovert feeling type', on the other hand, express more feelings than they actually have. They are objective. Such a man is apt to pride himself over his shrewdness in which he lacks. The polar opposite of this type is "the introverted intuition type". This seems to be, on the whole, the most gifted type. The prophets and seers belong to this type; no original work is possible without intuition. Prophets are essentially men of intuition, the priests, on the other hand, entirely lack it. Such a man is courteous, dignified, primarily subjective, given to reading between the lines. He appears unstable in friendship. This is temperamental.

'The introvert sensorial type' appreciates the good thing of life. He seems to be self-possessed but behind his apparent self-possession there is uneasiness. 'The extrovert sensorial type' is very much dependent on objective conditions. He is most easily bored. He is incapable of taking joy in the abstract. This is the least gift type.

'The extrovert intuition type' is after change. He has the reputation of being an optimist. He tends to over-emphasise the importance of certain points. He is essentially an opportunist, and he makes his way into the world by a combination of hopeful agility and childish obstinacy. This obstinacy is his only defence when he is faced with plain facts and direct logic. He is most dependable in times of emergency, for his quick decision helps effective action.

Exercises

1. What are the main components of a personality? Describe the importance of intelligence and character in the formation of personality.

2. Distinguish a stable minded personality from an unstable minded one. How do the two behave in a critical situation?
3. How does Jung classify personality? How would you know that a particular person has a personality of one kind or that of another?
4. What is the educational significance of studying personality traits? How can we remedy the defects of an introvert personality?
5. Write an essay on an *extrovert personality.*

References

1. Crichton Miller: *Psycho-analysis and Its Derivatives.*
2. Thomson: *Instinct, Intelligence and Character*
3. Jung: *Psychology of Individuation.*

15

Personality and Children's Adjustment Problems

The Learner and the School

Every school learner, from his beginning days in first grade until high-school graduation twelve years later, makes a long series of adjustments between the whole unique personality he is and the programme of the school. Each girl and boy is seeking to become an individual person having a healthy physique, a growing intellectual ability, a greater degree of emotional poise, an increased participation in social groups, and such other characteristics as enhance personality. At the same time, through its curriculum, the school is attempting to develop this person into as efficient a learner in the realms of modern living as the capacities of the girl or boy permit. Since the school represents society at large, the learners' adjustment problems can be regarded as one phase in the development of growing individuals and, hence, of society. Broadly speaking, the consideration of personality and learners' adjustment problems may be considered as the daily interaction between the particular developmental strivings of this girl or boy and the general educational programme of the school. Although in many instances modern schools have accepted responsibility for adjustment their programmes to the diverse needs of individual learners, the discussion in this chapter is concerned primarily with the kinds of personal, psychological adjustments the individual makes while under the guidance of teachers and other members of the school staff.

Nature of Adjustment

Although the actual nature of the personal adjustment of the school learner will become clearer as the discussion moves forward, a few preliminary suggestions may be useful in viewing the teacher's task as one of aiding learners in their problems of adjustment.

First, the learner adjusts actively in the school environment rather than passively adusting to the school's programme. When a learner enters a class, he does something to that group, just as the group does something to him. This concept of dynamic interaction between the individual and the group has roots both in modern interpretations of the learning process and in current studies of the psychology of group living. This view fits neatly also with the democratic philospher's insistence that each individual shall count as a contributor to his society as well as recipient of the benefits of sharing in the life of the group. As has been said elsewhere concerning the emotionally stable, person, "the organization of personality to the point of stability involves an active adjustment of the individual in his physical and social environment rather than a passive adjustment to or acceptance of his enviornment."[1] Unless some such qualification is made, the term "adjustment" may be misinterpreted. as, Lindgren[2] and others have pointed out.

Second, we do not mean here by adjustment any unhealthy twisting of one's personality through withdrawing from others, evading responsibility, or deceiving oneself, however much comfort may come therefrom. Rather, we here seek under the title "adjustment" healthy, energetic participation in group activity, grasping of responsibility, at times to the point of leadership, and, above all, avoidance of any self-deception in the adjusting. The well-adjusted child meets his school environment with the initiative appropriate to a full sharing with others and the optimum development of himself.

Third, since the personality of the individual, as depicted in the preceding chapter, is so largely a product of learning,

1. W.F. Bruce, and F.S. Freeman, *Development and Learning* (New York: Henry Holt & Company, Inc., 1942), p. 451.
2. H.C. Lindgren, *Mental Health in Education* (New York: Henry Holt & Comapany, Inc., 1954), pp. 93-94.

adjustment is essentially a process of re-learning. Although a variety of factors influenc adjustements, directly or indirectly, many maladjustments are primarily the result of unfortunate learning experiences.[3] When interpreted broadly as learning in the whole realm of personality, adjustment has both a negative and a positive aspect. From the negative side, the elimination or reduction of emotional maladjustments is sought; whereas from the positive side, the focus is upon healthy, realistic ways of thinking and acting. Since adjustment is not a peculiar, mysterious, psychological trick, but a learning process, the continuity of personality characteristics gives the teacher confidence in the effectiveness of changes made in any school learner's pattern of life. While the well-adjusted teacher begins by accepting each individual learner as he is, this preliminary acceptance is really a basis for helping the learner toward what he may become.[4]

Fourth, even the youngest school learner is already a personality. When the child of five or six years enters the first grade, he has already developed a self, for whose defense and protection he is deeply concerned. The young child has had many experiences through which he has fashioned particular habits or devices of adjustments, which serve him more or less usefully. For example, since the age of three or four he probably has been using the "sour-grapes" attitude when in need of comfort. Like the fox in the fable who excused himself from the effort of the big jump by the assertion that he disdained the grapes because they were sour, so the child expresses disdain for the follow-the-leader game he is actually afraid to play. Thus, even the young child, as well as older folk, attempts to protect himself form the ridicule of his peers and his own feelings of inadequacy by excuses whose weakness goes unrecognized by the person making them.

Also, the pre-school child has easily learned to put the blame on his sibling or playmate for any deviation from acceptable action, accidental or intentional, that occurs. Thus, he

3. See L.F. Shaffer and E.J. Shoben, *The Psychology of Adjustment* (2nd ed; Boston: Houghton Miffin Company 1956).
4. G.W. Allport, *Becoming: Basic Considerations for a Psychology of Personality* (New Haven: Yale University Press, 1955).

protects himself from the wrath of his elders by a device that under certain conditions the psychologists call a form of "projection". The condition that throws both the "sour-grapes" and the "projection" reactions into the defensive maladjustment category is that the child deceives himself into assuming that his dislike for the game is his real reason for not participating and that the blame for his own mishap really belongs to someone else.

Such examples of self-defensive twists in the young child's thinking are sufficient to indicate to anyone the considerable advance in the patterning of the personality that occurs in the pre-school years, without our necessarily agreeing with the Freudian emphasis upon the establishment of fixed patterns of personality in infancy. Thus, our inquiry into the nature of adjustment may be based upon evidence that the children whom the first-grade teacher greets are already making many adjustments in their social environment, and that insofar as each adjustment is a learning process, which may help or hinder his further development, the way is open for the able teacher to guide the adjustment made in school in a direction that strengthens personality.

Facing Reality on One's Own

The candid and courageous facing of reality, facing the actual conditions in one's environment and being aware of the quality of one's own existing capacities, is a prime characteristic of adequate personal adjustment. This ideal of facing up to the real situation—within and without the individual—is derived in part from contrast with the dodges by which a person unwittingly deludes himself, as in giving a "sour-grapes" excuse or projecting blame upon others. Although the human inclination to evade reality persists throughout life, the unsophisticated school learner is particularly susceptible to such maladjustment. The elementary-school child, especially, is very dependent upon his elders for accurate information about the wide world. There is so little he can see with his own eyes and bring within his own personal experience that many misconceptions creep into his interpretations. Even when his parents and teachers are doing their best to guide him to information, he becomes confused by the inadequacy of his background, as many a humorous instance of reporting by children shows. Certainly, the six-year-old can scarcely be expected to understand his own emotions or appraise fairly his own abilities, when most adults are still in the early stages of using psychological findings in practical ways to guide themselves. So, in putting forth the facing of reality as a prime objective for the learner and for the teacher who would help him toward adequate personal adjustment, we are taking a first step into the central problem of this discussion.

Progress in learning to make adjustments to actual situations involves dealing directly with one's own problems. The six-year-old has to make his own childish adjustments today, so that ten years hence he will be better able to make other more-or-less related adjustments peculiar to adolescence. In highly verbalized fields of study, such as history or even science and mathematics, teachers have been misled into assuming that pupils were learning when they were mainly repeating textbook statements on demand. Fortunately, more emphasis upon insight and understanding of original problems in science, for example, has done much to correct this misconception of the learning-teaching process. Those teachers who work in the field of manual skills as used in the applied or fine arts quickly learn the futility of words divorced from meanings. Such an understanding of learning is highly essential in guidance toward personal adjustment, for here the teacher is trying to help the learner into new ways of feeling, thinking, and behaving that run much deeper than memorized verbal rules of conduct. It follows that when each individual is dealing with his own unique, personal problem, he can do so only by a method that he is making his own as he goes along. The degree of similarity between emotional adjustment and understanding in art and social studies is such that the alert teacher may be able to detect some of the conditions within the school so that the learner can more readily meet his personal problems realistically.

The improvement of *the teacher's own social-emotional adjustment* is an essential aspect of preparation for helping learners in their personal adjustment problems. For the purposes of this discussion of teacher and learner adjustment, we assume a close working relationship among several practical ideals that have been variously designated as mental health,[5] mental hygiene,[6] and emotional stability,[7] as well as adjustment.[8] Insofar as the teacher of mathematics, biology, or American history needs general subject-matter preparation in his specialized field, does it not follow that every teacher needs special preparation in the more general and more difficult field of personal adjustment? Added to this logical conclusion is the fact that in the area of personal adjustment *what the teacher is as a person* seems equally important as *what he knows about personality and adjustment*. The point is that teachers can *learn to be* better adjusted persons.

Thus, "facing reality on one's own" is not as lonesome a venture as one might think, for learners and teachers may work together to discover favourable conditions for personality adjustment and for avoiding the deceptive ways of thinking and acting that our common culture inflicts upon us all. In a very real sense, every learner learns for himself, but, as we shall see, he derives essential support form his peers and his elders. His parents and teachers, in turn, can gain support in their efforts from a host of past and present thinkers in psychology and the related fields of biology, sociology, anthropology, ethics, and philosophy.

---

5. Association for Supervision and Curriculum Development, *Fostering Mental Health in Our Schools*, 1950 Yearbook (Washington, D.C. National Education Association, 1950).
   H.C. Lindgren, *Mental Health in Education* (New York: Henry Holt & Company, Inc., 1954)
   L.P. Thorpe, *Psychology of Mental Health* (New York: The Ronald Press Company, 1950).
6. L. Kaplan, and D. Baron, *Mental Hygiene and Life* (New York: Harper & Brothers, 1952).
   F. Redl, and W.W. Wattenberg, *Mental Hygiene in Teaching* (New York: Harcourt, Brace & Company, 1951).
   J.E. Wallin, *Personality Maladjustments and Mental Hygiene* (rev. Ed.; New York: McGraw-Hill Book Company, Inc., 1949).
7. Bruce and Freeman, *op. cit.*, Chap. 18, "Emotional Stability."
   W.F. Bruce, and A.J. Holden, Jr., *The Teacher's Personal Development* (New York: Henry Holt & Company, Inc., 1957), Chap. 3, "Personal Energy and Emotional Stability."
8. K. Cobb, *Problem Behaviour and Adjustment in Children* (Boston: Hougton Mifflin Company, 1951).
   Shaffer and Shoben, *op. cit.*
   L.C. Steckle, *Problems of Human Adjustment* (New York: Harper & Brothers, 1949).

Withdrawal from Reality

Like the clinical psychologists,whose investigations of maladjustment paved the way for our present understanding of adequate adjustment, we turn to a consideration of the devices used in withdrawal from reality. Our purpose is to learn how to avoid these personality defects and the conditions contributing to such evasive behaviour. Let us begin with the case of the withdrawn child, "the quiet one."[9] Fortunately, most teachers no longer pay attention only to those learners who draw attention to themselves, either by overparticipation or disrupting behaviour. The modern teacher has an eye out for the pupil who never volunteers, who never disturbs the class. Many schools have moved far toward giving serious concern to the withdrawn, reserved personality in the three decades that have elapsed since the pioneer studies of Wickman[10] showed how teachers or 1928 placed these kinds of personal problems low in importance as compared with transgressions against the authority of the school. The clinical psychologists, in contrast to the teachers, placed withdrawing and recessive behaviour very high as threats to personal development. Anyone can see that unless a learner faces up to his responsibilities in the class group he can scarcely learn sound social-emotional adjustments. The "quiet one" learns less than he might in both subject matter and in personality realms, partly because he does not test his ideas in the form of class discussion. Furthermore, with greater risk to his personal growth, the withdrawn child often is doing something else behind his mask of apparent apathy. So, the teacher's task of "drawing out" the withdrawn learner of six or sixteen years may involve at least the recoginition of some of the devices commonly used by the "quiet ones." It must be kept in mind, however, that not all "quiet ones" are maladjusted.

Daydreaming is widely recognized by parents and teachers, who may never think of classifying this behaviour as a "psychic

9. Films such as *The Quiet One, Angry Boy, This is Robert, Facing Reality*, and many others, throw vivid light upon the processes of adjustment.
10. E.K. Wickman, *Children's Behaviour and Teachers's Attitudes* (New York: Commonwealth Fund, 1928). (*See also* H. Berlen, "Teachers' and Clinicians' Attitudes Toward the Behaviour Problems of Children: A Reappraisal," *Child Development*, XXX (1959) pp. 9-25.)

mechanism" and labeling it "fanstasy" or "phantasy." The fact that a child seems to be a daydreamer may be relatively unimportant, but, on the other hand, it may be a symptom of drastic evasion of the real situation and the practical problems with which he should be dealing. Under such conditions, daydreaming becomes a menace to personal development and a serious obstacle to progress in school, for daydreaming may cover a wide range from long, long thoughts on a field of special interest leading to constructive action, or it may be a way of comforting oneself when frustrated from reaching goals a person has already accepted for himself. Therefore, the teacher's task in some cases is to discover the special interest and further it as a means of enlarging and deepening the learner's educational life. In other cases, with which we are here particularly concerned, the teacher has the far more difficult task of getting at least a glimpse of the condition frustrating the girl or boy's deepest desires. What does this young person want most? What are the hidden urges of which he himself is hardly aware? Daydreaming, besides being generally a time-wasting process, may be a symptom of some psychological maladjustment that progressively interferes with effective action and happy social relations. The teacher who recognizes daydreaming as a challenge to study the individual and to experiment with curriculum adjustments, regrouping within the class or school, and other ways of changing the conditions, may contribute greatly to the life of the over-quiet, over-withdrawn learner.

Regression is a form of withdrawl from reality by returning to behaviour appropriate at an earlier age. Teachers in the early elementary grades often point out "babyish" children, while parents and teachers are sometimes accused of "acting like adolescents." In order to avoid the responsibilities of maturity expected at a certain age level, the individual retrogresses to the standards set for a younger person. Instead of courageously grasping the developmental tasks of their age group, the girls and boys fail to face the reality of their own growing up. When such an attitude is taken without the individuals being aware of this backward slip in his emotional reactions to troublesome situations, the clinical psychologists designate the action by the term "regression," as a common mechanism of escape from reality.

A school may not be entirely blameless when many of its pupils show signs of regression. Teachers may well ask themselves: How well is the curriculum fitted to this age group? Are difficulty and interest related so that the learners are challenged? Are the methods of teaching appropriate for these boys and girls? Are the school tasks diversified enough to care for the four-year range of test intelligence and reading ability commonly found on each grade of the elementary and secondary school? When the school has faced and provided adequately for such realities in the learner group, then it is time to inquire about other causes underlying the behaviour of the girl or boy who gives evidence of regressive inclinations. The conditions these learners are encountering in their homes and among their peers may throw light upon the special factors influencing them toward emotionalized dropping below the intellectual and social standards they would otherwise exhibit.

Although it may be difficult for a teacher to distinguish between the learner whose low ability is due to a variety of environmental conditions and the learner whose present attack upon his school tasks is affected primarily by regressive tendencies, the teacher may well regard the inclination to revert to the easier ways of earlier years as a persistent threat to all learners. Certainly, the awareness of the recurring temptation to regress needs to be safeguarded by a recognition of various other psychological realities bearing upon the behaviour of both learners and teachers.

Negativism is another from of withdrawal from or avoidance of reality. As has been pointed out elsewhere, however, negativism, even in the young child, is not "an inevitable stage of temporary retardation in emotional development...traceable to a definite hereditary pattern,"[11] but a result primarily of adults using the child's slight acquaintance with the meaningful language to redirect him suddenly away from his own chosen activities. No wonder the normal child responds with a sulky "no!" to such frustration, especially if the adult has persistently tried to curb the child's adventures with "don't", don't, don't" and "no, no, no!" It is easier to teach negativism than to reestablish initiative. The alert teacher asks: How much negativism is being

11. Bruce and Freeman, *op. cit.*, p. 94.

learned in my class and in our school? How are learners helped in their adjustment as they enter elementary school, junior high school, senior high school, or college? Whether the negativism is learned early or late, the remedy lies in providing conditions favourable for learning to grasp reality along with its responsibilities. One of the essential conditions is that the teacher reduces his own negativism to reasonable proportions. Again, it is not a simple matter to distinguish clearly between a wise teacher's refusal, on the one hand, to be drawn into too many activities of the school and community, and, on the other hand, a blind, blanket refusal to participate adequately in school and community affairs. An awareness of the origins of negative attitudes in others and in oneself constitutes a safeguard against drifting unconsciously into the employment of this psychic mechanism. The negative individual is an immature person, whether at ten, twenty, or forty years of age.

Although clinical psychologists have identified as psychic mechanisms other forms of withdrawal from reality, giving them such distinctive labels as "insulations" "repression," the preceding discussion of daydreaming, regression, and negativism is without doubt sufficient to illustrate the fundamental principles of adjustment. In each form, the individual is unaware that he is avoiding reality, because he assumes that the situation actually is just the way it looks to him. These person who uses a psychic mechanism is making a pseudo-adjustment that satisfies and comforts him to some degree. While he daydreams in his particular world of fantasy, he is saving himself from the difficulties of his school tasks. By using the regressive device, a second-or-third-grader psychologically lowers the standards he sets for himself to those of the easy life of the first grade, or high –school student chooses the elementary-school teacher's close supervision over responsibilities of high school. In adopting a negative attitude a student substitutes an assertion of disinterest in a particular school subject and so tends to lighten his feeling of responsibility for the study. He erects a protective shell around himself that "insulates" him from the class group and its demands upon him for his just share of effort in the joint project. He "represses" his own deeper wish to do his part and so comforts his educational conscience. He "identifies" with some person who has made a great success in life, but whose biographer asserts that the hero was a failure in the formal school of yesteryear. Thus, by one device or another, or by a combination of psychic twists, many a pupil deludes himself into appraising his withdrawal from the realities of the school life as a reasonable adjustment to the situation. Such a learner fails to realize the character of the pseudo-adjustment or maladjustment developing in his personality and spreading from the school situation to the individual's life outside the school and into the years beyond school days.

Again, the teacher's task includes finding out what conditions inside and outside the school are inducing such a pseudo-adjustment in the learner's personality. If the teacher too quickly attributes school failure to the learner's personal maladjustment, then the teacher himself may be withdrawing from the responsibility of studying the contributing factors, much as the young learner may withdraw. Although the personal history of the persistently withdrawing girl or boy may throw light upon the underlying causes, the actual remedies most available to teacher control are usually related closely to what is happening this week and this day as the learner encounters his classmates and the teachers in school classes and extracurricular activities. In other words, consideration of "withdrawal from reality" may be more useful to the teacher as a guide to present conditions than when stretched too far into speculation about remote in place and time.

In the actual development of soundly adjusted personality, the learner and teacher together have to make judgements, based upon the past and present, as to which experimental changes in conditions are most likely to lead towards reduced withdrawal and a more complete facing of reality in the future. Since facing reality honestly and vigilantly is a contagious emotional attitude as well as an intellectual process of sensitive perception, teachers have the additional responsibility of setting an example of minimum withdrawal and facing of the stern realities involved in guiding all the youth of the community.

Substitution as a Pseudo-adjustment

Among the other ways in which school learners and even their adult parents and teachers endeavour to escape from the harder realities of life is the mechanism of substituting one goal for another. Clinical psychology offers two forms of substitution: compensation and sublimation. Under "compensation" are usually gathered those cases where the individual attempts to cover up his weakness in one area by exhibiting his strength in another. For example, the ten-year-old who is weak in arithmetic may be strong in annoying the fourth-grade teacher. In contrast, "sublimation" has been restricted by most psychologists to the behaviour of adolescents. The high-school boy or girl is supposed to redirect his or her developing sexual implulses into activities that are non-sexual and acceptable to their elders. Through considering these two forms of substitution in relation to each other, the general implications for teaching practice may become clearer than when "compensation" and "sublimation" are treated as distinct psychic mechanisms. The question is whether the avoidance of a real goal in education and life by substituting another objective is a necessary and temporary pseudo-adjustment that actually may lead on to healthy adjustment and further development of the school learner.

Compensation is a concept that may be very helpful to a teacher who is annoyed by the misbehaviour of pupil. Instead of quickly concluding that the girl or boy has inherited evil tendencies either as a phase of universal "human nature" reputed to be naturally sinful, or through a particular bad biological inheritance from degenerate parents, or by disruptive habits instilled by his low-class family, the teacher may be encouraged to spend a bit of time searching for the frustration that is driving the learner toward compensating acts. The youngster himself, in typical case of compensation, does not realize that his drive for status among his classmates underlies his search for a conspicuous accomplishment. A set of conditions inside and outside the school may be contributing to the learner's personal difficulties, and the teacher's realization of the possibilities of the compensatory twist in motive offers an approach to a revealing inquiry. What are the capabilities of the boy or girl? How does the family discourage or overstimulate study? Should the school adjust its requirements to the learner of show the learner how to adjust effectively to the curriculum, or a combination of both? Should more recognition be given to the learner's success in one field and fewer rebukes be given for weakness elsewhere? Isn't some behaviour bordering on compensation actually an asset in the lives of learners and their teachers as well, since few of us are strong in every field of endeavour? Are teachers sufficiently alert to the dangers of a learner's overcompensation for physical or social inferiority by a narrow devotion to those aspects of school studies that promise to bring high marks from the teacher? Whether or not compensating activity is helpful or harmful depends partly upon the degree of awareness or unawareness of the process by the person himself, and partly upon the indications that it is promoting or retarding further development in other areas of education and of life generally.

Sublimation is widely regarded as a behavioural adjustment that is essential and therefore beneficial to the adolescents of high-school age. This attitude seems sound, for example, in the case of the substitution of such adult-sanctioned behaviour as social dancing in the home or school (under sympathetic supervision) for non-sanctioned sexual behaviour. As has been said elsewhere, "The advocates of such substitutes maintain that adolescents have their sex impulses directed, without being aware of the process, so that the teachings of social control will be adequate."[12] Since these supposedly subtle methods do not always achieve their intended objective, as indicated by the amount of sexual activity really occurring among young people, high-school teachers may well reserve judgement concerning the all-round effectiveness of such substitution. Instead of advocating self-deceptive devices characterized by unawareness, a programme of worth-while social activities may be developed with awareness of its limitations as well as its values. Actually, many adolescent groups have learned to regulate their own social behaviour, for example, in regard to "petting." These adolescents are thus showing their own maturity in terms of facing the realities of life, so that more and more their parents and teachers may see how to share with youth the responsibilities of social conduct on a basis of self-discipline.

In the discussion of these two substitution devices, compensation and sublimation, perhaps it has become evident that when learners and their teachers mutually understand the

12. Bruce and Holden, *op. cit.*, p. 160.

purpose of a limited degree of substitution of a new objective for a related responsibility, favourable development of personality may eventuate. This understanding or awareness of the character of the substitution process tends to remove its aspect of unconscious avoidance of reality (against which clinical study of the maladjusted adult has warned) and brings it out into the very midst of educational and social realties. There appears to be, in the case of normal learners, a possibility of a continuum of change in behaviour and thought, by which a person may advance from unawareness toward awareness, from the avoidance of reality to a firm grasping of the pertinent conditions as they really exist. A favourable prospect may be detected by turning the psychic mechanism *other side up*.

Briefly, let us try our list of pseudo-adjustments "other side up." "Daydreaming" may be translated into rational planning for the future. "Regression" may be transformed into adjusting one's objectives to one's capabilities, even though at times one's sights may be temporarily lowered. Just as the bar for the high jumper must be set by trial within his range as a preliminary to raising it to his best effort, so the learner and the teacher may set goals appropriately without being dominated by "regressive" attitudes. Even "negativism" may serve to remind us that there are times when it is healthy to say firmly, "No!" "Insulation" may be reinterpreted as the "need for privacy," identified by Maslow[13] in his significant study of psychological health. There Maslow points out that "self-actualizing-people," who exhibit a high degree of adjustment as a group, are characterized by "a quality of detachment" to the extent of enjoying time to listen to music, think, and commune with oneself. Although such withdrawal into one's private spot may be mistaken, even by one's friends, for "insulation," it actually contributes greatly to a person's social adjustment when consciously planned as one aspect of a total life. Likewise, "repression" may suggest a reasonable control of one's speech and thought by consideration of the relations of the self to others rather than continuing as a deep hiding of one's shameful thoughts and guilt-producing memories below the level of awareness. Finally, "identification"

13. A.H. Maslow, "Self-actualizing People: A Study of Psychological Health," Chap. XIV in C.E. Moustakas (ed.) *The Self: Explorations in Personal Growth* (New York: Harper & Brothers, 1956).

with another person can be freed form its narrowing, emotionalized copying, which weakens the individual's responsibility for his self-development, as this deep regard may be transformed into an intelligent selection of the most worthy qualities of the person, with whom one has been tempted to "identify". Thus, we draw from a friendship general ideals without binding ourself blindly to one particular style of life.

Thus, all the psychic mechanisms mentioned may serve as warnings to the teachers of pseudo-adjustments to be avoided. The harm lies in the blind way in which victims misapply them; however, they may contain hints for positive, intelligent adjustment. As every legitimate coin has a head and a tail, so every maladjustment can be turned other side up, not by a chance throw, but by a thoughtful re-evaluation based upon studies of the negative consequences of drifting into psychic twists and upon consideration of the positive ideals of personality development in our democratically oriented society.

Other Devices that "Protect" the Personality

Among the other deceptive devices supposed to protect the self, or ego, we select for consideration three more of the psychic mechanisms identified in the psychological clinic: projection, compartmentalization, and rationalization. In addition to looking at the dangers to healthy adjustment these devices represent in the lives of learners, we may be able to see how three corresponding aspects of personality development may be fostered in the school.

Projection can be contrasted with "identification" to the degree that the latter implies a 'pulling in' to the self of the desires and motives of another person whom one admires. "Projection" is a tendency to "push out" upon another person one's own unrealized, frustrated ambitions, or to attribute to another one's own faults. For example, school learners are often the victims of their parents' projection of their former hopes for higher education and higher social status. The damage does not come from a father's hope that his son may have wider opportunities in life than he himself enjoyed, but from a blind drive toward a particular professional goal that may fit neither the sons's interests and capacities nor the real opportunities of the current scene.

Thus, the adjustment of the son to today's conditions is menaced by the father's "projection" of an adjustment suitable only to an earlier decade. Likewise, a teacher sometimes projects upon a favorite pupil an ambition that properly belongs to the teacher himself. Instead of doing the preferred pupil a favour, the teacher may thus, without being aware of the underlying, long hidden impulse, mislead the learner when giving educational and vocational guidance. In general, the adult guide may well pay as close attention to his own tendencies to project or use any other deceptive mechanism as to the learner's inclination to fall into projection, identification, or other psychic traps.

As far as the learner himself is concerned, "projection" sometimes takes the form of assuming that one's own motives, especially the lower, less generous sort, are the impelling forces in the lives of his peers. This process of attributing one's worst motives to the older fellow was almost reversed in a study by Wright[14] of eight-year-old boys and girls. Perhaps because they had not yet learned the ways of many adults, these third-graders attributed to their peers motivation by generosity in the same degree as themselves. Although it may be naive to attribute to others without discrimination the same motives as ourselves, it is a better basis for social adjustment in a group than ascribing to our fellows our own worst motives. When projection is considered as the establishment of intimate relations with others, it can be transformed into sympathetic understanding of one's associates, or even further into sympathetic understanding of one's associates, or even further into the "Golden Rule" of putting oneself actually in the place of the other person. The sensitive intelligence and human warmth consistent with the application of the Golden Rule contrast sharply with the unseeing projection of one's less commendable attributes upon others. Unless the projection tendency is reversed during the school years by guidance in fair, realistic treatment of one's associates, the coming generation is likely to still be filled with adults who continue to act and live in the obscurities of projective behaviour.

Compartmentalization is a device by which the human being in today's complex world attempts to simplify his problems by

---

14. B. Wright, "Altruism in Children and the Perceived Conduct of Others," *Journal of Abnormal and Social Psychology*, XXXVII (1942), 218-233.

dividing his life into separate parts or tight compartments. In learners this may take the form of having one pattern of life at school and another at home. Some children adopt a relatively mature way of behaving at school, while they reserve their "babyishness" for their family. The duty for the teacher is to try to help the learner make adjustments that carry through life as a whole. It is evident that in a matter as fundamental as personality adjustment, little can be accomplished unless home and school cooperate. Effective cooperation can be based only on a degree of mutual understanding. In a sense this means that teachers who are seeking to free their pupils from the grip of psychic mechanisms, such as compartmentalization, projection, identification, and all the rest, may find that one avenue lies in conferences with parents. Together, helpful methods of guidance may develop, and the teacher may take some leadership in pointing out ways of avoiding adjustment for the boy or girl under consideration.

Although not all teachers will care to delve into the deeper problems of compartmentalization such as Thayer[15] finds involved in the separation of state and church, nor the philosophic cleavages in our culture depicted by Bode and others,[16] every teacher can find ways of unifying his own life and of helping learners and their parents to unify theirs in the daily life of the school and community. Compartmentalization may serve here to call attention to the pervasive operation of maladjustment by misleading mechanisms operating throughout the community at every age level, and to the long history of such human misconceptions, some of which are peculiar to the Western world. Whether the learner and his teacher are aware of its insidious presence, compartmentalization is a persistent threat to the healthy, wholesome, unified life. What is needed is a clear recognition of the diversity of behaviour appropriate for home, school, church and vocation. Such adjustment to diverse situations can be made, however, in ways by which these several phases of life are related constructively, rather than destructively broken into separate bits by tight traditions.

---

15. V.T. Thayer, *The Attack upon the American Secular School* (Boston: The Beacon Press, 1951); see also, by the same author, *Public Education and Its Critics* (New York: The MacMillan Company, 1954).
16. See chapter by B.H. Bode in F.Burkhardt (ed.), *The Cleavage in Our Culture: Studies in Scientific Humanism in Honour of Max Otto* (Boston: the Beacon Press, 1952).

Rationalization is an all-inclusive psychological term under which might be included many of the devices already mentioned. In rationalizing one devises ostensible reasons to justify an act, opinion, or attitude that is actually based upon other reasons or motives. The rationalizer is typically not aware that he is putting forth "good" reasons and suppressing the real reasons for his behaviour. Rationalization may be distinguished from genuinely reflective thinking by the way in which suggestions are treated. Instead of pursuing alternative suggestions through a substantial period of consideration,[17] an inappropriate suggestion is quickly accepted under emotional motivation as the final solution. Then only the evidence favouring the preselected solution is gathered. This biased process is often further favoured by binding together firmly all the arguments on the side selected to be "proven" and then throwing their combined force against each opposition argument one at a time. This discounting of each element of the opposition argument is known as giving the *segregative* treatment to the side against which one is prejudiced. On the other hand, the *cumulative* organization of each side is the method of rational reflective thinking. In projecting blame upon others and in using other devices for proteaching the ego, much rationalization supported by cumulative-segregative bias enters without awareness upon the part of the person who deceives himself into believing he is adjusting to the real situation.

Through their endeavours to help learners make their personal adjustments, teachers are incorporating in their educative programmes a major responsibility. Whether or not teachers deal courageoulsy and intelligently with these vital problems of personal development, the problems exist and continually affect the learning process. Maladjustment and the employment of psychological devices are almost as prevalent as human emotion, and who can find or would want to teach a girl or boy who had no emotions? The more serious teachers consider their responsibilities for promoting intellectual development, the more attention they well pay to the underlying personality structure and its dynamic operation. This brief survey of some of the mechanisms that mislead both school learners and their adult parents and teachers now becomes a basis for the

17. L.E. Cole and W.F. Bruce, *Educational Psychology* (2nd ed.; Yonkers, N.Y.: World Book Company, 1958), Chap. 13.

consideration of a positive educational programme. We seek a programme that will promote more adequate adjustment by all concerned in the work of the school.

Security for Learners in an Age of Anxiety

Fundamental to healthy personal development is a feeling of security. It is essential, therefore, that the school programme promote feelings of security rather than of anxiety or worry in the learner; nor should the learners' worries be transferred to their teachers. Teachers, parents, and school-age learners all need a sense of security as they work together. To the degree that anxiety can be reduced, any person is less likely to resort to the misleading mechanisms discussed above. We seek conditions in which the facing of reality is supported by a sense of personal security.

How can the school promote, in all the people connected with it, a sense of security in these days, which can be characterized as "an age of anxiety" as realistically now as when the John Dewey Society so titled their 1953 *Yearbook*?[18] How can the school promote the freedom in education that the *Yearbook* recommends and also maintain a substantial degree of emotional security? How can one be both secure and realistic in times when the fear of political tension abroad and of economic and social tension within the United States makes the news headlines a daily threat to a sense of security? Insofar as we are correct in the identification of adequate adjustment and mental health with the facing of reality, the school dare not ignore the forces in the world and in the local community that really worry thoughtful persons, young and old. The modern school is too vital a part of society to function in isolation, to adopt the mechanism of insulation, or of compartmentalization. The school is dodging its responsibility if its builds a fantasy world in which learners are encouraged to daydream about a peaceful future in a world actually divided. No, the school must begin by accepting the current worries of the political, economic, social, and racial frontiers, as well as by developing resources of personal security as it makes its contribution to adjustment.

18. H.G. Hullfish (ed.) *Educational Freedom in an Age of Anxiety* (New York: Harper & Brothers, 1953).

Obstacles to Security in the School

This promotion of security for a complex personality—the school learner living in the midst of an insecure world—is no simple matter. Consider a positive statement of this broad programme for the school as put by Carolyn Tryon: "Thus the conditions of good mental health require that the school create a situation for all-day-long where good human relations between child and child and between teacher and child can flourish."[19] Notice that one condition of "good mental health," or adequate adjustment, is the sense of personal security in the school group with which we are here concerned; nor is this healthy emotional climate confined to a single class period in "personality" development" but an "all-day-long" condition in which the security is promoted largely by mutual support between each learner and his peers and his teacher. Even the teacher is assumed to be freed from worry, although in many classrooms certain boys and girls are a major source of worry to their teachers. How can a shift be made from worried learners and worried teachers to an atmosphere characterized by both freedom and security? Certainly "it takes time"[20] to learn to manage a school such that life in it is characterized by spontaneity, by genuine interest, by diligent effort, by good human relations between learner and learner and learner and teacher. What are some of the major obstacles to be overcome in moving towards better mental health, greater security in freedom, more courageous facing of reality, more adequate adjustment, greater democracy, or whatever phrase the reader prefers for this many faceted ideal?

The school mark is one obstacle that tends to separate teacher from learner, and learner from learner. However, some way of making, grading, and evaluating the pupil's school work seems necessary. The learner, though, is apt to be thrown out of democratic social adjustment to his teacher and classmates by

19. C.Tryon, "Some Conditions of Good Mental Health," Chap.1 in *Fostering Mental Health in Our Schools*, 1950 Yearbook (Washington, D.C.: Association for Supervision and Curriculum Development, National Education Association, 1950), p. 12.
20. M.I. Rasey, *It Takes Time: An Autobiography of the Teaching Profession* (New York: Harper & Brothers, 1953).

any mark, high, low, or medium. The high mark may be related to undue subservience to teachers' requirements or to exaggerated feelings of superiority over his peers. The low mark may lead to feelings of inferiority and to evasive excuses employing the mechanisms of psychic maladjustment. Even the medium mark may not be a guarantee of security or healthy attitudes toward classmates and teachers. In spite of the long persisting criticism of school marks[21] for unreliability as well as adverse emotional effects upon learners and teachers, we recognize the practical reality of certain contributions of school marks in deciding about promotion in a graded school system, in transferring pupils from school to school, in informing parents and pupils of scholastic progress, and in promoting the individual learner's own realistic conception of himself. Inasmuch as the substitution of other methods of reporting progress and of reconstructing the graded school are affairs that take much time, the teacher has the immediate and difficult task of promoting better human relations in the face of a school-marking reality that learners and teachers must accept more or less gracefully. Such acceptance does not mean, however, a kind of soft adjustment that discourages efforts to improve the process a evaluation in the school. Although it is a long road from an over-emphasis upon competition among pupils to fuller understanding of cooperation within a study group, many a class, under skillful teacher leadership, has made substantial progress in a single year. When a school system devotes its twelve-year opportunity to making adjustment in this crucial area a central concern of its parent-teacher, teacher-learner, and learner-learner personal relations, greater freedom and greater security can develop consistently.

Teacher anxiety is another obstacle to learner security. From the days of infancy throughout life, anxiety is contagious. As Harry Stack Sullivan, out of his long experience as a psychiatrist,

---

21. W.F. Bruce, *Principles of Democratic Education* (Englewood Cliffs, N.J.: Prentice-Hall, Inc., 1939), Chap. III, "Confusion over School Marks."
C.L. Drawhorne, "Relationship Between Pupil and Student-Teacher Interaction and Pupil Ratings of Teacher Effectiveness, "*Educational Administration and Supervision* XL, No. 5 (1954)", 283-296.
S.T. Hadley, "A School Mark - Fact or Fancy?" *Educational Administration and Supervision*, XL, No. 5 (1954), 305-312.

has reported: "The tension of anxiety, when present in the mothering one, induces anxiety in the infant."[22] To what degree this inducing of anxiety in a learner by a teacher occurs depends partly upon the intimacy of their contact. Certainly, the personally secure teacher, as leader of the class, imparts to all the members of the group, in many subtle ways, the freedom from anxiety that is his. Furthermore, the teacher who is free from worry is free to think clearly in planning the daily programme of learning and to adjust to the vicissitudes that occur each day.

Whereas the reduction of worry in any teacher's life is a very personal problem and in meeting it the teacher may well seek out his own sources of help among friends and counselors, two areas of worry related to the school itself may be mentioned. As has been pointed out, "Too often a teacher's anxiety is increased rather than relieved by careless use of ill-founded general terms, such as 'creativeness,' 'guidance,' 'supervision,' 'social class,' and even 'democracy.'[23] When we add to this list "security" and "adjustment," then we are bound by our further statement to do something toward "more specific defining of these words as each is used in a particular context." In this effort, we enlist the aid of the student of education, the reader, who may be able to interpret the limited suggestions of this discussion in ways applicable to his own problems of security – outside of as well as within the school. The defining of "security-adjustment" is an unending task, about which this whole chapter is concerned.

Misbehaviour of a few girls or boys in the class is often a major source of teacher anxiety. "If I could only get rid of those pests," many a teacher has despairingly exclaimed, "all my worries would be over." This kind of worry is no longer relieved easily by wielding any kind of hickory stick. Today, the teacher's anxiety is increased by an annoying conflict between two desires or responsibilities. For example, teachers feel responsibility for maintaining discipline, but they have an opposing desire to be popular with their pupils. The cumulative effect of this anxiety-

22. H.S. Sullivan, *The Interpersonal Theory of Psychiatry* (New York: W.W. Norton & Company, Inc., 1953), p. 41.
23. Bruce and Holden, *op. cit.*, p. 73.

producing conflict has been emphasized in a study of the central anxieties of beginning teachers by Travers and his associates.[24] The authors of this report believe that such opposing desires are apt to produce increasing emotional tension, "since whatever action is likely to relieve one is likely to accentuate the other." The teacher is being squeezed between two apparenlty opposing social forces, which he has incorporated into his single personality or self. Out of the past, and, indeed out of any clear recognition of the full meaning of democracy as a protection of the group, comes the demand for social order, for discipline of the individual when he trespasses upon the rights of his fellows. In school situations, the right of each learner to an education must be protected from disruption by one or two unruly class members. On the other hand, out of a current trend among middle-class Americans, the typical teacher is being forced, without any clear awareness on his part, into becoming an "other-directed" perosn,[25] that is, a person who is guided more and more by the views of others. Thus, a teacher's feelings about being popular with parents and pupils may have deep, partially concealed cultural sources. As relief from this conflict, there are two related possibilities. One source of help lies in teachers gaining awareness of the sources of conflict within themselves; the other is through teachers learning more about the motives underlying the misbehaviour of learners. If this referring of teachers' and learners' adjustment problems back to a study of the personalities of learners and teachers seems like circular thinking, we may remind ourselves that the road to adjustment is a complex daylong process filled with dynamic interaction. Understanding of personalities, of ourselves and others, underlies adequate adjustment.

Multiple Causation Means Multiple Remedy

The principle of multiple causation, of many factors contributing to a situation, suggests to the teacher that in the investigation of a learner's persistent misbehaviour, the search

24. R.M.W. Travers, W. Rabinowitz, and E. Nemovicher, "The Anxieties of a Group of Student Teachers," *Educational Administration and Supervision*, XXXVIII, No. 6 (1952), 368-375.
25. D. Riesman, "Teachers Amid Changing Expectations," *Harvard Educational Review*, XXIV, No. 2 (1954), 106-117.

is likely to reveal a number of underlying unfavourable factors. Although some particular event may be the "last straw" to precipitate rebellious action, this action is often a symptom of a network of culminating conditions. As Hymes says, progress in the teaching of discipline cannot be tied to "some one pet, personal method," but "you must determine the cause, and your action must be consistent with cause."[26] Since the causes are multiple, the effective remedies are also likely to be multiple. The teacher may well search for causal facts in the school itself—its methods, curriculum, and regulations. Another good place to look is the peer group outside the classroom, because there occur jealous and childish cruelties that are apt to be hidden in the teacher-supervised class group. Look also in the home, where relations with parents and siblings may undermine the disciplinary guidance of the school. Although reading about typical cases will help the teacher, he must be on guard against typing or classifying, as by saying: "That is just like my Bob," or "Exactly like my Betty," or "Now, I know just what to do." Rather than adopting too readily this attitude, the alert teacher reads between the lines of careful studies[27] to discover the multiple nature, and the uniqueness of the effective remedies employed. Thus, the multiple causation-multiple remedy principle again suggests the complexity of the process of adjustment, of teaching discipline so that it becomes self-discipline. This principle also suggests the many techniques that the able teacher can use in various combinations with judgement based upon real understanding of the underlying conditions.

Teamwork in the School

Personal adjustment, we reiterate, takes time. Fortunately, the school has time: twelve years commonly from first grade to

---

26. J.L. Hymes, Jr. *Behaviour and Misbehaviour: A Teacher's Guide to Action* (Engelwood Cliffs, N.J.: Prentice-Hall, Inc., 1955), p. 140.
27. R.J. Havighurst and H.Taba *Adolescent Character and Personality* (New York: John Wiley & Sons, Inc., 1949).
    C.V.Millard and J.W.M. Rothney, *The Elementary School: A Book of Cases* (New York: The Dryden Press, 1957).
    D.A. Prescott, *The Child in the Educative Process* (New York: McGraw Hill Book Company, Inc., 1957).
    J.W.M. Rothney, *The High School Student: A Book of Cases* (New York: The Dryden Press, 1953).

high-school graduation. Unforutunately, this continuity asset is not often used to the full. As Hymes[28] points out, teachers of succeeding grades of the elementary school often fail to share their understanding of particular individuals. Teachers in the diverse subjects of the high school seldom have or make opportunities to interchange their understandings except in the most crucial cases. When the school has a systematic plan for dealing with personal adjustment, then teachers and principal can work as a team. Closer connections between the elementary, junior high, and senior high schools so that they become better articulated, as John Dewey[29] long ago suggested, are still greatly needed today. In many schools the team may be strengthened by adding guidance workers, counselors, and school psychologists, and by using such facilities as community clinics. Broadly planned teamwork fits in with the broad character of the adjustment process. When teamwork in behalf of learners is organized with flexibility and warmth, much valuable help may be given. Nevertheless, the leader of the team, as far as the adjustment of a particular learner is concerned, is still the class-group teacher .

The Teacher and the Group

Fortunately, teachers deal with classes, the members of which may become related in an interacting, mutually adjusting group. The adjustment of any person involves centrally his adjustment to and with other human beings, his adjustment *in* a group. If schools were not organized into groups, they would not serve the full educational need of the individuals. The study of group dynamics now offers the teacher a number of techniques and understandings by which personal adjustment can be facilitated through the class group.[30] As the rapidly growing

28. Hymes, *op. cit.*, p.120.
29. J. Dewey, "General Principles of Educational Articulation" (Address before Department of Superintendents, National Education Association, Official Report, 1929), pp. 51-60.
30. See, for exampie:
K. Benne, "More Learning Takes Place," *NEA Journal* (Apr., 1954), 205-208.
——— and P. Sheats, "Functional Roles of Group Members," *Journal of Social Issues*, IV (Spring, 1948), 41-49.
G.E. Jenson, "School as a Social System," *Educational Research Bulletin*, XXXIII (1954), 38-46.

study of group dynamics becomes more closely integrated with the study of individual personality, a new and highly useful resource will become available to alert teachers and administrators. The teacher will find that, although individual counseling has its distinctive place in the development of adjustment between learner and teacher, very great possibilities lie in the human relationships of the class group under the guidance of a teacher who is also a student of group dynamics. Such an informed teacher will devise ways of grouping within his own class, and of dealing with the whole class as a group, that will not only increase effectiveness in subject learning but will multiply the opportunities for learning mutual adjustments of a social-emotional character. Thus, the teacher may become a group hygienist who discovers how fully the tolerance and justice offered to individuals promote effective study and social stability in the group as a whole.

The Teacher's Own Adjustment

Although the teacher's own personal adjustment is a lifelong process, with its unique turns for each individual, as has been stated elsewhere in detail,[31] its effects upon the adjustment of the learners can scarcely be overemphasized. A most cogent admonition is: "Be yourself !:" In other words, each person, with whatever aid at hand, must work out his own adjustment in his own way. Being oneself, however oneself, however, does not mean staying where one happens to be, in a particular month or year. When the teacher treats himself *as a member of the study group,* he will learn much about adjustment in the classroom. The teacher has other group resources, however in his adult friends, in his professinal associates, in his family and in other groups. Balancing his thinking about his own personal development with substantial activity in groups where

______, "The Social Structure of the Classroom Group: An Observational Framework," *Journal of Educational Psychology,* XLIV (1955), 362-374.

______, and M.R. Goodson, *The Formal Organisation of School Systems* (Minneapolis: Burgess Publishing Company, 1956).

H.A. Thelen, "Educational Dynamics: Theory and Research, " *The Journal of Social Issues,* VI (1950), 2-93.

______, "Group Dynamics in Instruction: Principle of Least Group Size," *The School Review,* LVII (Mar., 1949), 139-148.

31. Bruce and Holden, *op. cit.*

adjustments are learned in realistic situations, the teacher may thereby enhance the quality of his leadership toward personal adjustment Our whole concern with learners' adjustment problems may be reflected in and promoted through the teacher's own developing self-adjustment. As the teacher learns, so will he teach.

—*William F. Bruce*